Alastair Morrison

FAIR LAND SARAWAK

SOME RECOLLECTIONS OF AN EXPATRIATE OFFICIAL

Kayan child at Long Miri in the Baram

Alastair Morrison

FAIR LAND SARAWAK

SOME RECOLLECTIONS OF AN EXPATRIATE OFFICIAL

STUDIES ON SOUTHEAST ASIA

Southeast Asia Program
180 Uris Hall
Cornell University, Ithaca, New York
1993

Editor in Chief
    Benedict Anderson

Advisory Board
    George Kahin
    Stanley O'Connor
    Takashi Shiraishi
    Keith Taylor
    Oliver Wolters

Editing and Production
    Donna Amoroso
    Audrey Kahin
    Dolina Millar

Studies on Southeast Asia No. 13

© 1993 Cornell Southeast Asia Program
   ISBN 0-87727-712-5

*Dedicated to the memory of my wife
with whom I enjoyed so many
happy years in Sarawak*

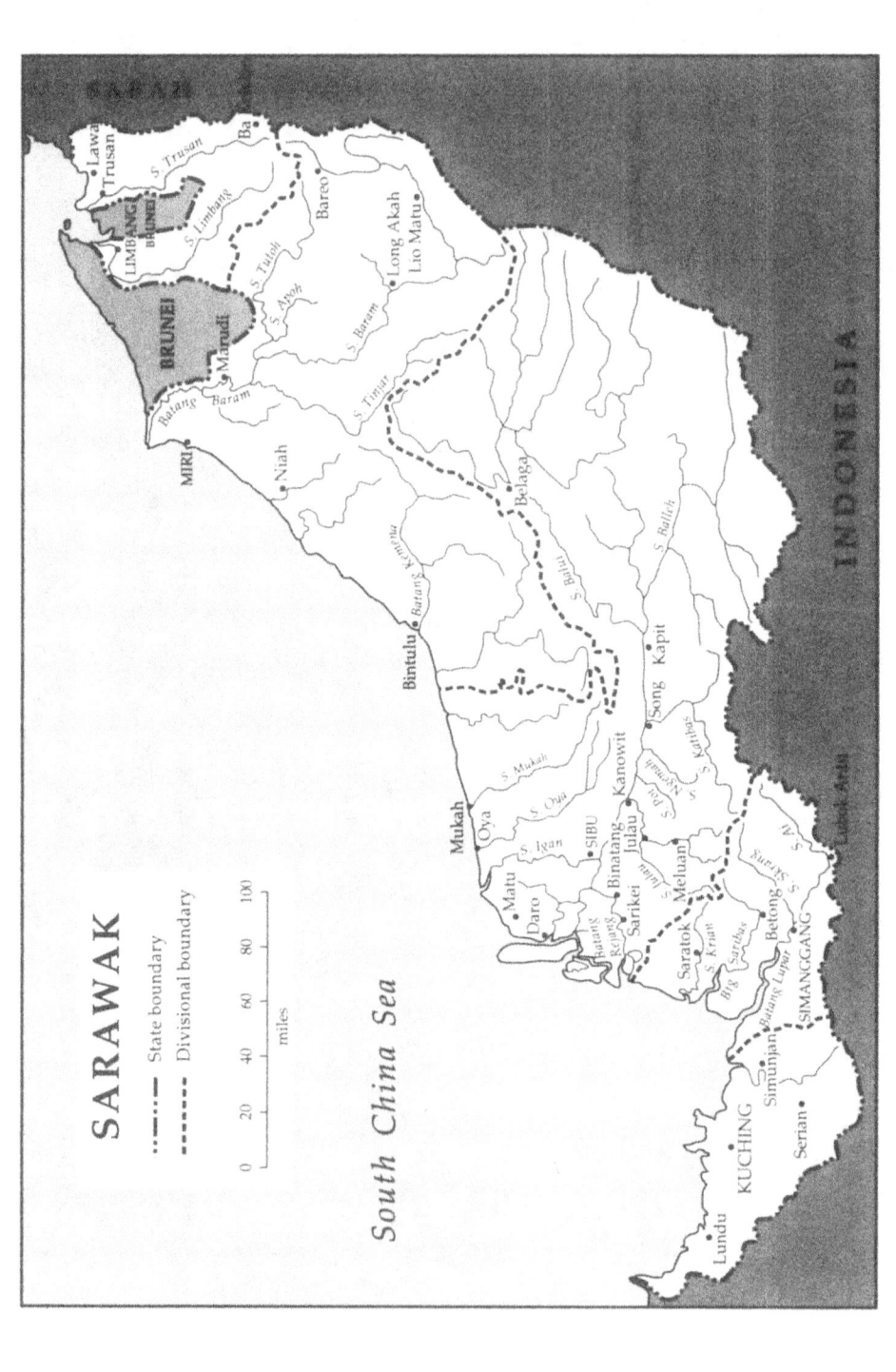

CONTENTS

List of Illustrations ix

Foreword xiii

1. The Backdrop 1

2. Early Days—Sarikei and Binatang 17

3. Lawas 39

4. Kanowit 57

5. Baram 75

6. The Secretariat 93

7. The Information Office 113

8. Establishment of Malaysia 131

9. The Last Lap 149

Bibliography 179

List of Illustrations

Kayan child at Long Miri in the Baram	Frontispiece
Map of Sarawak	vi
Ngu Ee King in his village shop near Sarikei. A 12-bore shotgun did wonders for his fortune.	20
Melanau girl of Kampong Rejang	21
Dayak longhouse in the 3rd Division	23
John Barcroft (right), my first Resident, watching the Sibu regatta with Sir Charles Arden Clarke and Miss Jennifer Arden Clarke	26
Our Major-Domo, Bolhi, feeding an orphan Maias	31
Chong Choon-nyen, a leading citizen of Lawas	40
Hedda with the party of Lun Bawang who took us over from the Trusan to the Limbang (photographed by the author)	52
Racha Umong, a hunter and notable Lun Bawang personality who led our party from the Trusan to the Limbang. He has since served as a member of Council Negri and as Chairman of the Evangelical Church of Borneo.	53
Asun, the last of the great rebels against Brooke authority	58
Ex-Penghulu Naga. I had to find his replacement	59
Keeping in step with the police. The author with Datuk Abang Haji Marzuki after the opening of the new Julau Chinese school.	67
Temenggong Koh, the paramount Dayak Chief in the Rejang, addressing the 1952 Conference (Aum) on Customary Law	68
Kasi, the powerful hostess of Long Teru, sings a song of welcome to my Resident, Alan Griffin. Between them is Kasi's husband, Penghulu Lawai	90

Looking westward over Kuching town and the Mosque 94

Tom Harrisson pays a Hari Raya call on Datuk Taib Mahmud and his
Australian born wife, Datin Leila 97

Tun Mustapha, later Chief Minister of Sabah, calls on the Tunku for the
first time in 1959 105

John Wilson talking to a group of Dayaks in Budu 109

The good Morshidi, who introduced me to rural Sarawak and was later
my Deputy in the Information Office, at his farewell party 114

Abang Razaleigh bin Abang Haji Jaya 115

Ivor Kraal, who taught me about the press 116

Typesetter in a Chinese newspaper 117

The Governor, Sir Anthony Abell, and the Chief Secretary, Derek Jakeway,
confer in the Chief Secretary's office, below a bust of James Brooke 123

Sir Alexander Waddell talking to Penghulus at the opening of the Batang
Lupar District Council offices 124

Carruthers 126

The Governor distributing discharge scrolls at the Brooke Memorial
Settlement for lepers 129

Ong Kee Hui, pioneer politician and member of a family with a great record
of public service, at a meeting of the Malaysia Solidarity Consultative
Committee 133

The Cobbold Commission. From left to right: Sir Anthony Abell, Sir David
Watherston, Lord Cobbold, Dato Wong Pow Nee, Tan Sri Ghazali Shafie.
Standing next to Ghazali are three Sarawak officers, Michael Sadin,
Yao Peng Hua, and Siaw Jun Chin 135

Abdul Rahman Yakub, the outstanding Sarawak politician. After service in
the Federal Ministry, he returned to the state to become Chief Minister and
later Governor. He was successful in bringing the communist insurgency to a
peaceful end 139

Sir Omar Ali Saifuddin, the former Sultan of Brunei, shortly after his ascent
to the throne 146

Sir Alexander bids farewell to his successor, Tun Abang Haji Openg 148

Portrait of a successful midwife: Duncan Sandys at the Malaysia Day celebrations in Kuching	150
Two of the soldiers: Major General Tan Sri Abdul Hamid, Malaysian Chief of Staff, and Brigadier Patterson	151
My first Malaysian Director, Encik Sopiee, with Peter Ratcliffe, the Sarawak Director of Broadcasting	154
Tony Shaw (center) talking to a senior Malayan official (right) and Datuk Teo Kui Seng, a leading Kuching Chinese personality	156
Rural settlement—new style. View over the Land Development Scheme at Melugu in the 2nd Division.	160
One of the Long Jawi widows whose husband was killed by the Indonesians	162
Temenggong Jugah and Bubu (Lt. David Rowe)	163
The Gurkhas had been teaching the girls Nepali dances	164
But the Temenggong thought they should learn some ballroom dancing too. Notice the pictures of the wrong royalty on the wall behind.	165
Stephen Ningkan, Sarawak's first Chief Minister, with his brother, Simon Ningkan. Simon was killed in the Indonesian attack on the 17th Mile Police Station.	169
Datuk Penghulu Tawi Sli, Sarawak's second Chief Minister	172
Tony Shaw's successor as State Secretary, Tan Sri Gerunsin Lembat, with his wife, Puan Sri Racha	173
The end of the British presence. The final parade in Kuching.	176
Major General Ibrahim, the first Malaysian Director of Operations in Borneo, with Royal Marines after the parade	177

*Fair land Sarawak
We will never cease
To honour thee
From your high forest hills
Down to the open sea
May freedom ever reign
Men live in unity*

(from the former State anthem)

Foreword

This is a book of personal recollections about nineteen happy years which my wife and I had the good fortune to spend in Sarawak. It does not attempt to provide a complete account of that period of Sarawak history but will, I hope, convey something of the way of life that we enjoyed and of some of the people, both Asian and European, whom we came to know. I hope that it may also provide some picture of an episode in British colonial disengagement. It was not one of the biggest episodes of this kind, but it was carried out under some difficulties and ultimately brought to a successful conclusion. Such success that it achieved was due in large part to the amiability and understanding of the Malaysian peoples involved and to the great regard and affection which those characteristics aroused in the expatriates who came to be involved in winding up this chapter of colonial history.

The narrative may appear lighthearted in places, but this is not due to any lack of a serious side to life in Sarawak. Rather it seeks to reflect the good nature and humor which are some of the most abiding impressions those who know Sarawak have always taken away with them.

I have sought to provide a short general account of Sarawak as the first chapter. If this appears to some as the dead hand of the ex-Government Information Officer at work, I apologize, but it is intended to allow the personal narrative to flow with fewer explanatory digressions. Those who know Sarawak do not need to read it.

I make no apology for offering a few critical observations. I do not think that any authentic account of this kind can gloss over happenings or developments with which one has disagreed or about which one may entertain misgivings.

I would draw attention to some points of style and terminology. I have used the word Native frequently and this is in no way disrespectful. The term is in everyday use in Sarawak and is there defined in law. In simple terms, it means indigenous and non-Chinese. It is not an entirely satisfactory term, because some Chinese have longer roots in Sarawak than some of the peoples classified as Natives, but the meaning is clear and it is a term in general use. In its Sarawak context it should normally be spelled with a capital letter in the same way as Chinese and Indian.

I have used the term Dayak as being synonymous with Iban, the largest of Sarawak's ethnic groups. There is also a smaller and distinct group known as Land Dayaks or Bidayuh, but in any mention of them I have referred to them as such. The Indonesian usage of the term Dayak is different and generally refers to all non-Malay Bornean indigenes. In certain cases where Malay spellings have changed, I have used the spelling in use at the time written about.

The photographs, except where otherwise stated, were taken by my wife. They do not attempt to duplicate the contents of three comprehensive collections of her photographs of life in Sarawak which have already appeared in print.

It is customary in forewords to acknowledge help and assistance of various kinds, but I find it impossible to compress my acknowledgements in this way. They should go to so many people that I knew in Sarawak in every walk of life. My gratitude goes to them all, colleagues and country people, businessmen and journalists, policemen, politicians, and missionaries and to a host of others for the tolerance and kindness they extended to us. I hope that what I have written may be regarded as some small tribute to a multitude of people who gave us their friendship.

1

THE BACKDROP*

Stretching for some 500 miles along the low-lying coast of northwestern Borneo, where great silt-bearing rivers reach the sea through immense and intricate deltas, lies the Malaysian state of Sarawak. It is by far the largest state in Malaysia.

Sarawak covers an area of some 48,250 of Malaysia's total of 130,000 square miles and is divided into three principal regions. These are the low-lying and often swampy areas of the coast; a region of low rolling hills lying behind the coastal flats; and a vast area of steep and jungle-covered mountains covering much of the interior. The population is found largely in the first two of these regions. Settlement in the mountainous interior, except for a few small wandering groups of jungle dwellers, is confined to the river valleys and some upland basins. For administrative purposes Sarawak was, until recently, divided into five Divisions numbered 1–5 from west to east; the capital at Kuching, in the 1st Division, lies some miles up the Sarawak River from which the state derives its name. The large 3rd Division has recently been divided into three.

Sarawak is the greenest of green countries with a heavy rainfall. It continues throughout the year though it is heaviest during the northeast monsoon, known in Sarawak as the "landas," which occurs from October until February. Over most of the country the rainfall averages from 120 to more than 200 inches each year.

This high rainfall is coupled with high humidity but lower temperatures than are found in many tropical countries. The mean surface temperatures vary between 72 and 88 degrees Fahrenheit. The European visitor generally becomes acclimatized very quickly. Except in the stuffiness of the towns, the climate is a pleasant one and the nights are cool.

The heavy rainfall is responsible for Sarawak's great river system. It is, in a very special way, a land of rivers, some of them of great size. Until the construction of roads began in quite recent years, it was the rivers which provided the main highways of the country and dictated the pattern of settlement. With rare exceptions they are navigable by various kinds of vessel, from ocean-going ships and big launches in the lower reaches to canoes powered by outboard engines further upriver and, finally, by small canoes which are paddled and poled in the shallow headwaters. The waterways have provided a remarkably satisfactory system of communications, only interrupted during periods of flood or drought.

The rainfall has also contributed to a less satisfactory feature of Sarawak. Its soils are generally poor and made worse by the leaching away of soil nutrients by the con-

---

* Editor's Note: This memoir was completed in the mid-1970s and has been published without revision.

tinual wetness. When the forest cover is first felled a misleading impression of fertility is created because over the centuries decaying vegetation has built up a rich but shallow layer of humus on the forest floor. When the protective forest is cut and burned magnificent crops can be grown for a brief period but the humus is quickly washed away and fertility correspondingly reduced.

The mountains of the interior do not attain great heights. The highest point, Mount Murud, has an altitude of 7,950 feet. But the mountain ranges have many heights of 4,000 to 5,000 feet. They are exceptionally steep and consequently unsuitable for agriculture.

The forests are very extensive and comprise many species of tree. Only in rare instances are uniform stands of one predominant species to be found. It is a mistake to think of the tropical forest as consisting entirely of giant trees. These are scattered and most of the forest consists of small to medium sized trees often festooned with various kinds of creeper and climbing palms or rattans. The trees mostly belong to the great tropical family of hardwood Dipterocarps. There are only isolated stands of tropical conifers. The shoreline is generally fringed by stands of the tall and graceful casuarinas. There are many flowers including some fine species of orchid and the curious parasitic Giant Flower or Rafflesia which grows as big as a man's head, but it is not a country where flowers are generally conspicuous.

Animal life is rather poor. The only large animals were the rhinoceros, wild cattle, and Rusa Deer. Unfortunately the harmless, slow-breeding rhinoceros has been hunted into extinction for the sake of its horn, much valued in Chinese medicine, and only a minute number of wild cattle remain. The Rusa is, however, fairly common. There is a small species of bear, the Honey Bear, and a small and harmless leopard, the Clouded Leopard, both of which are still to be found in dry jungle areas. Wild pig are abundant in the interior.

Sarawak has two kinds of anthropoid ape, the Maias or Orang Utan and the Gibbon, and several kinds of monkey. The Maias, although nominally protected, is now very rare. The numbers of Maias, Gibbons, and monkeys have been greatly reduced by shooting. Not only are Sarawak people the most obsessive of huntsmen, but they have been allowed to acquire an extraordinarily large number of shotguns. The effect on animal and bird life has been very severe indeed. There are many small animals, especially squirrels and other kinds of rodent.

There are several hundred species of birds including some unusual species confined to the island of Borneo. One of the best known birds is the Rhinoceros Hornbill, which plays an important role in traditional Iban or Sea Dayak ritual. There are some fine species of pheasant and the great mud flats of the coast are the haunt of immense numbers of migrant waders during the winter. Despite the large river system, ducks are surprisingly rare, due apparently to a lack of suitable food supplies.

Crocodiles occur in the rivers but have become rare. Turtles breed in considerable numbers on some small islands off the coast of western Sarawak and their eggs, which can never be hard boiled, have traditionally been harvested for food. Fishlife in the rivers has been severely affected by over-fishing with the deadly Japanese-made nylon nets, and sea fisheries are poorer than might be expected. Various large species of sharks and rays occur but are not considered a danger to human life.

There are vast numbers of insects including, unfortunately, large numbers of ones which bite, particularly mosquitoes and sand flies. Most of these, however, are not carriers of disease. The malaria vector is a comparatively rare species of mosquito, and nowadays malaria itself has been brought under almost complete control.

Sarawak has a varied population though it is not a large one in relation to the area of the state. The census of 1970, conducted under difficult security conditions, gave the state a total population of 977,438. This was a somewhat lower total than an earlier projection based on the 1947 and 1960 census figures. Various Native groups make up some two-thirds of the population, the balance consisting predominantly of Chinese. It is growing at a rate of 2.8 percent per year.

The biggest racial group consists of the Sea Dayaks or Iban who numbered 302,984 in 1970. They are a well-known people of Borneo because of their piratical forays out to sea in the early part of the nineteenth century and their former custom of taking and keeping the heads of their enemies. The Iban probably arrived in Sarawak in the seventeenth century, pushing overland from the Kapuas valley of Kalimantan (Indonesian Borneo) where other Iban groups live to this day. Iban tradition indicates that there were also two smaller migrations by sea but the main migration was overland into the valleys of what is now the 2nd Division of Sarawak. Here they absorbed or destroyed small populations of jungle-living tribes, the Bukitan, Seru, and others. The Iban were an aggressive and warlike people living in longhouse communities, that is villages under a single roof. Groups of longhouses, generally living in a single valley, combined under notable leaders. The Iban pattern of life was egalitarian and any outstanding personality could achieve distinction in the community. There was no sense of unity among the various river valley communities, and there were no great tribal leaders able to weld these groups of peoples with a common language and culture into a larger whole.

The Iban planted hill rice, following a shifting system of swidden cultivation. The jungle was felled and burned and on the rich humus so exposed they grew abundant crops. Their only domestic animals were pigs and chickens. The rivers and the surrounding jungle provided fish and game and so an ample supply of protein. The headman of the longhouse is normally elected. Women enjoy a respected position in the community, play a considerable part in village discussion and have equal property rights with the men.

The longhouses were and are substantial though not permanent buildings, each family with its private quarters and a share in the great communal room or ruai which stretches the whole length of the house. Up to fifty or more families might live together although the average number in my time was twelve to fifteen. They enjoyed a highly social existence which also, in the past, provided for protection. Before and after the harvest or in connection with the departure or return of war parties and on other lesser occasions great festivals would be held at which vast amounts of rice beer or tuak would be consumed. But although the Iban well understood how to make alcohol and this was the basis of their festivals, they did not drink as a regular part of their life and habitual drunkenness was unknown. It is still rare.

They had no writing—although certain memory tablets used in invocations to the spirit world came close to being an early form of graphic script—but they had retentive memories. Genealogies and folklore were well preserved in this way, especially by many bards who recited myths and legends and traditional history. Their most striking art form consisted of the weaving of colorful and lively cotton blankets and they also achieved a considerable degree of excellence in carving.

Life revolved around relations with the spirit world, with the planting cycle, and especially with the practice of warfare and the acquisition of enemy heads which were believed to confer great benefits on the longhouse community. In particular, the possession and taking of heads were important in providing fertility for the people and for the agricultural cycle. The Iban showed great bravery in some of their activities as fighting men, as for instance in their encounters with the Royal Navy, but there was little that was romantic in headhunting. The head of a child or an old woman brought as much benefit to the community as that of an enemy warrior killed in equal combat. Many of the heads were acquired in treacherous surprise raids on unsuspecting neighbors.

In the nineteenth century the process of Iban expansion continued. There was movement over the watershed into the Rejang valley and many war parties pressed boldly out to sea. It was the contact so established with western sailors which led to their being called Sea Dayaks.

They came into head-on conflict with the first Rajah, Sir James Brooke, and he only succeeded in overcoming them with the help of the Royal Navy. They largely made their peace with the Rajah although intermittent warfare continued until well into the twentieth century. The process of expansion continued. Iban became strongly established in the Rejang valley and are now to be found in every Division of Sarawak as well as in Brunei. Although some remain animists, most Iban today are Christians.

Today their wanderings are over. Many still live in longhouses in the valleys which their ancestors settled. They still plant rice, but nowadays most Iban families own rubber gardens. They play a very important part in the life of the state. There have been a number of Iban Ministers and all sections of the government service, as well as the Federal Army, contain numbers of them. To achieve this has meant a very intense educational effort, but like all the other peoples of Sarawak the Iban have shown remarkable determination to catch up educationally in order to modernize their community.

Neighboring the Iban to the west, entirely in the 1st Division of Sarawak, are another group of inland peoples, the Bidayuh or Land Dayaks. They numbered 83,276 in 1970. While they follow the same general pattern of life as the Iban, they are physically distinct, being a shorter and more round-faced people; they speak an entirely different language, which is itself split into several distinct dialects, and they have far more sedentary and less aggressive characteristics. They have never spread out from their homelands in the hill regions of the 1st Division which adjoin areas inhabited by similar peoples in Kalimantan.

Their villages consist of clusters of rather small longhouses with a special, high-roofed, separate building for the unmarried men and for visitors. They too plant hill rice, but through continuous cultivation their land has been exceptionally overworked and degraded. A swidden cycle of fifteen years or so, which allows a fair measure of regeneration before the secondary growth is cut again, is a fairly efficient way of making productive use of poor hill land. But when the population pressure builds up and the cycle falls to ten, eight, or even less than five years, the degradation of the soil is rapid.

The Land Dayaks have been largely converted to Christianity, the Roman Catholic, Anglican, and Seventh Day Adventist Missions all being at work amongst them.

After the Iban the largest Native community is that of the Malays who make up about seventeen percent of the population. Some Malays originated in Brunei during the period when the Brunei Sultanate had dominion over the whole coastal region as far as Kuching. But many of the leading Sarawak Malay families had come from the west, tracing their ancestry to Sumatra. Malay numbers have been augmented by conversion of and intermarriage with indigenous peoples. Conversion to Islam results in very rapid acculturation.

The Malays live largely on the coast and in the estuaries. Most of the larger towns have extensive Malay settlements or kampongs. They occupied a very special position under the Rajahs, who were heavily dependent on Malay support. It was the Malays who provided the Rajahs with junior administrative officers, sailors and policemen, and armed levies when the need arose. Today they still provide a large and important section of the government service, while in the countryside they are industrious rice planters and fishermen. Malays are now politically dominant.

They live in individual and often very elegant and elaborate houses. They are devout Muslims but at the same time a very tolerant community. The Mosque is the principal center of community life. The Malay New Year or Hari Raya, which ends the month of fasting, is celebrated in a very grand manner. Rich and poor alike keep open house to entertain their friends from all communities.

In the swamplands of the 3rd Division to the north of the Rejang and in parts of the 4th Division live a distinct people known as Melanau or Likau. They number rather more than 50,000 and are an indigenous people related to the Kayan and Kenyah of the interior. Having settled in the coastal regions, they early came into contact with Islam and a majority are adherents of that faith. However, some Melanau remain pagans and others have been converted to Christianity. They have a distinct language of their own though it varies greatly from river to river.

While they are also fishermen and padi planters and are today of importance as timber industry workers, the Melanau traditionally specialized in the cultivation of the sago palm which is planted on the alluvial river banks. The pith of the sago palm is a source of starch and in the early days was an important article of trade with Kalimantan (the Indonesian name for Borneo, which means Sagoland). It is also a useful source of food, especially when the sago is mixed with small quantities of rice bran to form sago pellets. The tall sago palm is not cut until it is nearly ready to flower at the age of thirteen years or so. Then the trunk is towed in sections to the village where the sections are split and the inner pith rasped and trampled while water is poured over it to carry the starch to settle in a trough below. The trampling was traditionally done by women.

Nowadays so many cheap sources of starch are available that sago is no longer a highly remunerative crop in world markets. The Melanau areas are consequently somewhat depressed. The Melanau, although superficially resembling Malays, have a much more complicated and stratified social structure. They have unusual and elaborate ceremonies designed to cure sickness.

In the Baram valley and at the head of the Rejang live the related Kayan-Kenyah peoples who, in the nineteenth century, were the great rivals of the Iban. Like the Iban, the Kayan and Kenyah are also people who moved in from adjoining areas of Kalimantan. They are an entirely distinct people as are their languages which are fragmented into a number of dialects. They have an aristocratic system of social organization and the power of the hereditary chiefs is very great. Unlike the Iban, where the headman's section of the longhouse is generally indistinguishable from that of anybody else, the Kayan and Kenyah chiefs and other aristocrats occupy much larger sections in the center of the house.

Although 100 years ago the Kayan and Kenyah were strong enough to present a serious challenge to Iban expansion, their power was crushed by a large-scale and very destructive expedition mounted against them by the Rajah's government in 1863. They were subsequently decimated by disease, by epidemics of cholera and smallpox, and above all by malaria. Their numbers are increasing rapidly once again and in 1970 they totalled more than 20,000.

The Kayan and Kenyah are famous for their singing and dancing, for wood carving, and for elaborate and charming beadwork. They follow the same pattern of life as the Iban, planting hill padi and brewing rice beer for festive occasions although the latter, known as borak, is far more bitter than the Iban tuak.

As with other longhouse communities, the Kayan-Kenyah longhouses are in some places tending to break up, a move that is regretted by some and advocated by others. Certainly a well-knit longhouse is a very advanced form of social organism where people cooperate with one another and where no one is ever lonely. However, even the best longhouse is left empty for much of the year when the people are in their farming huts in the padi fields. These generally lie at a considerable distance from the house. The longhouse no longer serves any defensive purpose, and although an administrative convenience for chiefs and government, it tends to act as a brake on progress, instilling uniformity and retarding the development of individual ideas. One of its greatest defects is the regularity with which longhouses burn down, destroying in the process all the property of its occupants. The longhouse is unlikely to disappear from the Sarawak scene, but it is gradually decreasing in importance.

In the Kayan-Kenyah areas live small groups of people known variously as Penan and Punan. There is argument about the correct terminology but in general it may be said that the Punan are settled people living a life that is very similar to that of the Kayan and Kenyah. The Penan are a jungle-living people who live by hunting and collecting jungle produce. Their principal foodstuff is wild sago. They exchange the produce for such things as cloth, salt, tobacco, matches, and ammunition through the medium of certain Kayan and Kenyah chiefs. They are tending to break away from their jungle life and to form permanent settlements. They are skilled craftsmen, making excellent parangs (swords), blowpipes, and fine mats, and their services are much in demand though liable to be exploited. The Penan still make some use of the blowpipe and poison darts, but they are increasingly acquiring shotguns. Manufacturing the blowpipe is a very skilled process since it involves the accurate boring out of a piece of selected timber five to six feet long.

At the head of the Baram, living largely in a beautiful vale 3,000 feet above sea level, are the Kelabit, a distinct, small group of people who are some of the best agriculturists in Sarawak. They plant large areas of both irrigated and hill rice. They are tall and energetic people possessing considerable wealth in buffaloes and ancient Chinese jars which have been laboriously carried up from the coast in days gone by.

Chinese jars, some of them hundreds of years old, are in fact objects of value throughout Sarawak, though nowadays their value is declining. They are generally tall, brown jars, often decorated with figures of dragons and are by no means attractive to western eyes. But their age and scarcity renders them valuable, and from the practical point of view they are excellent containers for brewing rice beer.

At the end of the war Australian forces landed by parachute in the Kelabit country and the Kelabit played a particularly worthy part in operations against the Japanese. At that time the Kelabit were so isolated that only a tiny handful could even speak Malay. Today they are some of the most progressive and education-conscious people in the state.

Related to the Kelabit and living not far away in the valley of the Trusan are the Lun Bawang. When we were in Sarawak they were referred to as Murut, but this is now considered to be a derogatory term. The Lun Bawang are also sometimes known as Lun Dayeh. They are a medium-sized group who are also very successful padi planters and rich in terms of buffaloes and cattle. They are amongst the most devout Christians in the state and by far the most dedicated teetotallers. Until the early 1930s the Lun Bawang were in a state of decline. They were pagans and notorious dipsomaniacs, converting their abundant rice crops into vast quantities of borak. Drunkenness was so universal and the results so squalid and degrading that when Christianity was introduced into the Trusan, at first by evangelists from the then Dutch side and later by Australian missionaries of the Borneo Evangelical Mission, virtually the entire population was rapidly converted and entirely abandoned the drinking of alcohol. Their conversion in the 1930s probably saved the Lun Bawang from extinction; nevertheless its rapidity and the utter repudiation of alcohol are remarkable by any standards.

In a remote corner of Lawas District in extreme northern Sarawak are a small community of Tagal, people related to the Lun Bawang, though their language and customs are different. They are best known for the curious sprung dancing floors in their longhouses. Their numbers in Sarawak were insignificant. There are much larger numbers of Tagal in the neighboring state of Sabah, where they were known as Murut.

There are only two other indigenous groups in Sarawak, the Kedayan and the Bisaya. The Kedayan probably number about 10,000 and are confined to the 4th and 5th Divisions. They are Muslims and perhaps of Javanese extraction. Tradition says that they were brought to Borneo by one of the early Sultans of Brunei. There are a considerable number in Brunei. They live in small farming communities and resemble Malays in appearance. They provided the backbone for the Brunei revolt of December 1962 which spilled over into the adjoining areas of Sarawak.

The Bisaya are a small group living in the Limbang valley with a few more in the Baram. There are larger numbers in Sabah and Brunei. They live on the alluvial flats and own large numbers of buffaloes. Their exact relationship with other groups remains uncertain. It is possible that they are related to the Visaya of the southern Philippines. It is also said that they have certain language features in common with the Kadazan of Sabah and with the Melanau.

Many of the Sarawak peoples have immigrated to the state. The most recent immigrants are the Chinese although today the vast majority—probably more than eighty percent—have been born in Sarawak. The Chinese, said to number 294,020 in 1970, have come from all over south China. The original immigrants settled in the state as traders, gold miners, and farmers. The earliest arrivals were Hokkien and Teochew from Amoy and Swatow, who were traders and came by sea, and Hakka gold miners who came by land from the neighboring gold-producing areas of Sambas in Indonesian Borneo, where they had established themselves in the eighteenth century. Other groups followed: Hailam from Hainan Island who specialized in the restaurant and coffee shop business; Cantonese who have undertaken much pepper planting; and the last comers, Foochow, who came to plant padi but took up rubber planting instead and have since become prominent in the timber industry.

The Chinese are both urban dwellers and farmers and are to be found in every District in Sarawak. Although restricted in the amount of land they can acquire, they are the most efficient and skilled agriculturists in the state and have undertaken much rubber and pepper planting. Retail trade is almost entirely in their hands as is the export of agricultural commodities. They do not, however, have such a large interest in the import business. They provide a large proportion of the professional men and women and of the public servants.

The European population of Sarawak is small, consisting of businessmen and oil industry technicians, a few technical and professional officers still in the government service, educationists, and missionaries. There is also a small Indian population, most of whom are employed in the government service or work as traders in textiles or as restaurant proprietors.

Until recently Sarawak was not a rich territory and despite periodic booms, beliefs that it was always proved illusory. But valuable oil and timber resources exist and are now being exploited. As mentioned earlier, the soils of the state are generally poor. Despite the large areas of land available, it is not even self-sufficient in rice production. The peoples of the interior nearly all plant hill rice but relatively few villages produce enough for their own domestic needs. There are some fertile alluvial areas where irrigated rice can be grown successfully but most of the swamplands are either too wet or have a great depth of peat which is entirely unsuitable for rice cultivation. The development of additional irrigated rice lands is possible but it is very expensive, calling for much costly drainage and irrigation work. Sarawak regularly imports quantities of rice from West Malaysia, Thailand, and mainland China.

The only other wetland crop is sago. The commercial sago palm grows extensively in marshy places where there are alluvial soils (it will not grow on peat), and in the past it has been an important export crop. Nowadays sago flour is still exported in considerable quantities, but prices are low and the livelihood of sago producers is a depressed one. Sago starch has certain special qualities and it is possible that improved processing might bring substantially higher prices, but although such improvements have been talked of for many years, they have never been achieved in practice. A smaller species of jungle sago is an important source of food in some parts of the interior.

Rubber grows well in Sarawak and is the mainstay of the rural economy. It is an almost ideal crop for smallholders because of its hardiness and comparatively long life. It is readily tapped and processed. Unfortunately, the quality and yield of most Sarawak rubber is low. There are no large estates; the Brookes discouraged large-scale alienation of land to foreign investors. Although there is a considerable scheme for the subsidized planting of high-yielding rubber, which is also being planted on new land development schemes, it has yet to be shown that most Sarawak farmers have the necessary skill to make good use of high-yielding trees. These are far more delicate than the common, low-yielding seedling rubber. Even at low prices, however, rubber must remain the main cash crop for country people in Sarawak. Production of rubber fluctuates greatly in accordance with its price.

Pepper grows well and is planted mainly by Chinese. But it is a high cost, intensive crop whose price fluctuates wildly. It is also very destructive in its effect on the land where it has been cultivated.

Valuable tropical crops such as tea and cocoa are now being planted in small quantities. Some soils are suitable for oil palms in the 4th and 5th Divisions but they are not extensive. Furthermore, oil palm cultivation calls for very expensive factory installations.

Timber is by far the most valuable produce of the land, but most of the timber is exported as logs and this brings benefits to only a limited section of the population. Exports of timber have vastly increased since 1963, but it is open to question as to how long the Sarawak forests will be able to sustain production at the current rate. Periodically the forests produce great quantities of a valuable nut, rich in vegetable oil, called the Illipe Nut or Engkabang. Unfortunately, the nut-bearing trees only set fruit profusely at irregular intervals.

Agricultural development is complicated by the land system. In order to ensure that Natives did not dispose of excessive amounts of land to the energetic Chinese element of the population, the latter have only been permitted to acquire land in what is known as the Mixed Zone, which covers an area of about 4,000 square miles. In the Mixed Zone, people of all races can acquire leasehold title to land, though much of the Zone remains under customary tenure. In addition there are some 2,500 square miles of Native Area land where only Natives can acquire title. In the rest of Sarawak no titles are issued and apart from 11,000 square miles of forest reserves most of the land is held under customary tenure, the right to use the land belonging to the descendants of the man who originally felled the jungle. No land rights are conceded over primary forest.

This policy has protected Natives from disposing of their main assets to non-Natives but it has also meant that many Chinese farmers have had genuine farming activities restricted; it has meant that the cash value of Native land is very low; and it has meant that there is a good deal of illegal leasing of Native land, mainly for pepper, to Chinese who, however, have little interest in keeping such land in good heart. They use it and pay very high rents until the fertility of the soil is exhausted. They then move elsewhere.

Sarawak's main source of mineral wealth consists of petroleum. A small oilfield at Miri in the 4th Division was worked for many years but has now been exhausted. Since the early part of this decade, however, considerable quantities of oil—about 5,000,000 tons per year—have been won from offshore fields and a large field of natural gas lying off Bintulu is being exploited.

Otherwise mineral resources are very limited. Gold, antimony, mercury, and coal have been worked and a little gold is still produced. A small bauxite deposit on the coast of the 1st Division was exploited for a time after the war but is no longer worked.

Industrial production is small and Sarawak's small internal market and expensive sea communications with other countries make it unlikely that any substantial development will take place in the foreseeable future.

Written history does not extend very far back in Sarawak, but archaeological investigations have shown that the state has, in fact, been inhabited since a very early period of man's evolution. The evidence for this comes largely from the limestone caves at Niah in northern Sarawak where abundant evidence has been uncovered of various phases of human occupation dating from perhaps 40,000 BC to the immediate pre-Christian era. Here not only have human remains been unearthed but also remarkable numbers of stone tools. Some of the more recent phases of human occupation are characterized by long-hidden wall paintings and ships of the dead. In all probability, similar remains at one time existed in other Sarawak caves, but the evidence has been destroyed in recent times through the removal of bat guano.

Later evidence of human activity has been unearthed on the coast, particularly at Santubong at the mouth of the Sarawak River. Here there are indications of Indian and Chinese trading contacts which archaeologists believe to date from about the sixth to the eleventh centuries of the Christian era. The existence of many Chinese jars at burial sites shows that trading contacts continued for many centuries. This continued until the arrival of western influence and the harsh and restrictive trading practices of western nations. These practices disrupted the former extensive and peaceful trading connections across the South China Sea and converted prosperous trading communities in the island world of Southeast Asia into nests of pirates since orderly trading was no longer profitable.

The picture which emerges for the first 1500 years or so of the Christian era is of growing trading contacts. These were mainly with Chinese but also with Indian and Arab traders. A sparse but active population of largely jungle dwellers traded jungle resins, rhinoceros horns, hornbill casques, monkey gallstones, fine hardwoods and rattans, and probably some gold dust in exchange for cloth and jars, iron and ornamental beads, and other goods. Such trading probably took place at the mouths of many of the rivers but only a few sites are known.

With the arrival of Islam and the establishment of a strong Sultanate in Brunei the picture began to change. Brunei became the paramount power in the area. This power did not extend inland but Brunei came to control the trading posts and river mouths. Some trade with China continued.

While the Brunei were establishing their authority on the coast and converting some of the coastal peoples to Islam, the great Iban and Kayan-Kenyah migrations were taking place inland, destroying or absorbing many of the former much less organized occupants of the land. Sago starch became a valuable export from some of the rivers, and pepper and gambier (a vegetable extract used for tanning which is no longer cultivated) were planted by Chinese planters.

Brunei power declined steadily from its peak in the sixteenth century. Although nominal control of the Sarawak coast continued, it came to be exercised largely by semi-independent Malay chiefs, many of part Arab blood. Trade became increasingly difficult though some trading contacts with the people of the interior continued. Slaves captured by the war parties of the expanding Kayan-Kenyah confederacy and by the Iban groups became an increasingly important article of trade. From the Baram the Kayan devastated the Limbang valley and the Iban put to sea and so extended greatly the range of their operations. The Chinese traders disappeared and European trading vessels ran great risks when they ventured into Bornean waters, not only from open piracy by the people of the coast, but also from the activities of pirates coming from the Sulu Islands and Mindanao.

This was the position in the 1830s when the Brunei Governor of Sarawak was Pengiran Makhota. In 1836 a rebellion against Brunei rule broke out among Sarawak Malays and Land Dayaks of the hinterland led by a prominent Sarawak Malay chief, Datu Patinggi Ali. The Sultan's uncle, Rajah Muda Hassim, was sent to Kuching to pacify the country although Pengiran Makhota retained his governorship. Rajah Muda Hassim was unable to restore order, and it was at this point, in August 1839, that an English adventurer, James Brooke, arrived in Kuching.

Brooke was thirty-six at the time. As a young man he had served in the East India Company's army and had been severely wounded in the first Burmese war. He later visited China and the Malay peninsula. By nature a romantic and an adventurer, he made up his mind to seek his fortune in Asia after his father died in 1835 and left him an inheritance of £30,000. He set out from England in his yacht *Royalist* in 1838.

During a visit to Kuching in 1839 he was well received by Rajah Muda Hassim, but after touring the coastal areas of what is now the 1st Division, he sailed on to Sulawesi (Celebes). He returned to Sarawak a year later and at this time helped to secure the submission of the rebel leaders. Disagreements with Makhota followed. Makhota was removed and in 1841 Brooke was himself installed as Rajah of Sarawak, his authority extending from Tanjong Datu to the Samarahan River. Brooke enjoyed the support of the Sarawak Malays and in 1842 reinstated their chiefs, or Datus, who had so recently been in rebellion against the authority of Brunei. Later in the same year his appointment as Rajah was confirmed by the Sultan of Brunei. Such was the small beginning of Brooke rule.

Although Brooke enjoyed the support of the Sarawak Malays and the Land Dayak peoples, the problems of piracy, the depredations of the Suluk and Illanun from the Philippines and the Iban war parties, together with the intrigues of Brunei chiefs who feared an extension of his authority, would probably have been too much for his slender resources had he not been able to enlist the support of the Royal Navy. Piracy being a threat to British commerce in the South China Sea, Captain Keppel of the ship *Dido* gave Brooke naval support in actions against the Iban of Skrang and Saribas in 1843. Such support continued for several years but was almost entirely withdrawn after a major engagement off the mouth of the Kalaka River in 1849. In this engagement a large Iban war party was trapped by the forces of Brooke supported by two Royal Navy ships and was defeated with severe loss of life.

This marked a turning point in Brooke's career. He had become a popular hero in England and had been knighted in 1847, but he now became the object of attack by a section of the opposition Liberal Party. This attack, by parliamentarians led by Joseph Hume and by the newly formed Aboriginal Protection Society, was one outcome of the 1849 engagement off the Kalaka River. Another was the Royal Navy's claim for £20,000. This was in accordance with the naval regulations of the day, at a rate of £20 for every pirate killed and £5 for every pirate said to have been present at the Kalaka engagement. The Royal Navy eventually received these rewards, but naval support for Brooke in Sarawak was withdrawn while the personal attacks on his name left him disappointed and embittered.

However, Sarawak was now sufficiently well organized to stand on its own feet. The Iban of Skrang and Saribas made their peace with the Rajah and many of these hitherto hostile peoples became loyal supporters of the regime. With solid Malay backing the Brookes were in future always able to enlist enough Iban support to overcome any opposition, although the state was nearly overthrown in 1859 when the Chinese gold miners of Bau District rebelled and succeeded in capturing the capital. The area from Sadong to Kalaka was ceded to Brooke by the Sultan of Brunei in 1853 and a large extension from the Rejang to Kidurong Point beyond Bintulu in 1861. Sarawak was recognized by Britain as an independent state in 1863. James Brooke died in England in 1868.

He was by any count a remarkable man. Although an adventurer out to make a place for himself in the world, he was also a man of high principles with a great capacity for arousing the affection and respect of those who knew him. He was unbusinesslike, autocratic, and resentful of opposition, but at the same time he was a brave and jovial man with real understanding and sympathy for the Asians with whom he came into contact. He was a gradualist who sought to change practices of which he disapproved, such as slavery, by persuasion and rational argument. Contemporary accounts leave no doubt as to the affection and regard in which he was held.

His successor and nephew, Charles Brooke, was a very different man. He was the son of James Brooke's sister and had changed his name to Brooke by deed poll. Born in 1829, he had joined the Navy at the early age of twelve and had seen active service in Borneo waters. He joined his uncle in 1852, seeing much service in small outposts, particularly in the 2nd Division. He was the virtual ruler of Sarawak after 1863 when James Brooke left the state for the last time.

Charles Brooke was a hard, self-educated, austere man (though with a healthy appreciation of pretty women). He was devoted to Sarawak and its people. He was not an easy man to work for but to a remarkable extent enjoyed the respect of his officers.

Under his strong rule Sarawak continued to progress in very much the same way as it had during the latter years of James. There were periodic clashes with Iban, generally to suppress outbreaks of tribal warfare. The pattern of suppression was always the same. An expedition would be mounted, commanded by a handful of European officers and with a core of Malay levies or a detachment of the Sarawak Rangers, an early para-military force. The force would be supplemented by numbers of unpaid Iban volunteers from another river or group who would take part in the expedition for the excitement and the loot which they could acquire. Generally the loss of life was small, but the houses of the rebels would be looted and burned and the people scattered. This was generally followed by formal submission.

In retrospect it was not an attractive system and some highly destructive expeditions were carried out by Native Chiefs without any supervision whatever. But it was in fact the only system open to a small and poor state which did not have the resources to maintain permanent security forces. The number of European officers was tiny. Much of the administration was in the hands of the almost entirely Malay junior administrative service.

Despite the periodic expeditions, the state was a peaceful and stable one, with a high degree of personal security for its inhabitants and a steadily developing economy. There were further extensions of the state's borders at the expense of Brunei. The extensive Baram valley was ceded in 1883 and the Trusan, on Brunei Bay, in 1885. Limbang was ceded in 1890. Finally Lawas District was acquired from the British North Borneo Chartered Company in 1905. It was certainly the intention of Charles Brooke to absorb the remainder of Brunei, with the possible exception of Brunei Town. In 1899 the people of Belait (today the site of Brunei's great oil industry) and Tutong rose in revolt against the Sultan and invited the Rajah to occupy their districts. The British government, however, decided otherwise and instead installed a British Resident in Brunei Town in 1905.

In 1869 the Rajah had married a young and attractive girl called Margaret de Windt. There are some grounds for believing that James Brooke had suggested that his nephew marry Margaret's mother, a rich widow, but whatever the truth of this, Charles opted for the daughter. They were in most ways an ill-matched couple, the husband a hard and autocratic man, the wife young enough to be his daughter, gifted, vivacious, and artistic. They had several children, the first three dying tragically of cholera at a tender age. Three sons survived.

Rajah Charles remained active until almost the end of his long life, dying in England in 1917. He had hoped to be buried in Sarawak, in Simanggang, but the wish was not honored by his successor.

He was one of the most unusual and in his way one of the greatest Englishmen to play a part in the affairs of Southeast Asia. The country which he ruled was a small one, but few men gave more devoted service to an Asian people or had more progressive ideas. Although a stern man, he had remarkably enlightened and liberal views. He was described by his children's tutor in 1887 as an extremely nice and kind man, "but a fearful radical." He detested the flag-waving manifestations of latter-day imperialism and in 1907, in the evening of his life and the heyday of the British Empire, he wrote: "All our possessions are too much Anglicised. Where good and friendly feelings—I might almost say love—existed in the early part of the last century, when black and white were combined in feeling, there has been a falling-off, a separation, in consequence of the English developing into higher civilisation—as it is termed—among themselves with wives and families and European luxuries, and so it has happened that though we govern, we only do so by power, and not by friendly intercourse of feeling. My own opinion is that before we reach the middle of the century all nations now holding large Colonial possessions will have met with severe reverses."

The last of the Rajahs, Vyner Brooke, received the conventional education of a young English gentleman at Winchester and Trinity College, Cambridge. He was good looking, lighthearted, shy, and rather weak. He was different in almost every respect from his father, except perhaps that they both appreciated attractive women. His brother, Bertram Brooke, on whom he came to rely very greatly, was a very much stronger personality.

Vyner Brooke joined the Sarawak service in 1897 and saw service in all parts of the state. But there was little love lost between the young Vyner and his father, and Charles' last years were marred by some ugly personal squabbles with his heir. When the third Rajah finally succeeded his father in 1917, he had been well groomed for the post, having a wide knowledge of his country. Sarawak was peaceful and prosperous, despite feeling the strain of the great depression. There was the occasional outbreak of headhunting, which was dealt with in the traditional manner (the last expeditions took place in the 1930s).

But although quiet and prosperous, it was to a large extent a period of stagnation. Sarawak went to sleep. The government continued to operate in the traditional manner, with some innovations introduced, particularly in the administration of the law, but the Rajah lacked the drive and the ideas of his predecessors. The atmosphere was easy going, punctuated by periodic purges of officials who became too independent.

The Rajah's main contribution to new thinking lay in the constitution, which he granted at the time of the centenary celebrations in 1941. Under the constitution the Rajah divested himself of his supreme powers. Council Negri, an advisory body which had existed since 1867, was given legislative and financial control, and the Rajah undertook in future to govern with the advice and consent of a Supreme Council. Membership of the new Council Negri was entirely by appointment, but it marked a major step forward in political development.

However, less than one month after the new Council Negri had met for the first time, the Pacific War broke out. Miri was occupied by the Japanese on December 16, 1941 and Kuching on December 24.

The Japanese occupation was a very unhappy period. The Japanese had neither the resources nor the capacity to provide a fair and efficient government. The entire population suffered severely. All the Europeans were interned and many lost their lives. The few who sought to remain at liberty were either rounded up or killed. Sarawak was eventually liberated by the Australian forces in September 1945 with the help of an active partisan movement amongst the peoples of the state.

The Rajah, who had spent the war years in Australia, was now seventy-one, a tired and disillusioned man. His three children were all girls and the heir apparent was Anthony Brooke, the son of his brother Bertram (the third brother, Harry Brooke, died in 1926 and played no part in Sarawak affairs). There had been serious differences between the Rajah and his brother and nephew. The Rajah decided that the best thing to do was to wind up the period of Brooke rule and cede the state to the British Crown. Apart from any personal considerations, the Rajah appreciated correctly that in the postwar period he would lack the resources to provide Sarawak with the services and the development which it would need.

After some tortuous and regrettably discreditable negotiations, the Cession Bill was approved by a narrow majority in Council Negri, entirely through the votes of appointed European officers. As a result Sarawak became a British Crown Colony on July 1, 1946. It was probably the right decision but certainly taken in the wrong way. It was opposed by a large section of the Malay community with eventually tragic results.

After cession the Rajah played no further part in Sarawak affairs and indeed cut himself off from all contact except with a handful of his old officers. His regime was not the most distinguished in Sarawak's history, but it would be unjust to be overly critical. The 1941 Constitution was a genuinely enlightened move and not the result of political pressures. He handed over the state with all its considerable funds and reserves intact. The Rajah died in 1963, shortly before the establishment of Malaysia.

Brooke rule had its good points and its bad. Sarawak had something of the qualities of a well-run English country estate with a good relationship between the squire and the tenantry. In social matters there was much to be commended. Good communal relations existed and there was a good and direct relationship between European and Asian. The worst feature of Brooke rule was the failure to appreciate the need for education. The only government schools were for Malays and were of a poor standard. The Chinese were left to organize their own schools to the long-term detriment of that community since it induced a considerable measure of separate development and encouraged Chinese racial parochialism.

The missions ran schools, some of which were of good quality. Most of the pupils were Chinese. There was no proper development of Native education and this meant that the state was to enter the postwar years of rapid change almost entirely unprovided with a balanced and educated elite.

Sarawak's first years as a colony were marred by the dispute over cession. This had been resented by many Malays who had constituted the governing class under the Brookes. Nearly all the Native members of Council Negri had voted against cession. A movement came to center around the person of the Rajah's nephew, Anthony Brooke, and a large number of Malay officers resigned from the government service.

The first British Governor was Sir Charles Arden Clark, a man of strong personality and long colonial experience gained in Africa. During his governorship there was considerable material and administrative progress and the foundations were laid for educational, economic, and local government development. The cession movement was not suppressed but the issue was treated as closed. Cession was in fact acceptable to the vast majority of the non-Malay population, but it caused deep divisions and bitterness in the Malay community.

This was the state of affairs when I came to be appointed as a Colonial Service Cadet to serve in Sarawak at the end of 1947.

2

EARLY DAYS—SARIKEI AND BINATANG

Like so many of the good things of life, going to Sarawak was not a planned affair. After I had been demobilized in 1947, I had expected to be appointed as a government Public Relations Officer in Hong Kong where I had spent my last period of army service. But when I applied to the Colonial Office, I was told that the post I sought had been given to the PRO in Aden but that I could probably have his job if I wanted it. This offer had no allure and I applied for an administrative post in Asia. Having firmly, if brashly, indicated that I would not accept a post in Africa where most vacancies existed even if I did not get one at all, I was lucky to be offered an appointment in Sarawak and accepted it with alacrity, though I knew very little about the territory. And so it was that my wife Hedda and I arrived in Kuching early in November 1947.

Our first view of Borneo was shortly after daybreak, our ship quietly at anchor just within the entrance to the Sarawak River at Muara Tebas, a broad stream with sunlight playing on brown water, the banks lined by stands of graceful Nipa Palms backed by faraway blue mountains.

From Muara Tebas to Kuching takes several hours. In those days the Sarawak Steamship vessels docked almost in the middle of Kuching town. The business and shopping area of the town was on the right bank, the Malay kampongs on the left bank, with the Astana, or Government House, on higher ground almost opposite the Steamship Company wharf. The town itself had narrow winding streets of Chinese shophouses with the dignified, old-fashioned single-story government offices near the river bank.

We were very kindly received in Kuching. We were the guests of the Chief Secretary, R.G. Aikman and Mrs. Aikman in the Chief Secretary's fine old rambling mansion, an immense two-story structure built mostly of ironwood, the floors polished with coconut husks to a mirror-like and extremely slippery finish. From our vast bedroom we descended to the bathroom by hazardous ladder-way. There was modern sanitation but no hot water. We bathed in the traditional manner—dipping cold water out of a tub and pouring it over ourselves.

Aikman was a kind host and very willing to answer the innumerable questions which Hedda and I fired at him. He had come to Sarawak in 1925 and had served in many Districts. He had an encyclopedic memory and a special interest in the Melanau peoples of the coast. During internment by the Japanese it had been his responsibility to pass on to the camp inmates the world news obtained from a secret radio. Nothing was ever committed to writing. Aikman was told the news and it was his task to recount it verbally.

Those first few days passed quickly. We met many of my colleagues and were taken to the club, and we hired a car and drove along the poor little road which led to the first longhouse we were to see, a big Land Dayak settlement at a place called Benuk, some twenty miles from Kuching. In those days roads were almost nonexistent. Apart from the road we took, there were others—little more than tracks—to the District Headquarters of Bau and Serian. Nearly all travel in Sarawak was by water.

We ourselves were quickly shipped off to Sibu, the capital of the 3rd Division, on our way to my first permanent posting in the Lower Rejang at Sarikei. We left Kuching in the evening in an uncomfortable little vessel built for northern climes. Early next morning we were in Sarikei, a small bazaar on a swampy promontory between two left-bank tributaries of the Rejang. Bob Snelus, the District Officer I was to serve under, was away traveling and so we made our way to Sibu after a stop at another little bazaar called Binatang.

The Rejang is an immense river draining a vast area of high rainfall country. Where it debouches in the sea it has built up a great delta of swamplands through which emerges the occasional patch of higher ground. Sibu, itself built on swampland, is where the delta commences. The area was originally almost totally unpopulated and is the stronghold of the Foochow Chinese who were introduced by a Methodist missionary at the turn of the century. The idea was that they would plant rice, but after a hard struggle to survive, the Foochow found that they could do much better planting rubber. From this they have prospered mightily and have now branched out into every kind of business, especially the timber business.

Sibu was the administrative capital of the 3rd Division under the control of a Resident who was responsible to the Chief Secretary. The various Departments—Medical, Education, Public Works, Land, and so on—all had representatives here. The Resident, John Barcroft, had newly arrived to take over the post from an officer of almost equal seniority, John Fisher, who remained as District Officer. We stayed in the resthouse and I was given the job of inspecting Chinese schools in the District, which I did by bicycle.

The Chinese Chamber of Commerce gave a dinner to welcome the new Resident and to bid farewell to the District Officer Philip Jacks who was being transferred to the 2nd Division. The Chinese Chambers of Commerce are the best of hosts and in Sibu there was a tradition of heavy drinking. It proved to be a highly alcoholic evening. The tradition was of long standing. In prewar days it had been a rule that no officer could leave the Island Club in Sibu until the Resident left. On Saturdays everyone adjourned to the Club after work and there were times when the Resident did not leave until Monday morning. I am glad I never had to endure such idiocies. At Chamber of Commerce dinners the hard-drinking members of the Chinese community—of whom there were more than a few—were put beside the Europeans; the non-drinkers watched patiently. There were innumerable speeches. I was myself called on to address the dinner in Chinese, of which my command is less than marginal. It was at the height of the anti-cession controversy and one of the guests was Mrs. Anthony Brooke, the charming wife of the Rajah's dispossessed heir. Her husband was barred from Sarawak, but she had been permitted to tour the country and was the Resident's guest. Barcroft called on her for a speech—hardly a judicious move—and John Fisher kept telling him to sit down and stop being a bloody fool. Mrs. Brooke did the sensible thing and thanked the Chamber of Commerce for a very nice dinner. The Superintendent of Police stood up to make a speech and was literally speechless. Though not by any means a teetotaller, I began to wonder what sort of a place I had come to. A few days later we moved down to Sarikei.

Here we lived in one of a pair of large bungalows on the first hillock behind the swampland on which the settlement is built. Behind each bungalow was a large water tank to hold the rain water, there being no piped water in the station at that time. The DO Snelus and his young wife Margot lived in the other bungalow. The bungalows looked out over rubber gardens planted on the peat land. Rubber grows quite well for a time on peat, but drainage causes the peat to shrink, leaving the roots exposed and subject to salt water flooding. Although the Foochow Chinese settlers had prospered planting rubber, the peat land is only good for one crop and even then only when the trees are young. When the trees grow old the yield is poor and the land is never of much use for anything else. The only other peat land crops are pineapples, green-skinned oranges, and pomelos planted on mounds of peat.

In front of our bungalows there was a narrow road which in those days ran for a few miles inland. It was little more than a mud track but brought the Chinese gardeners to market and to do business in the settlement. Some Iban also used the road, always walking in single file, a habit derived from the narrow paths of the areas in which they live.

I went to work in the long, low, government office. Snelus sat at one end and I at the other, next to the Senior Native Officer, Morshidi, with the various clerks and departmental officers in between. Life at first was not too easy—my relations with the DO being somewhat distant. He was a capable and experienced officer who had joined the Rajah's service some years before the war. Later we were to become good friends, but at first he seemed to resent having as his first Cadet a man almost as old as himself. I was told little but had to find out for myself. Snelus had been DO in Simanggang, the capital of the 2nd Division, when the Pacific War broke out. He could easily have made his escape through Dutch Borneo as several others did, but it was his duty to stay at his post and stay he did until captured by the Japanese. He was devoted to Sarawak and I learned a great deal about administration through watching him at work.

I had a much closer and warmer relationship with Morshidi, a small, chubby man in the Native Officer's Service—the junior administrative service staffed largely by Malays which provided the Rajah's government with much of its organizational strength. He had previously been in the clerical service. He was patient and good-natured, with a ready sense of humor. He it was who first took me traveling and it was through his wise, kindly, and humorous eyes that I formed many of my first and most formative impressions of Sarawak. Morshidi was a man of modesty and compassion. His wife was the adopted daughter of an old English mining engineer who, about a year after I went to Sarikei, fell on evil times and suffered a stroke which rendered him entirely paralyzed. The Morshidis cared for him with the utmost kindness and devotion for the rest of his life.

The work was certainly not arduous. I had to check account books and deal with applications for travel documents and land transfers and, in theory, to supervize the local jail and even the police. The latter, at the time, was a poorly developed service. The jail was small but generally had a few inmates. The old and humane traditions of the Rajah's government still applied. A jail sentence was a period of unpaid work for the Government. There was no stigma attached. Once, before the war, a prisoner ran away from the Sarikei jail and the DO sent the other prisoners off to bring him back. There was one escape during my stay in Sarikei, by a young Dayak who had not been properly brought up. The warder was deeply affronted. The escapee crawled through a ditch, though he could more readily have walked out of the front door which was rarely closed.

We started to get to know the area, sometimes walking, sometimes bicycling along the small paths built and maintained by the Chinese gardeners—Chinese smallholders are for some reason never referred to as farmers but always as gardeners. I collected a few birds to familiarize myself with an avifauna new to me, and Hedda rigged up a little makeshift darkroom and found much to interest herself in the everyday affairs of the District.

Some of her earliest studies were of a Foochow pepper gardener called Ngu Ee King, who had a small village shop and some 500 pepper vines about three miles up the road. Pepper is one of the traditional crops of Sarawak; it grows extremely well there and has a particularly fine flavor. It is made from the berries of a creeper which is trained to grow up hardwood posts. Black pepper is the berry after it has been dried; white pepper has the skin or pericarp first removed by soaking the berries in

Ngu Ee King in his village shop near Sarikei.
A 12-bore shotgun did wonders for his fortune.

water. The plant needs to be well tended and the vines had largely died out during the war. There were only a few thousand vines in Sarawak in 1947 and Ngu Ee King had one of the best gardens.

I was of some small service to Ngu in getting him a shotgun, which he said he needed to protect his padi farm against pigs and monkeys. He did extremely well out of pepper, hit the top of the Korean war commodity boom, got out of the crop before it slumped, and went into the textile importing business. The reward of his industry was a degree of modest affluence, and he was able to send his children overseas to be educated.

We called on him not long before we left Sarawak—he has since died—and reminisced over days gone by. I reminded him of the gun which he had needed to protect his padi farm. Ngu chuckled. "It was not the padi," he said, "it was the pepper. I had great difficulty because thieves were always stealing my pepper cuttings. But after you helped me to get that gun I had no more trouble with thieves."

Melanau girl of Kampong Rejang

Our first tour took place not long after we arrived in Sarikei. I was sent, with Morshidi, to conduct the annual boards of survey in three small sub-district offices at Rejang, Daro, and Matu. The Annual Board of Survey was a sacred ritual of British colonial administration. No matter how unwisely you might have celebrated New Year's Eve, the very next day you counted the cash and the postage stamps and in large stations all sorts of stores to see that what was held tallied with the books. I always questioned its usefulness—everything was always in order—but it was a duty that had to be done.

We took the launch assigned to the District, a squat, roomy, thirty-eight foot Australian workboat with a crew of four and went downriver to Rejang near the river's mouth. The sub-district office was in those days a tumbledown office adjoining a large Melanau kampong. Morshidi and I checked the books, and Hedda wandered off into the kampong and took some portraits of quite delightful girls. We then went on through narrow, Nipa Palm-lined channels to Daro, which lies on another branch of the Rejang to the north. It was a muddy place and often flooded, but it catered for an important padi-producing area. That night we were treated to an extraordinary display of fireflies.

The next morning we continued to Matu, a much larger place and at one time an important District Headquarters, though this was discontinued after the Foochow settled in Sarikei and Binatang. There was an enormous, gloomy half-ruined DO's house some way downriver from the settlement. It was thought to be haunted—the last DO went out of his mind there—and the launch crew and our servant hated to stay there. We normally camped out in the old Court Room.

Matu is a very pretty place even though it is in a swamp. The fast-flowing stream is chocolate brown in color, contrasting with the lush, vivid green foliage and the generally calm blue sky. We often visited there later. The people worked sago—trampling the rasped pith and pouring water over it to extract the starch—and planted padi.

Launch trips were always fun. To have a substantial launch and a crew of four may seem a trifle extravagant but that traditionally was the way one traveled in the downriver areas of Sarawak. Apart from the government boats, there were innumerable Chinese launches—many of them fine, stately, two deckers—which operated very efficient services up and down all the larger rivers. They were slow—always stopping at little landing places made of floating logs which rose and fell with the stream level. Hedda made many trips on them and I too when we traveled on locally taken leaves. On the smaller streams travel was by outboard-powered longboat or prahu. The building of prahus is a most ingenious process. Starting with a log of suitably durable timber, the builder roughly shapes the sides and scoops out the middle until the log looks like a trough. Then comes the highly skilled part. Fires are lit against the sides and this causes the wood to warp outwards. As this happens stout wooden cross-members are inserted to hold the new shape. When the heat process has been completed the shell has assumed its final shape. For small prahus the shell alone may be used, but generally plank sides are built on so as to provide freeboard. For the largest boats a roof is added. It is not difficult to attach an outboard engine at the rear but the boats vary greatly in stability. On the main rivers speedboats made of plywood are much used, but they are useless on small streams where the boat must often be dragged through shallow reaches.

It was in a longboat that I set off with Morshidi to make my first Dayak tour after I had been in Sarikei for about seven months. I was really very much of a passenger for, although I had by then learned to speak a little Malay, I had no Iban and this was the language one needed to work efficiently among that people. Iban is a dialect of Malay but a very distinct one. Many words are common to both languages but spelled and pronounced differently. Few Iban in those days spoke Malay. They expected government officers to speak to them in their own language and took a poor view of those who did not.

Traveling meant taking the Government to the people. In every house visited you would take a simple census, give medicine and first-aid to those needing it, encourage the people to maintain their houses well, check the presence of visitors and unlicensed traders, settle disputes, and enforce a rule which then existed that no recognized longhouse should contain less than ten families. It was an arbitrary regulation designed for the convenience of government officers and Penghulus—the elected chiefs for a number of longhouses. You warned the houses in advance that you were coming to ensure that as many people as possible were present and you avoided the padi growing season when most of the people were living in their farming huts which are often far from the longhouse.

I still have all my traveling diaries. You would take the Penghulu with you and drive upriver to the first longhouse to be visited. At the landing place you would be met by the headman or Tuai Rumah and generally by a group of his longhouse elders. After shaking hands you would proceed to the longhouse and probably be

Dayak longhouse in the 3rd Division

offered a drink or drinks of tuak, the Iban rice beer, by some of the girls. By Dayak custom it was obligatory to take a little of the tuak, but by the same admirable custom you could pass the glass back to the girl offering it who had then to drink it herself. Then up the often rickety notched log giving access to the longhouse. You would sit down on the section of the communal room belonging to the Tuai Rumah, which was generally decked with all available Iban cotton blankets, a very ornamental form of woven textile. As soon as politeness permitted you would get on with the job of taking the census. This consisted of listing the family head of each door, or family section, of the house and details of how many adults and children there were in each door. You looked at gun licenses and checked the details of visitors. On a properly planned trip, while this was going on, the Dresser you had with you would be holding a clinic. This was always a matter of some difficulty because apart from the genuinely ill, so many others wanted to be given medicine.

Taking the census generally brought out most items of current interest in the house—the husband who had been away traveling for the last year without providing for his wife and family, for example, or land disputes. Many of these were in the jurisdiction of the Penghulu. If he could not settle them on the spot, the parties would generally appear at our nightstop for a fuller hearing. Many requests would come for permission to open village shops which often meant that the applicant was in reality a front man for a Chinese trader. Once the business was completed the Tuai Rumah would generally offer the visitors a drink. The more hospitable the people the more quickly was government business despatched. And so on to the next house. You would try to visit four or so in a day. If there was a lot of business and a lot of tuak it could be a very exhausting process.

Visitors were often given chickens; on very important occasions or at houses which excelled in hospitality you had to spear a wretched pig lying prostrate at the foot of the ladder. Fortunately this did not happen very often—pigs were too valuable. You ate the rice of the house and your cook would produce an instant chicken stew which was generally very tough indeed.

At the nightstop you could take things a little more easily, rest a little, and have a bath, taken at the communal bathing place on the bank of the often muddy river. But subsequently the proceedings would be much more protracted. The more important disputes would be settled in the evening and the most important item of business was often the last to be raised. The DO would sit with the Penghulu. Proceedings were informal and sometimes hectic. An experienced Sarawak Judge used to say that the only rule of court in a longhouse case was that not more than seven men should speak at once. The women played an active and vociferous part in discussions too.

When formal business was completed there would often be a party, with beating of drums and gongs, more tuak, and much stylized war dancing, which no one, no matter how unversed in the art, could avoid. It would probably be the early hours before you could escape to your camp bed, generally put up in the communal room, and the party would probably go on till dawn. It did not greatly matter because you would grow so weary that you could sleep soundly with gongs being beaten within a few feet of your head. Not all longhouses had the resources to entertain on a grand scale, but the hospitality was nearly always of the kindest. Even when all seemed quiet you were liable to have your slumbers interrupted by dogfights and by cocks crowing. Along the walls of the longhouse were generally tethered the treasured fighting cocks. At any time of the night one of these muscular birds was liable to wake up, imagine quite wrongly that it was the dawn and crow loudly. This would awaken all his fellows who in turn would crow. On a quiet night the din could be deafening and then the cocks would go to sleep again more readily than the visitor.

My first day's travel will always remain embedded in my memory. We had with us Penghulu Andin, an elderly and very tall Iban, a dignified countryman with something of the air of a well-regarded English squire. Our first house was Rumah Mambang, quite close to Sarikei Bazaar, a large house of nineteen doors. We did the census and found that one man had moved without paying the customary fine and left his door in disrepair. It was rather a poor community, short of padi, and only half of them owned any rubber, the main generator of cash flow in country areas. The next house was Rumah Engkulau, about the same size. Lively and vociferous people, they were short of padi but were renting out farmland to Chinese. They also had a good deal of skin disease. On for lunch to a small house called Rumah Jilan prettily situated on a hill overlooking the Nyelong River. It was below the regulation ten-door minimum size and the Tuai Rumah was trying to find another family to join.

After lunch we went on to a little temporary house or dampa called Rumah Andin. This was a very prosperous group who had broken away from Rumah Mambang with whom they were in dispute over farming land. The house was far below the regulation size, and the Tuai Rumah gave us a splendid reception with most attractive and well turned out young women wearing their silver and with tuak of most excellent quality flowing freely. I was quickly reduced to the state experienced by those drugged henchmen of the Old Man of the Mountains, persuaded that they had been transported to paradise. I was prepared to stay in Rumah Andin forever, but the less impressionable Morshidi insisted that we had to go. And so I floated out from Rumah Andin to walk to our nightstop Rumah Chuat, having sent the boat ahead. The way led through an interminable swamp along slippery logs and I fell off one and barked my shin most painfully. And then there was a violent downpour of icy rain which soaked us to the skin. It was a rude awakening.

Rumah Chuat was a very large and very prosperous house of twenty-eight doors built largely by Chinese carpenters. Nearly all the doors had rubber. The people had even tried to start their own little school, an unusual initiative in those days, but were unable to find a teacher willing to stay. Morshidi and I were able to get to bed a little after midnight but the Penghulu had no sleep at all. It was his own fault. He had been lazy and had never visited the house, though Penghulus were expected to tour their houses regularly. Consequently there was a great deal of business for him to deal with.

And so it went on for nine days. The Penghulu put on a great reception at his own house where I had to spear a pig and where both Morshidi and I took part in a harvest ceremony to bless the whetstones. At some houses we were paraded in to the beating of gongs; at others we were greeted with the firing of old brass Brunei cannon, which always terrified me because they sometimes blew up. We crossed over into the area of the next Penghulu, Giman, a small, rotund, and energetic businessman and went some way up into the upper reaches of the Sarikei River where the stream was clear and rippling and the people's health generally better than in the muddier reaches further down.

It was the first time that many of these houses had been visited by a European officer since the war, and this to some extent accounted for the rather special nature of the welcome we received. Many little children were brought to see the Tuan and few failed, after one horrified glance, to burst into vociferous lamentations.

In general it set the pattern for many more tours which I had the good fortune to make in Sarawak. A feature of such traveling was that you felt you were traveling among friends. Your personal security was complete. You never carried weapons; you never had a guard. Nothing was ever stolen. If you were wise you never took a policeman with you—they were liable to engage in petty extortion—unless he was a welcome personality, popular in the area, and a jolly traveling companion, or a man going back to his own village for a visit.

I made several such trips in Sarikei and I put it to the DO that I should be able to take Hedda with me on my travels. This had never been the custom in Sarawak although there was no regulation forbidding it. I submitted a formal request through Snelus that this should be permitted. I heard nothing for several months but towards the end of my stay in Sarikei it was approved and thereafter I rarely traveled on my own. It worked very well. People seemed glad to see a European wife and it greatly increased Hedda's photographic range. I was under the impression that approval had been given despite the objections of Snelus and that we were particularly indebted to Barcroft for getting the proposal through the Secretariat. He was always very kind to Hedda and although I had my ups and downs with him, I was really very grateful for what I believed to have been his good offices.

John Barcroft (right), my first Resident, watching the Sibu regatta with Sir Charles Arden Clarke and Miss Jennifer Arden Clarke

Several years later I was to discover that nothing could have been further from the truth. Going through a stack of obsolete files when I was Principal Assistant Secretary (Defence), I came across one entitled, "Wives accompanying Officers on tour." Here was my original application together with the covering letter from Snelus, who, despite some personal misgivings, had been entirely correct and fair in putting the pros and cons of the case. But Barcroft, far from acting as our benefactor, had in fact attacked the proposal in the most vitriolic terms. The file had circulated through the Secretariat where almost everyone seemed to have appended his views. They were generally helpful. The decision was left to the Governor, Sir Charles Arden Clarke, who had minuted in gubernatorial red—only governors write minutes in red ink—"I do not agree with Mr. Barcroft's misogynistic sentiments. Mrs. Morrison may accompany her husband on tour." Thus are great principles enunciated. And it was just like Barcroft to have enjoyed years of gratitude for something which he had done his utmost to prevent!

He was a strange, lonely man. He had a commanding presence and a military look about him. Endowed with a good brain and uncommon abilities, he was yet wayward, mischievous, autocratic, and unpredictable, drowning his loneliness in drink. In the morning he was courteous, thoughtful, and constructive. In the afternoons, after his midday libations, his mood was liable to be less certain. His brow would grow black, his temper short. It was his European colleagues who generally, though not always, caught the backlash of the abrasive side of his nature. He could be charming and at times extremely offhand. Wherever he had served he was well remembered, and when he eventually died of a heart attack, his funeral was attended by an extraordinarily large number of Asians. I had no doubt that their attendance was motivated by genuine feelings of sorrow. Of all the Europeans I knew in Sarawak I doubt whether any were regarded locally with more genuine esteem.

Government officers were expected to pass exams in various subjects, the most important ones being law and the Malay language. For those joining the Colonial Service immediately after the war and straight from the services, there was no training. You had to plan your studies yourself. A simple knowledge of the law was not too difficult to acquire because in criminal matters it had been reduced in Sarawak to two remarkably concise works based on the Indian codes—the Criminal Procedure Code and the Penal Code. In those days there were no lawyers in private practice, and for the vast majority of the population it made little difference. In civil matters one spent a great deal of time trying to persuade parties in dispute not to go to court. A great many disputes were settled by arbitration privately. There were examples of miscarriage of justice but they were rare. As the courts developed later, a great gap widened between the judges and, at any rate, the country people whose cases came before them. The Senior Administrative Officer, speaking local languages and understanding a good deal of the way of life of the people, often dispensed better justice and worked much harder than some of the professionals who replaced him.

I realize that lawyers do much to help people understand and secure their rights. Nevertheless, the growth in legal work in Sarawak as the number of lawyers increased was an astonishing spectacle. One might be forgiven for concluding that there is some kind of natural law that litigation grows to meet the needs of the legal profession.

I set out to learn Malay, the language in which the government exams were held. This was a matter of some difficulty in Sarawak, particularly in the lower Rejang where the Malay population was small. The most common language was Iban, and many Chinese spoke no local language or were embarrassed to use what they had in conversation with a government officer. The fact that I spoke a little Chinese quickly became known, and one of the first occasions at which I was to officiate as a government officer took place just after we arrived. I was invited to present the diplomas at the annual prize-giving ceremony of the local Chinese secondary school. I made it very clear that I was not prepared to address the students in Chinese and that I would require an interpreter. One was promised—a clerk in the local office of the Borneo Company.

When the day arrived I presented myself in the school assembly hall and was greeted by the elders of the Chinese community and with them took my seat on the stage. The children thronged the seats below us neatly decked out in their plain black and white school uniforms. The Foochow Headman or Kapitan—a term apparently acquired from the Dutch—gave a long speech in Foochow, and having satisfied myself that my interpreter was positioned as arranged near the front row, I let my mind wander and mused of other things.

Eventually I noticed that there was a pause in the speechmaking and taking stock of the situation I found that all eyes were upon me. The Kapitan smiled and bowed and indicated that it was now time for me to give my speech. As I rose to my feet I was warmly clapped, but looking for my interpreter, I was dismayed to find that he had disappeared. For one moment I thought to make a bolt for it but then launched into a very poor, stumbling talk in Chinese to say how happy I was and how glad I was to know that the children had all studied hard. It was a ghastly few minutes and I am sure that not a word was understood. But the applause was loud and prolonged and I acquired great face. The local Chinese newspaper said that the Assistant District Officer gave an admirable speech in the fluent Mandarin which he had acquired during his long residence in Peking. My interpreter had in fact ducked down out of sight behind the seat in front of him while I dozed on the dais. This was almost certainly by prearrangement with the Chinese elders.

The Chinese are intensely education-conscious and had shown remarkable industry in developing their own school system. This was common to all the British territories of Southeast Asia. Despite the praiseworthy nature of this educational effort, it was a most unfortunate thing and did the Chinese community much harm, for the pattern of education which they established kept them apart from the Malays and Dayaks among whom they lived. The Rajah's government accepted few responsibilities in the field of education. Some help was given to English-medium mission schools which accepted both Christian and non-Christian pupils. The government also established a number of Malay language primary schools. The education-conscious Chinese were left to do pretty well what they pleased.

Consequently, wherever groups of Chinese lived, whether in the bazaars or in the countryside, Chinese-medium schools grew up. They were generously supported by the Chinese community, but a great deal of the finance was obtained by mobilizing superior Chinese economic power and organization. Traders would agree to provide a small percentage of their turnover, but since many of their customers were not Chinese, it meant in effect that they were exacting a levy on members of other communities. The local steamship company which traded with Singapore had an arrangement with the Chambers of Commerce which also benefited Chinese education. In return for an agreement to use that company's services exclusively, the shippers received a deferred rebate which was paid directly to the Chinese schools. The schools tended to develop as little Chinas, their methods and curricula drawn from China and oriented towards that country.

The same thing happened throughout the territories which now comprise Malaysia. Failure to provide for a uniform and non-communal system of education was a serious failing of British administration in the region. It kept people apart and differences became institutionalized. The successor governments had the difficult and unenviable task of providing a national system of education in their place.

We found the climate in Sarawak to be a pleasant one. The nights were cool—we never during our entire stay felt the need for air conditioners or fans in the houses we lived in—and the mornings extraordinarily beautiful. The best time of the day was the two or three hours after dawn. Gradually the day would heat up, and usually in the afternoon great storm clouds would roll in and there would be a heavy downpour of rain, often accompanied by the most frightening thunderstorms. The frequent heavy rain has the effect of washing everything down and keeping dust to a minimum. There were very few flies. Mosquitoes there were in abundance, but the ones which bite you in the evening do not spread disease. The malaria carrier is a rare species with peculiar habits, emerging late at night. There was a malaria problem, but its effects had been felt most in some of the upriver areas. We never took prophylactic drugs, and the only malaria I ever had was a recurrence of something I had contracted in south China during the war. The most tiresome insect pests are the sandflies, small biting insects which can make life disagreeable at times. They are, unfortunately, often to be found in seaside areas and along the rivers.

Sarawak is affected by both the southwest and northeast monsoons but the former is hardly noticeable. The northeast monsoon, known locally as the landas season, brings strong winds and heavy rains from about November to February. It makes travel at sea difficult, and in days gone by meant that government posts along the coast were cut off for long periods.

Our first encounter with the landas was a rather dramatic one. The small Jerijeh lighthouse at the entrance to the Rejang went out of operation. A temporary light was installed and the Marine Department asked Snelus to check whether it could be clearly seen from the sea. I was told to carry out the necessary inspection and nothing loth set off for Jerijeh in the government launch, taking Hedda and our cook Bolhi, intending to stay the night in the Jerijeh schoolhouse. We visited the kampong, called on the Tua Kampong, and at seven went out to sea for what we thought would be a brief sortie.

We found when we moved out of the river mouth that the landas was blowing strongly and soon there were heavy gusts of rain. We went several miles out to sea and were able to confirm that the light was visible though not very brightly. The launch was rolling heavily and we were not sorry to turn back for the shelter of the river mouth. The rain squalls now grew heavier, periodically blotting out the now dim and distant temporary light. It was not long before they blotted it out altogether. The seas grew rougher, the launch pitched and rolled, and in order to see better, the

Juragan (launch captain) stood on the instrument counter with his head and shoulders through the hatch above, steering with his feet.

The situation was now becoming more than a little alarming, what with the movement of the launch, the yells of the crew, and the roar of the wind. Then we started bumping and I thought we must turn turtle. The steering jammed and it was noticeable that the man who dived under the stern sheets to free it was not the engineer or his mate, whose job it should have been, but Le the sailor, a happy-go-lucky young man who had the reputation for being lazy and often absent from duty. By great good fortune, the bumping was the prelude to our running hard aground and right side up. We looked out and there was water all around but it was only a few inches deep. The crew jumped over to find that the launch was entirely undamaged. Bolhi jumped out too and trod on a crab. A little later the tide went out altogether and we were left resting on the great sand flat which lies off the coast here at low tide. Hedda and I decided that it was time for a brandy and we asked the Juragan whether he and the crew—all good Muslims and normally teetotallers—would like some too. "On occasions like this," said the Juragan with feeling, "we would all like some brandy."

When the tide came in, the wind had abated and the Juragan got us off the sandbank without difficulty, and we made our way back to Jerijeh. Here we all walked out to the light and scrambled to the top with the lighthouse keepers where Hedda took a souvenir picture of us all on the light platform. I learned later that the logbook of the launch ran as follows:

1900 hours	Put to sea with Assistant District Officer to inspect Jerijeh light.
2030 hours	Inspected light from the sea. OK.
2130 hours	Anchored off Jerijeh Point.
0530 hours	Raised anchor and returned to Jerijeh.

The account in the logbook was not entirely accurate but the Juragan was a tactful man. The Director of Marine was devoted to his launches and there was no need to worry him unnecessarily.

Sarikei was not the most attractive post for one who wanted to see much more of Borneo than was possible in the District. I put in a request for transfer out of the Lower Rejang. In response to this request Barcroft moved me to Binatang, the only other European-manned station in the Lower Rejang. It bore many similarities to Sarikei, built on a swamp between two left-bank tributaries of the Rejang and populated by the same kinds of people. Still it did mean a little more independence and I was not sorry to move.

The officer I succeeded, Ian Urquhart, moved to Kapit, in the upper Rejang, taking with him an assortment of pets, including a baby Maias which he had impounded. Maias had at one time been found all the way from the Rejang southwards, but much of their habitat had been destroyed by Dayak farming methods and they had been hunted relentlessly by the same people. There was still, however, a small pocket of the animals in an area of swamp forest in Binatang and Sibu Districts. The baby in Ian's care had allegedly been found in a padi field. More probably the parent animal had been killed. It is a sad fact that virtually every wild-caught anthropoid ape in captivity has been obtained by killing the mother, a fact

Our Major-Domo, Bolhi, feeding an orphan Maias

which is blandly ignored by the zoos and other institutions whose insatiable greed for these animals is today the main cause of their growing rarity and approaching extinction in the wild.

Ian was a forthright, extroverted, outspoken individualist. He had won the Military Cross at Imphal. We shipped him off to Kapit, but not before he had left a most tiresome problem in my hands. We had spent a day together in the Binatang office during which Ian had adjudicated on a Chinese adoption case. Adoptions, especially of Chinese girls, were quite common in Sarawak. The children were usually adopted when they were tiny infants and often by Malay families. There was generally some financial settlement. The little girls were brought up as members of their new family and were lovingly cared for. The process of adoption has resulted in a significant though concealed amount of inter-racial marriage.

Adoptions had to be properly registered in a government office and during the Japanese occupation this had not always been done. In the present case, an old

Chinese lady had adopted a child, but the adoption had never been registered, though it had been done quite properly insofar as Chinese custom was concerned and there had been a financial settlement. The child was now about five years old and the father wanted her back. In a rather painful scene, Ian gave a decision in strict accordance with the law, ruling that the adoption was invalid and returning the child to the father. She was dragged screaming from the office and the police had to break up a near fight outside between supporters of the two parties.

I thought that this was not necessarily in the best interests of the child and allowed the case to be reopened. But the cunning father, having swindled the old lady, saw to it that the little girl was well and truly spoiled at home. He also, I learned later, told the child that it was the old lady's intention to "sell her to the Dayaks." The Foochow Kapitan and I heard the appeal and talked to the child in closed court. It was quite clear that nothing but force would now take her back to the old lady, though there was no reason to suppose that she had been other than well treated by her. So she stayed with the father.

Binatang was far too close to Sarikei on the one side and Sibu on the other to be a viable town, but with the inexhaustible optimism of the Chinese trading community an elaborate new bazaar was being built. Another mud road stretched out beyond our bungalow, which was on a knoll in swampland. One of the first outings which Hedda and I undertook was to go out by longboat to the place where the road was supposed to end with a view to walking back to the house in time for Sunday lunch.

It would have been wiser to make a few inquiries first because in fact the road was so overgrown that no one ever used it. It took us many hours to get through and we arrived at dusk, tired and footsore and much scratched from ploughing our way through tall grass, in time to meet a police party going out in search of us. Our thoughtful Bolhi was carrying a large pomelo for Hedda and a bottle of beer for me. I never tired in later years of touring the roads which were built over the countryside which I had earlier covered on foot. In those footslogging days Sarawak seemed so very much larger than it did later on.

Our bungalow was in a grove of rubber trees which subsequent DOs happily cut down, leaving the surroundings bare, hot, and uncomfortable. There was at that time no electricity supply line to the bungalow and we used pressure lamps. Through the wide front door at night would come a procession of amiable toads to catch the insects which were attracted by the light while the walls and ceiling had more than the usual number of chichaks, the little house geckos, small lizards with suction pads on their fingers enabling them to run upside down on the ceiling. When there was heavy rain and the surrounding swampland was flooded, we had rather less welcome guests in the shape of numerous snakes which sought refuge on the higher ground. Most of these were harmless, but we had the occasional cobra and we feared for the safety of Bolhi's numerous family.

My Malay was making a little progress and I successfully surmounted the first part of the government exams, though in some subjects by a fairly narrow margin. In my oral Malay I had a conversation with the Senior Native Officer of the Division, Datu Abang Yan, a distinguished looking Malay Haji—a man who has made the pilgrimage to Mecca. The Haji introduced the subject of our cook, Bolhi, a lively man who liked to travel and spoke excellent Iban. I spoke well of Bolhi, whom I liked, and perhaps it was just as well for I found later that the Haji was his father-in-law.

We spent our second Christmas in Sarawak in Binatang and took the opportunity to visit a Dayak house which still adjoined one of the few remaining patches of primary jungle in the area. The Tuai Rumah was a kind man called Sawing. I spent my time collecting birds and Hedda taking photographs. Sawing took me shooting in his little patch of forest. It must long since have been cut down and reduced to the prevailing status of scrubland. One especially vivid recollection that I have of the visit was being soundly berated by Sawing for the gross solecism of bringing some rice into his house. Inflicting ourselves on his longhouse for Christmas and knowing that the people were short of padi, we thought that we should at least not be a burden on the house in respect of food. However, while the people did not mind one bringing foreign styles of food, Sawing felt hurt that we had also brought rice and expressed himself on the subject in no uncertain terms.

We only made one Dayak tour in Binatang but it was a notably exhausting one. The area of Penghulu Nyipa contained twenty-seven houses—many large in size—and we visited them all in six traveling days. It was just after the harvest, most of the houses had had a good harvest, and in twenty-five of the twenty-seven houses we were plied with tuak, often of excellent quality. The best tuak is a clear, slightly sweet drink of about the same potency as a light white wine. From this pitch of excellence it varies in a descending scale to an unpleasant looking white broth, sweet and sickly with flabby rice grains and heaven knows what besides floating in it. Courtesy requires that you take some of the bad as well as the good, even to the detriment of one's liver, for the kind thought behind the tuak is the same in each place.

Nyipa was small and elderly and a little old-fashioned. He carried with him what appeared to be a bronze wand of office, which I thought to be some rare heirloom, but which I found on closer examination to be part of a brass bedstead. He was much perturbed when we left one longhouse, he and the Tuai Rumah bringing up the rear as we made our way down to the boat. Two small birds flew across their path in opposite directions which they interpreted as meaning that any regular visitor in the party who did not return to sleep in the longhouse would never see the longhouse again. This genuinely worried the Penghulu for he seemed to be the person most directly affected. I offered to change the itinerary and have the whole party spend the night there instead of going on to the next house, but after some consultation it was concluded that it would be enough for the Penghulu to leave behind his official khaki jacket trimmed in red. This was done and everyone seemed satisfied.

Most of the problems in this area concerned guns or land. The people were relatively well-off for guns, but most of these had been recovered from the river where they had been dumped by the Japanese. The Japanese had taken away all the Dayak guns they could lay their hands on and towards the end of the war thrown them all into a deep reach of the Rejang not far from Nyipa's area. Many guns had been recovered by diving, and where ownership could not be established the finder was allowed to retain them. Nothing earned the Japanese more dislike among the Dayaks than this action. It did little to help the Japanese from the security point of view, because after several years of the occupation there was virtually no ammunition in Sarawak.

Interest in owning guns, especially on the part of the Dayaks, was intense, and gun problems provided a large proportion of the work load for the District Administration. When I first arrived in Sarawak there were none for sale and the fate of salvaged guns was a burning issue. Shortly afterwards a trickle of poorly made single-barreled 12-bore Belgian guns started to reach the market, followed shortly afterwards by much larger supplies of good American guns. The rule at first was that guns would be restricted to one-gun-per-three-doors. But with the vast rise in rubber prices due to the Korean war, most country people had plenty of money with which to buy guns. One-gun-per-door was soon reached and there were many exceptions even to that. The District Offices had to control both gun and ammunition purchases. The used ammunition had to be produced and the casing slashed or cut in two in front of an administrative officer before the license holder would be permitted to buy more. There were gun transactions of astonishing complexity to unravel. The most ingenious reasons would be advanced for wanting to sell a gun and buy another one. One man told me that he had to sell his almost brand-new gun because it was no good. I asked him what was wrong and he replied that he could not hit anything with it. This seemed reasonable and I approved his application for a new one.

Although Dayaks were the most gun-mad, guns were made freely available to other peoples too. When Confrontation eventually came upon us, there were about 55,000 licensed shotguns in Sarawak. Chinese shotguns were then called in, but the resourceful young men of the communist movement set to work and made their own with lengths of piping. Ammunition remained more readily available. For purposes of assassination these homemade shotguns were quite serviceable weapons.

The effect on wildlife has been deplorable. Pigs, deer, monkeys, and large birds were quickly eliminated in settled areas and life became very hard for squirrels. Soon there was very little of consequence to shoot, but shotguns were always taken to the farm or on boat journeys. They were an essential article of adornment for the self-respecting male.

Land problems never failed to be a subject of discussion. In Sarawak land was not traditionally owned outright. Although the distinction often became blurred, it was only the right to use land which belonged to the individual who felled the original jungle and to his descendants. The felling had often taken place in the distant past; there might be many descendants; people had moved away and come back again. The inevitable vagueness of ownership provided grounds for innumerable disputes. Some of them were of great current interest but others were of ancient lineage, adjudicated years before and revived every time there was a change of District Officer. If it was feasible, you would look at the position on the ground and walk the bounds of the dispute and try and reach a settlement in the field. But people always feel strongly about land. No matter what your decision, appeals were frequent.

In the area of Penghulu Nyipa was one particularly vexing problem concerning an area of good alluvial soil on the northern side of the Rejang called Pulau Bunut. The downriver areas and the deltas of the great rivers of Sarawak are peculiar in that, although they cover large areas, they contain very little good agricultural land. There are large areas of peat on which are to be found valuable and specialized stands of timber, but only in a few places are there deposits of fine alluvial soils suitable for padi and other crops. Pulau Bunut was one such area—an extensive tract of fine alluvium which had been improved during the Japanese occupation by the cutting of a drainage canal. Many Dayaks had moved onto Pulau Bunut, but its traditional owners were communities of Malays. At the time there was much argument about ownership and it had eventually to be divided.

The people farming on Pulau Bunut had excellent crops. This was reflected in the quantity of tuak which made its appearance, and at one of the Pulau Bunut houses I acquired some local fame. It was the house of Tuai Rumah Tuah, a very courteous and popular Tuai Rumah with a large and contented longhouse. Here, towards the end of the tour with Penghulu Nyipa, the tuak flowed as I had rarely seen it flow before, and it was with real regret that we eventually made our departure, being escorted down to the landing place by the entire population of the house.

Next to our own longboat we found a small trading boat belonging to a member of a small Bugis agricultural settlement which existed near Sarikei. The Bugis people come from Sulawesi and Bugis communities are to be found all over Malaysia. Hedda had visited their village and had in fact photographed the very attractive wife of the trader whom I now met for the first time. Furthermore, he told us that his wife was with him but sitting under the boat's raised roof. In my euphoric state I felt it my duty to greet the lady, but stepping onto her boat from ours, missed my footing, and to the delight of the crowd went headlong into the river. It was the only really popular thing I ever did in Sarawak.

Another of my duties in Binatang was to explain to the people the meaning and importance of the Local Authority which had been introduced in the District the previous year. This was an attempt to establish local government bodies throughout Sarawak. Initially they were mostly racial authorities and the Lower Rejang Iban Local Authority was one of the first to be established. The idea was simple enough. The Dayaks paid a head tax of $1 per adult male. This was continued but supplemented by a matching grant from the Government paid to the Authority which consisted of the area Penghulus. This provided the funds which they could use to undertake simple development of a social nature, especially the establishment of rural schools. At that time schools amongst Dayaks were virtually unknown except in areas where mission influence had made itself felt, but the demand for education was beginning to develop. The difficulty was that the Penghulus themselves were almost totally illiterate and had little understanding of what they were expected to do. The traveling government officer had to explain, to encourage the people to think of education, and to tell them to put their requests to the Authority.

To begin with, progress was very slow for there was an almost total dearth of teachers until the Batu Lintang Teacher Training Centre, newly established in Kuching, began to turn some out. This in itself was a slow process because, for the communities which had never had schools, there were no literate individuals capable of being trained as teachers. For its first few years Batu Lintang had to provide crash education courses to bring teacher trainees up to the point where they were capable of being trained. The early schools had to depend on a handful of untrained teachers obtained from the Mission schools. It was difficult for an elderly gentleman like Penghulu Nyipa to understand what the Government was trying to achieve, but he and the other Penghulus did their best and schools of a kind did start to appear in places where they had never existed before.

In practice it was found that the racial authorities were too weak to be successful and Sarawak soon turned to Mixed Local Authorities whose areas usually coincided with District boundaries. These authorities were more successful and eventually became responsible for planning and administering primary education in their areas as well as providing some other services. A rating system was gradually introduced and Local Authority elections were held in 1959.

In many ways it was a remarkable effort. The officers who were responsible for Local Authorities were great enthusiasts and hoped to lay a sound foundation for the growth of democratic practice. To a point they were successful, but eventually the system became too complicated for the people the Authorities were intended to cater for. The District Administration tended to divorce itself from the supervisory role that was needed and there were financial problems. The Chinese paid their rates but a great many others did not. Arrears of revenue became very high and no one was prepared to incur the odium of ensuring that firm action was taken against defaulters. The Authorities, or District Councils as they have come to be known, still exist but are no longer very effective. They were relieved of their education responsibilities in 1972.

Towards the end of our stay in Binatang I took the first of many local leaves. Expatriate officers were generously treated in regard to leave. They were given home leave—so many days per month of resident service plus travel time and travel expenses—and local leave as well. For the latter you received only a small grant towards travel expenses. Local leaves enabled us to see far more of Asia than we otherwise could have done.

On our first leave we decided to visit the upper Rejang to see something of the very different peoples who lived there and to return via the 4th Division. We traveled upriver to Kapit by one of the old-fashioned double-decker Chinese launches which plied the Rejang. They made leisurely progress upriver, and if you were not in a hurry they provided very pleasant traveling. In Kapit we stayed with Ian Urquhart, whom I had replaced in Binatang, and then obtained a lift by government longboat up to Belaga. This is a long journey and involves porterage past large rapids at Pelagus, not far upstream from Kapit. Boats have to be dragged through rapids which have taken many lives.

This was the scene of a Dayak attack on the Japanese during the war. A Japanese party withdrawing inland was wiped out here by a party of Dayaks who were helping them through the rapids. Unfortunately, a number of prisoners being used as porters—loyal government officers mistrusted by the Japanese—were massacred too. In their excitement the Dayaks did not distinguish between friend and foe.

At Belaga there was a small, tumbledown bazaar. Hedda, who had photographed opium dens in Japanese-occupied Peking, sniffed the air and said it reeked of opium. Above Belaga the main stream of the Rejang is known as the Balui. We went a little way up the Balui to stay in the house of a Kejaman Chief called Lassa. The Kejaman are related to the Kenyah of the Baram. All these headwaters once supported a large population of Kayan, Kejaman, and other peoples who are known collectively in Sarawak as Orang Ulu, but their numbers have greatly declined. In 1863 the Government mounted a massive expedition against the area, which had harbored the murderers of two Europeans, Fox and Steele, who had been killed in Kanowit the previous year. The Ulu people had thought that no expedition could surmount the Pelagus rapids, but many thousands of Dayaks did so and brought destruction to a great area even beyond Belaga itself. In later years the population was decimated by disease, especially cholera and smallpox, and there is much endemic malaria.

We spent some time in Lassa's house. I made a small collection of birds in the neighborhood and Hedda photographed the people of the house. The Orang Ulu personality is quite different from the Dayak. They are quieter and less extroverted, and their arts, culture, and languages are very different. We were to come to know them better when I served in Baram District, which adjoins the Belaga Subdistrict.

From Belaga we traveled up the Belaga River and then over a low watershed to Tubau in the upper Kemena which reaches the sea at Bintulu in the 4th Division. The DO Bintulu, Philip Jacks, was visiting Tubau when we arrived, and we traveled with him down to Bintulu, a charming coastal settlement which at the time was being rebuilt. It had been destroyed, quite unnecessarily, by the Australian Air Force during the war.

By great good fortune, Philip's launch had to take an eminent Malay personality, Datu Tuanku Taha, on a visit to Niah further up the coast, and so we were able to accompany the Datu and to visit the remarkable Niah caves. These caves are located in a massive limestone massif some way upriver from the small settlement of Niah. The caves are enormous and inhabited by vast numbers of bats and swiftlets. They were later found to contain very important remains of early man who lived in the caves when the sea reached much further inland than is now the case.

The return to Bintulu was very rough. It was so rough that the Juragan thought it prudent to put into a small river to allow the weather to improve. I was much impressed to observe an old Chinese launch which was following us press boldly on. I learned later that this was not a matter of superior seamanship, but was due to the fact that the launch skipper feared that if he turned towards shore, he would capsize.

From Bintulu we went on to Mukah and Sibu by another Chinese launch. Mukah is another pleasant coastal settlement, the river on which it lies an important producer of sago. The Chinese launch was crowded with a party of Dayaks returning to the 3rd Division from working in the oil fields. We slept like sardines on the hatch cover. One of the Dayaks kept talking to himself and during the night kept trying to take possession of Hedda's pillow. We thought him a little dotty, but the next time Hedda saw him after our arrival in Mukah, he was being carried to the government dispensary tied horizontal to a pole. He had, after arrival in Mukah, made a violent onslaught on his companions, who had to tie him up and take him to the local Hospital Assistant for advice.

3

Lawas

We had been in Binatang for about six months when I learned that I was to be transferred to Lawas, one of the two Districts in the 5th Division and the most northerly part of Sarawak. I took an early opportunity to break the news to Bolhi because I was not sure whether he and his family would want to move so far. "Bolhi," I said, "I'm being transferred to Lawas." "I know," he replied. "What do you mean, you know?" I demanded. Bolhi grinned. "I knew some time ago," he said. "My friend works in the telegraph office in Sibu. Sure, we like to come to Lawas."

We went to Kuching to catch the small government coaster, the "Lucille," which maintained communications with the 5th Division, but the "Lucille" was delayed, and I went ahead via Labuan while Hedda came later with our belongings.

Lawas is a small District on Brunei Bay. The township where the District Office was situated lay some miles up a small river. It was a charming place with views inland to the mountain ranges, which in this part of Borneo came down quite close to the sea. It was the last piece of territory to become part of Sarawak, having been acquired from the British North Borneo Chartered Company in 1906. It adjoined the Trusan Valley, which had become part of Sarawak some twenty years earlier. The Chartered Company parted with Lawas because it was troublesome to administer and seemed unlikely to pay its way.

The District Office was a rambling old wooden building built on a hill which overlooked a well-kept padang (lawnlike open space) with government quarters grouped around it. The DO's quarters were on the first floor as was the Court Room. The bazaar was a temporary one and lay just beyond the padang. The old bazaar had been destroyed during the war by the Royal Australian Air Force in the totally erroneous belief that it was occupied by the Japanese. The RAAF, with some help from the Americans, destroyed every bazaar and virtually every government office in North Borneo, Brunei, and northern Sarawak, and there have been few more futile exercises of misguided bomb happiness. The Japanese were not so stupid as to billet themselves in bazaars. They in no way suffered from the bombing. The main sufferers were the Chinese business communities and the public generally. After the war it took years to rebuild the bazaars and even longer to replace the government records which had been lost. In North Borneo all the Land Records were lost. Such are the sacred idiocies of air power.

I had a prolonged takeover period with the departing DO and was much alarmed by what he told me about the nonavailability of local supplies. Nothing, he told me, was to be had locally. You had to bring in all your supplies yourself. I cabled Hedda, who was still in Kuching, to stock up with supplies, and she spent a large amount on tinned foods. Once we had settled in, however, we found that we had been misinformed. There were lots of good things to eat locally. They included a never failing supply of succulent prawns, good fish from Brunei Bay, and a large amount of game. In those days there were plenty of deer and pigs in the vicinity. A hunting party of the office staff led by the Chief Clerk, Hugo Low, used to set out almost every fine afternoon and rarely returned empty-handed. We developed a gentlemanly barter system. They provided us with fresh meat, mostly venison, and we provided sweets for their children. We never ate better than when we were in Lawas.

Lawas had a varied population of Malays and Kedayan downriver and Lun Bawang in the ulu. It is the only District which has no Iban population except for government servants. The Chinese population was comparatively small and largely used Malay as a lingua franca. Hugo, for instance, whose father had been Chief Clerk in Lawas before him, could hardly speak Chinese. The District is unique in Sarawak because although the Trusan is a major stream, neither it nor the Lawas river are navigable for any distance and nearly all the traveling was by foot. Not far

Chong Choon-nyen, a leading citizen of Lawas

upriver was one of the only European rubber estates in Sarawak, run by an old-time Scottish manager called Jock Maclaren and two assistants. Eva, Mrs. Maclaren, was a highly qualified surgeon and was a tremendous asset to the District. Because the nearest hospital was a whole day's journey away, Eva often performed difficult and complicated emergency operations without any proper operating theater to work in.

There was also a small community of Indians including two families of Sikhs. I have a great respect for Sikhs, an energetic and resourceful people, but one maladjusted Sikh can be a source of singular discord. One of the Lawas Sikhs, Jitha Singh, seemed to feel that the world was against him—especially all DOs—and coupled with this was an undeniably quick-tempered and aggressive personality, especially when primed with brandy. Eventually I established a reasonable relationship with Jitha Singh and a fair degree of peace in the bazaar ensued. But one particular recollection which I have of Lawas concerns the dismay with which I discovered, in checking Customs documents, that Chop Jitha Singh had imported a case of brandy. I forthwith called for Jitha Singh to appear in the office (after office hours so as not to embarrass the poor man) and lectured him severely on the evils of drink, especially as it affected him. Jitha Singh listened courteously and expressed his appreciation at the interest I had taken in his problems. "But surely," he said, "you don't imagine that this brandy is for me. Why nothing could be further from the truth. The fact is, Tuan, that my wife is expecting a baby and it is very important for her to have plenty of good strengthening soup mixed with brandy." I was doubtful whether this story was entirely true, but there was no further outburst while I remained in Lawas. Later on, I am afraid, his temper got the worst of him and he eventually had to leave Sarawak. He was not exactly the most popular man in the District but you could not help liking him.

One of the tasks which I found I had inherited in Lawas was to rebuild the road to Trusan, fifteen miles away. A simple road had been built before the war but had largely disintegrated, and an optimistic government had allocated the sum of $20,000 to rebuild it with the help of the Lawas Tua Kampong, Haji Zainal Abidin. With his loyal followers armed with hoes and barrows the TK set to work, and I used regularly to walk out in the early morning to see how work was progressing. We got to about Mile 3 and then the money ran out and no more was provided. The road was later built at a cost of about one million dollars. It is possible to build quite good roads by hand if you have enough good labor and pay them very little or nothing at all. Such roads have been built in China and New Guinea, and even in adjoining North Borneo good bridle tracks were built in this way through the highlands. But generally in the tropics it is a waste of time and money to try to do anything of this kind. The roads are quickly washed away or, if used, become impassable bogs.

A little way upstream from the District Office and on the other side of the Lawas river the Borneo Evangelical Mission had their headquarters. It was a small Australia-based mission dedicated to the establishment of an indigenous church among the interior peoples of Borneo. The Mission had started its work in Limbang District among the Iban in the 1920s but its work had not prospered there. In the early 1930s the Lun Bawang turned towards Christianity, largely stimulated by pioneer work by missionaries on the Dutch side and in reaction to the degraded state they had reached through obsessive drinking. BEM missionaries went over to Lawas and nearly all the Lun Bawang accepted Christianity with a rare degree of fervor. They threw off drink entirely.

Although I thought the BEM was a little over strict in some of its ideas, in some ways it acted with a remarkable degree of foresight. Reliance on foreign missionaries was minimal; a truly local church was established; simple Malay, together with the local languages, was used extensively for the work of the Mission; the Mission did not engage in running schools and hospitals and they made remarkably efficient use of aircraft to overcome the problem of travel in Borneo. The Mission had realized that the only way to counter the high cost and slowness of surface travel in Borneo was to use light aircraft. As a result, small airstrips were built all over the interior, initially by local effort, and the Mission maintained contact with light aircraft flown by efficient and skilled missionary pilots. When I was in Lawas their first aircraft arrived—a little Aeronca—and I was convinced that it would quickly crash. I watched it taking off, skimming the tree tops as it climbed out of the valley. When I told the pilot, Bruce Morton, that it looked dangerous to me, he replied airily, "So it might appear to a layman." The Mission achieved a remarkable safety record—but the pilot always said a short prayer before take-off.

There was a small jail in Lawas containing a solitary prisoner called Man. He was serving a long sentence for his part in the brutal murder of a hawker. Imprisonment in such a place as Lawas was far from arduous. Man's sojourn in the actual jail building was largely nominal in nature.

Not long after we arrived in Lawas, Hari Raya, the festival day marking the end of the Muslim fasting month, was observed. On this day it was—and is—the pleasant custom in Sarawak for Muslim citizens to call on the local government head after the morning Mosque service. Afterwards the Governor, Resident, or DO as the case may be returns their calls and visits as many of his Muslim friends and colleagues as possible. On this particular morning a well-dressed young Malay arrived, wished me the compliments of the season, and proceeded to help serve refreshments to my guests. It took me a few moments to realize that this was Man, my solitary prisoner. Where he kept his party clothes I never knew and it seemed tactless to ask. We became quite attached to Man and he used sometimes to escort Hedda on her photographic rambles. Later on the wheels of progress caught up with Man and he was transferred to the main prison in Kuching. Personally I thought that the old Sarawak system had much to commend it.

The DO lived very close to his work in Lawas. At times it was almost too close, the post office being immediately under our bedroom. One night during a holiday season I found it hard to fall asleep because of what I took to be a cow mooing repeatedly and at short intervals somewhere very close by. Descending to investigate, I found that it was no cow but the policeman on duty, fast asleep and emitting snores of a herculean kind. He was very indignant when I called his Sergeant to witness the lapse. We also lived very close to nature. Two large toads had their daylight lair behind Hugo Low's safe. And Hedda had a darkroom where she once found herself enjoying the company of a large though very sluggish Banded Krait, a snake said to be deadly, though usually inoffensive in Borneo. Lawas had great charm but lacked modern conveniences, including water-borne sanitation. The toilet was an earth closet reached by a little path along the hillside. One day when we had a guest staying with us, I was the third person to visit the toilet but the first to notice that there was a fair-sized python curled up behind the throne, peacefully digesting one of our chickens.

The special interest in Lawas lay in the long walk up to the head of the Trusan. We did this twice. It was particularly enjoyable touring because you had a long walk between each Lun Bawang village, generally crossing the watershed between the right hand tributaries of the Trusan in which the villages lay. You walked through fine old jungle unscarred by felling until you emerged in the green and beautiful cultivated valleys, surrounded by jungle-covered mountains and watered by rushing mountain streams. The Lun Bawang are a somewhat taciturn people and lack the extroverted spontaneity of Dayaks. They are tough, solid hillmen and some of their taciturnity stemmed from past neglect. They were not highly regarded by the Rajah's government, which paid them little attention. Once they had overcome their drink problem they were quick to turn to education. The Lun Bawang girls are some of the most attractive in Borneo.

Travel in the Lun Bawang country involved the same sort of routine as elsewhere. One took the census and talked about maintaining the main track which led from Lawas to the Indonesian border, a matter of some difficulty as it was continually churned up by the movement of buffaloes and cattle, the most valuable and mobile form of produce in the ulu. There were problems because the authority of the Penghulus was weak. The Lun Bawang were particularly keen to see the establishment of schools and simple medical facilities. They were hospitable, but having given up alcohol, their hospitality lacked something of the gaiety which one encountered in Dayak communities. Their houses were not adapted for this anyway for they had largely given up living in longhouses and lived instead in quite small and detached village houses. A feature of their villages was the singing of hymns before dawn and last thing at night. The Lun Bawang were not very musical but made up in stentorian vigor what they lacked in harmony.

The Lun Bawang country had seen a good deal of activity during the latter stages of the war. The Australian SRD (Services Reconnaissance Detachment—the Australian equivalent of the British Special Operations Executive) mounted an elaborate operation into central Borneo in early 1945. Parties landed in the Kelabit area, which lies at the head of the Baram and adjoins the Ulu Trusan. From here they fanned out into North Borneo and the 3rd, 4th, and 5th Divisions of Sarawak. It was a bold and imaginative operation into a little known area. It was largely the brainchild of Tom Harrisson, who later became the Curator of the Sarawak Museum. Whether the operation achieved very much is open to question. It has, over the years, received a lot of publicity, but the Japanese were not greatly inconvenienced by it. The hard and bloody fighting had still to be done by the Australian Army. The most impressive and least known achievement of SRD was, in concert with Native Chiefs, to help keep thousands of wildly excited Dayaks in the 3rd Division from slaughtering Chinese in a massive resurgence of headhunting.

The Lun Bawang were amongst the best and steadiest supporters of SRD. Their homeland was also affected by two extraordinary Japanese withdrawals. It was the Japanese intention in Borneo to make a final stand in the Tenom area of North Borneo. The several hundred Japanese in the Brunei and Miri areas were told to withdraw to Tenom and this they attempted to do overland. One party from Brunei moved up the Tengoa tributary of the Trusan and cut straight over the mountains to the Padas Valley and Tenom. It was an extraordinary effort for their way led them through exceptionally wild and broken country. They were harried by SRD and lost many stragglers, but most of the party reached their destination. The other group traveled up a tributary of the Baram and over into Limbang and so over into the head of the Trusan. Here they eventually surrendered to SRD.

The Trusan provides the nearest route to the coast for a large population of Lun Bawang living in Indonesia and also for the people of the Kelabit area. In those days movement was free and a steady stream of travelers from these areas used to come down to Lawas to trade, bringing cattle and rice with them to sell and taking back with them cloth and other consumer goods. The Malaysian government no longer allows such movement from Indonesia all the way to Lawas, with the result that the Lun Bawang of the upper Trusan, who have well developed business instincts, have established a lucrative trade as middlemen.

One of the problems I had to try and settle in Lawas was the compensation due from the Kelabit for the murder of some Lun Bawang in the middle Trusan by a psychopath who ran amok. The Lun Bawang, although nominally Christian, demanded blood money, and the Kelabit agreed to pay several head of cattle and some valuable old jars in compensation. A partial handover was done in Indonesian territory with the cooperation of the local Indonesian official or Kiai and I witnessed the event. The Lun Bawang went up later to the Kelabit country and collected the rest. It was an object lesson to me in the complexities of such negotiations. The details had largely been arranged by Harrisson, but there was still room for much argument as to the correct custom, where the handover was to take place, the value of the cattle, the condition of the jars, the value of the murderer's beads destroyed by the Lun Bawang, and extraneous matters such as a sudden and unexpected demand for additional parangs. It was finally settled, although nowadays no Sarawak Kelabit would dream of walking to the coast. They prefer to travel by air.

We returned from our first visit to the head (ulu) of the Trusan via the Tengoa Valley, which leads down to the limit of navigation on the main river. In days gone by there was a small government post at the mouth of the tributary which gave access to the then turbulent ulu. It was one of the most leech-infested walks we ever made. Leeches abound in old, wet jungle. Their bite is not painful but sets up an irritation which can easily become infected and lead to painful tropical sores. You have to stop regularly to remove leeches. In the Tengos I removed thirty-one at one sitting. At the river mouth there was a poor little longhouse of some Indonesian Tagal, who are related to the Lun Bawang. It was remarkable for the overpowering smell of urine from a horde of incontinent hunting dogs. We were not sorry to depart and canoe gently downriver to Trusan Station where a fine old ironwood fort was in a state of gentle decay.

Here we received our first intimation of the assassination of the Governor, Duncan Stewart. He had only just arrived in Sarawak to succeed Sir Charles Arden Clarke. On his first tour to Sibu he was, on December 2, 1949, stabbed by a young Malay and died from his wounds some days later in Singapore. The murder cast a great gloom over us. No one had thought that such a thing could happen in Sarawak, a belief which simplified the task of the misguided young man who did the stabbing.

This unhappy event was the culmination of the anti-cession movement, the predominantly Malay opposition to the cession of Sarawak by the Rajah to the British Crown in 1946. A White Raj was obviously an anachronism long before the war and subsequently it was a totally unviable form of government. The Rajah correctly recognized this; in addition, his own children were all girls and he had serious differences with his nephew, the heir apparent, Anthony Brooke. The Rajah was an old man with neither the interest nor the resources to continue to hold the reins of government. Cession was acceptable to the vast majority of the population but failed to take into account the likelihood that it must affect the position of the Malays, who were the main prop to the Rajah's authority and who provided much of the administrative service. Added to this was the dishonest and clumsy manner in which cession was brought about. If the Rajah had taken the trouble and had been sufficiently patient, he could quite probably have persuaded the leading Malay personalities that there was no realistic alternative to cession. At least there could have been some mitigation of the resentment which arose. But cession was pushed through by methods which were both autocratic and devious, and the final vote of Council Negri approving cession was only carried by the votes of European officials. A large number of Malay officials declined to sign a declaration of loyalty to the new government and were compelled to resign from the government service. There was agitation, focused on the figure of Anthony Brooke, but it achieved nothing except to engender acute frustration and seriously divide the Malay community.

The anti-cession leader in the 3rd Division was a former Customs Officer called Awang Rambli (he had been dismissed from the service prior to cession). He it was who presided over a small group of extremists who called themselves the Rokon Tigabelas (the Thirteen Elements) and proposed that the only solution was to voice their dissatisfaction by killing the British Governor. This was easy enough. There were no proper security precautions when the Governor arrived in Sibu. After the Governor had inspected a Guard of Honour and was walking past a line of schoolchildren, a well-dressed young Malay from among the spectators darted forward and stabbed him. A second man sought to do the same but was prevented.

There was nothing personal about the attack on Stewart, an amiable and capable man who had only just arrived in Sarawak. There was, however, some personal animus directed towards his predecessor. Arden Clarke was a tough man and he had taken a tough line towards the anti-cession movement. He was not very sure of himself when he first arrived in Sarawak—all his service had been in Africa. He was much mellowed by the time he left and went on to develop a much more understanding relationship with Nkhrumah in Ghana. Although I doubt whether it made much difference to the final tragedy, Arden Clarke had clashed personally with Rambli. He had on one occasion granted Rambli an interview in Sibu. At this, far from trying to listen politely and to reason patiently, he had proceeded to upbraid Rambli to the great embarrassment of Barcroft and Fisher, both of whom were present and knew Rambli well. This was simply not the way things were done in Sarawak. Years later John Fisher told me he had never been so depressed in his life. After the interview was over, he and Barcroft adjourned to the Island Club and gloomily drank together. They were too depressed to say a word to one another.

Rambli and three others were hanged. Up to the last, Rambli expected some miraculous intervention by Anthony Brooke. The trial itself had some unhappy aspects, for the prosecution was led by the Sarawak Attorney-General, who was a KC, but no qualified lawyer was appointed to conduct the defense. The task was given to my colleague John Pike, who, although one of the most able and intelligent men that Sarawak has seen, was at the time the most junior administrative officer in the service and had no legal qualifications. The evidence was clear enough and Pike probably did as much as anyone could have done. Nevertheless it was a shabby episode, and when the trial was over, relatives of the accused bitterly rounded on Pike and he narrowly escaped at the very least a serious assault.

The assassination of Duncan Stewart did, however, lead to the rapid disappearance of the anti-cession movement from the scene, although old animosities aroused by the movement persisted among the Malays for years afterwards. The Malay community was horrified and shocked. No matter how strongly they felt about cession, the vast majority had never advocated violence. The assassination led surprisingly quickly to a large measure of reconciliation, a process which was much helped by the remarkably successful tenure of office of Duncan Stewart's successor, Sir Anthony Abell. Anthony Brooke was also shocked by the turn of events. He withdrew from the political scene and became an advocate of Moral Rearmament.

Fortunately, cession had made very little impact in the 5th Division and life there continued very much as it had done before. Amongst other things, we started to keep chickens, which are a particularly useful form of supplementary supply for the outstation DO. The foundation of our flock was a very pretty and tame little grey hen which we had been given on our first ulu journey and which I could not bear to eat. We brought it back with us, and the idea occurred to me that I would establish a flock of all grey chickens, which could not be confused with the chickens of anyone else, grey chickens being rather unusual in Sarawak.

I let it be known that I wanted to buy grey chickens but ran into some difficulties as a result of my poor command of Malay. I thought the word for grey was kurus, but kurus means thin. The word for grey is kelabu. The people of Lawas were greatly surprised at my insistent demands for thin chickens. They were used to the oddities and idiosyncracies of European DOs but this was something new to them. The situation was eventually resolved by a Malay elder who took me aside and asked me to explain just what it was that I wanted. We then acquired a fine collection of grey chickens, but unfortunately, grey seems to be a genetically unstable color in fowls, and the birds we bred from our flock proved to be every color of the rainbow.

Soon we were in the throes of preparing for the first visit to the Division by the new Governor. I was able to learn quite a bit about the plans for the visit because our wireless operator, Ali, used to monitor the traffic to Limbang, the Divisional Headquarters. Ali was a thin, elderly, bespectacled Malay who generally had a cigarette drooping from the corner of his mouth. He was an inspired wireless operator; he had but to kick his old B2 wartime radio set for it to start immediately transmitting impeccable morse at 150 words a minute. He used to listen to what was going on in Limbang. If he could not fully understand a message he would take it upstairs and consult Hedda. My Resident, John Fisher, was a fine organizer for whom no detail was too small and the Governor's visit was planned with great precision. At one point Fisher inquired whether the Governor liked shellfish—the Limbang prawns were particularly good. As an afterthought, remembering that the Rajah had had an aversion to dogs, requiring them to be locked up when he toured, Fisher further inquired whether the Governor minded dogs. The reply which was promptly despatched read "SHELLFISH AND DOGS OK IF COOKED SEPARATELY." Ali was much astonished and immediately sought the advice of Hedda who had worked with the American Red Cross and understood such matters. She explained to him that it was an obvious error in transmission and must refer to hot dogs.

The visit was carried through with much state and Hedda, for the first and last time in her life, was required to wear a hat and gloves. I too had a bad moment when, having lined up all the notables from Lawas District who were to meet the Governor, I discovered, as the Governor was about to arrive, that the line had been joined by a sinister-looking and somewhat disheveled betel-chewing figure. Thoughts of assassination were very much part of one's thinking at that time. But it was too late and it would have been too embarrassing to have him thrown off the line. The Governor shook hands with him as he did with the other notables. He turned out to be a middle-aged Dayak who happened to be down in the bazaar. Dayaks are not notably shy and this man, seeing the commotion and the line of visitors, saw no reason why he too should not greet the Governor.

So began our long association with the new Governor, an unconventional, enthusiastic, and humane figure who did much good in Sarawak. He had exactly the right personality for the time and place and he had the advantage of being a bachelor. Abell came to us from Nigeria. He was not one of the most senior potential appointees but it was an inspired choice.

He was a prime example of the intelligent flexibility of the Colonial Office, which assessed men primarily on character. He must have been somewhat wild in his youth and was sent down from Oxford. But his merits were recognized and somehow he was found a post in the Colonial Service. The appointment may have been made to some extent on the old-boy basis but it was a highly beneficial one.

What impression he took away from that first visit to Limbang I do not know, but it could have been a little confused. John Fisher, the Resident, and his wife Ruth were splendid hosts and the food they provided was magnificent. Nor was Fisher a man to be mean with the drinks. He followed the old Sarawak custom whereby as dusk fell, shortly after six, you started to drink whisky. At 7:30 or later you went and had your bath and this was followed by a number of pink gins. John was also known to fall fast asleep at dinner. On this occasion, much to our embarrassment, he fell asleep over the soup. The meal proceeded, the Resident slumbering peacefully at the head of the table. He awoke during the fish course and after glaring sternly about him, he rose to his feet and said, "Gentlemen, the King." It certainly was one of those evenings.

At breakfast that morning in the Residency there had been a minor crisis when the milk tasted odd. Ruth was aghast and attributed it to silver polish. But it was worse than that, for Fisher's experienced nose led him to the discovery that the powdered milk had inadvertently been mixed with gin.

Fisher was a tall, spare man with a bushy military moustache. His manner of speech would have done credit to the Brigade of Guards. These externals concealed a remarkably sharp mind though he did not always make full use of it. Two of his uncles had been well known Residents in the Rajah's service before him.

Indicative of his approach to problems was his handling of a small disciplinary problem on an Australian troopship. He was put in charge of a troopdeck on an Australian transport returning to Australia from Borneo at war's end. The Officer Commanding the Troops was particularly concerned that there should be no smoking below deck, not an easy rule for a very British British officer to enforce. Fisher solved the problem by lighting a cigarette himself when he went to see his troops. After establishing some personal rapport with the occupants of the deck he took his departure, but not before he had told them to smoke as much as they pleased, but please to be careful because there were explosives loaded in the hold below. There was no smoking—nor were there any explosives.

He had been in an Empire flying boat shot down off Timor in January, 1942. The flying boat captain later recounted, that as the survivors swam about while Zeros zoomed overhead, "Mr. Fisher, who was suffering from two broken ribs, remarked to me when he saw me, 'Jolly sporting of them not to shoot us up in the water.'"

Back in Lawas there was always plenty to do. The DO was expected to supervise all the Departmental operations going on in his District. We were building a new hospital and police barracks. There was an extraordinary proliferation of small Customs posts in the District because of its location on Brunei Bay and these had to be visited. Court work was light but there was always land work to deal with. I completed a census of the District. The total came to just under 10,000 and I was pleased to be able to locate a little lost kampong which gave the District five-figure status. There were war damage claims to be investigated and medals still to be distributed.

One of the latter caused me some perplexity. It was a King's Medal for Courage awarded, on the recommendation of Harrisson, to an intrepid Chinese guerrilla called Miaw Sing, Headman of Sipitang, the Sabah District which adjoins Lawas. Miaw Sing was said to have organized a mixed force of Chinese and Pagans and to have operated with much success against the Japanese in his area. But no one had ever heard of the man. The problem was eventually solved by one of my assistants who found that Miaw Sing was in fact a corruption of Mat Yassin, the shortened version of Mohamed Yassin. Mohamed Yassin was a Malay official who had indeed operated successfully against the Japanese. He had been awarded the same decoration by the Sabah government. He later became a prominent Sabah politician and holds the distinction of being the only man to have been awarded the KMC twice. But Miaw Sing the Chinese guerrilla chief lives on in the literature. Harrisson gave him a splendid write-up in *International Affairs*, the Chatham House publication.

We had a crocodile scare in the river and a professional crocodile catcher called Brahim caught a number in the river near the bazaar. Brahim was a fisherman and coconut planter who lived not far from the sea. We visited him in his pleasant house. He had started life as a houseboy in Sabah, but he learned to catch crocodiles on the East Coast and had made a profession out of it. His last years were, however, to be marked by tragedy, for his son was killed by a crocodile, and Brahim himself and many others thought that this was supernatural retribution.

It was about the time of the crocodile scare in August 1950 that I was to have an experience which too could be explicable to some in terms of the supernatural. I was very fit at the time, but one morning I was struck by a most violent headache. Never before or since have I known anything like it. It was so bad that I had to go and lie down until it passed away. The next day I received the news that my brother Ian, to whom I was very attached, had been killed in Korea the day before. As far as I could make out subsequently, his death (he and three others were killed when their jeep ran into a South Korean minefield) must have occurred at about the time that I was stricken with sudden, almost blinding pain far away in Lawas. We had not been in close touch and I did not even know that my brother was in Korea. I thought he was in Europe.

One of the things which the Government was trying to do was to introduce cocoa to the 5th Division, including the Ulu Trusan. There was a need to introduce some crop which had a relatively high value in terms of its weight, and it was thought that the ulu area would be suitable for cocoa cultivation. Various cocoa plots were established in the lowlands, and I had the task of sending up cocoa seedlings to Long Semado in the middle Trusan, about five days walk from Lawas. The seedlings had to be carried up and I found a number of Indonesian Lun Bawang who undertook to do this in return for payment in advance, so that they had more money to spend on goods to take home. Some seedlings did reach Long Semado but they arrived in poor condition. Sad to relate, the men I contracted with decided on their journey that while they had indeed contracted to carry up the seedlings, they had not necessarily contracted to carry all the earth which went with them. They accordingly lightened their loads to the detriment of the cocoa. Actually cocoa failed to do well in the 5th Division and the problem of providing a more valuable crop in the ulu remained unsolved. Tobacco would have been by far the best prospect but this was frowned on by the Borneo Evangelical Mission.

It occurred to me that one way to improve the economy of the Trusan would be to build bridle tracks and introduce pony transport as had been done in North Borneo. I suggested that it would be desirable for me to see for myself what bridle tracks were like and to assess their suitability for Lawas. I was allowed to combine a part-official, part-local leave visit to North Borneo which took us along the bridle tracks from between Tenom and Keningau northward through the Interior Residency to Ranau and then out to the coast again at Kota Belud. Hedda had earlier traveled this route by herself and it was one of the most delightful journeys that I have ever made. I walked most of the way; it was very pleasant going on the well-graded track with the great mountain of Kinabalu appearing and reappearing around bends in the track. There were simple resthouses along the way but not many villages; these generally lay off the track. I concluded that although in theory bridle tracks were feasible for Lawas, the availability and willingness of labor on the Sarawak side ruled them out. The North Borneo tracks had been built largely on a cooperative or voluntary basis. They ran through comparatively thickly populated areas and had cost little to build.

The visit to North Borneo achieved little but it was a memorable experience. Between Ranau and Kota Belud the track climbs over a shoulder of Kinabalu and we made the ascent of this most beautiful mountain, at 13,455 feet by far the highest mountain in Borneo. It does not reach the snow line, but the tops are open granite and on a clear day you can see all over North Borneo. We also went round by ship to Tawau on the east coast and visited the great Gomanton caves near Sandakan.

We paid a second visit to the Ulu Trusan in 1950. It was again a very pleasant experience, especially because we now knew quite a few of the people and had a greater understanding of their way of life. Much of my time was spent trying to unravel disputes involving buffaloes and cattle. The 5th Division is the only area in Sarawak where there are a fair number of these animals and buffalo problems provide a fertile field for argument. Some of them were ancient disputes but still taken very seriously. Since the animals themselves were generally no longer available for inspection, the problems relating to them were well nigh insoluble. The nature of these problems may, perhaps, be gauged from the following accounts culled from my traveling diary.

THE CASE OF SIA MURANG'S COW

Abai Semawai is a blind man from Indonesian Borneo and a very skillful negotiator. He came over as spokesman some time ago for a group of eleven Indonesian Lun Bawang looking for work. Sia Murang, of Long Kerbangan, contracted with them to build a sawah (irrigated rice field) for him and promised a cow in payment although as a matter of fact he was already involved in a dispute over the animal. So the eleven men went to work on the sawah. Abai went down to Lawas to get some goods and on the way he interested Paril Kadang Bugu of Long Tuyoh in the cow and Paril gave him an advance of $80 on the animal, balance to be paid when he had seen it.

When Abai came back from Lawas he and Paril went up to Long Kerbangan where the sawah had been built but in the meantime Sia had replaced the original cow which was a large one worth about $100 with a small bull worth only about $50. Paril refused to accept this but did not get his $80 back. Now the eleven men are back in Indonesian Borneo and both Sia and Paril have died. Abai wants to take action against the estate of Sia.

THE ESTATE OF SEKELAN NAWA

Sakai Balang is the son of Balang Lun by his first marriage. Later Balang Lun married a woman called Sekelan Nawa who owned some land and also had a daughter Yamu Tadam by a previous marriage. Sekelan died about twelve years ago. Now the Lun Bawang custom is that if anyone dies and another person kills a cow at the funeral, that other person is entitled to some part of the property of the deceased. Balang Lun killed a cow and so did a relative of Sekelan's called Boya Tadam. Boya asked for a gong from the estate of Sekelan but Balang Lun would not give it to him. He received instead the loan of the land. All the children of Sekelan by Balang Lun died and eventually Boya returned the land for the use of Yamu Tadam and he received a gong from Balang Lun. Finally Balang died, about six years ago. About a year later Sakai Balang laid claim to the land because his father too had killed a cow at Sekelan's funeral. Sakai has ever since been making use of the land over the protests of Yamu who claims that the land rightfully belongs to her. Penghulu Ating Mugang has decided that Sakai has a valid claim and has ordered Yamu to give Sakai one small cow in full settlement of the claim. Yamu will not do this and wishes to appeal.

I was unable to settle either of these cases before I left the District and bequeathed them to my successor. They could well be unsettled yet.

Nor was I able to settle the matrimonial problems of a good-looking young Lun Bawang who some time before, in a Christian ceremony, had married a very attractive girl who adored him and in rather short order bore him a child. The young man claimed the child was not his, maltreated the wife, and finally separated from her. He demanded a divorce; she demanded restitution of conjugal rights. But the marriage was not in accordance with Native Customs and the Mission opposed divorce. Just to complicate matters further the Christian ceremony had not been properly registered. I felt sorry for the couple, who had been caught up in a period of social change without fully understanding its implications. The man had done well during the war but died of pneumonia not long afterwards. I remember him especially for having claimed exemption from head tax because he was a schoolboy, although he was in fact one of the biggest and strongest men in the District.

One complicated family case which I was able to settle concerned a respected Chinese vegetable planter in Lawas who had married his adopted daughter. He and his wife were childless and had adopted a little girl. When she grew up the man married her. It was a somewhat unusual thing to do, but the wedding had been celebrated in a properly conducted Chinese ceremony and according to the old custom. This came to the attention of the police, and the Police Sergeant and the Senior Native Officer concluded that under the provisions of the Penal Code this constituted incest. I had to admit that according to the strict letter of the law this seemed possible. I was, however, most reluctant to take action against this couple.

In my dilemma I consulted the local Puisne Judge, Mr. Lascelles, who resided in Miri. He was one of the most senior of the remaining Brooke officers but being a qualified lawyer had moved to the judiciary after the war. He was a wise and humane man. He may not have been the most erudite of lawyers, but he brought to the bench what was later nearly always lacking, real knowledge and sympathetic understanding of Sarawak and its people.

He replied to my inquiry that, having given all the facts which I had brought to his attention careful consideration, he concluded that a possible solution to the problem might be for me to ask the Resident to use his powers to annul the adoption! This solution had not occurred to me. On his next visit the Resident held a formal inquiry attended by both wives, the younger one now very much in a family way, established that annulment would be with the agreement of all parties, and duly pronounced the adoption annulled. In the course of the proceedings, the old wife told the Resident that she had no objections to her husband taking a second wife. Later on I looked up the Court Notes recorded by the Resident which read somewhat on these lines:

Q. Did you, Lau Ping Nui, agree that your husband, Lau Meng Fook, should take Wee Ping Nui as his second wife?
A. I, Lau Ping Nui, did indeed agree that my husband, Lau Meng Fook, should take Wee Ping Nui as his second wife.

Actually what the old lady said was simply, "bulih," which might be translated as "can do."

On our second ulu trip, we had with us Heng Kia Hem, a Senior Hospital Assistant, to look into health problems. Kia Hem was an extraordinarily capable man. Had he but enjoyed the education to which his talents entitled him, he would have been a brilliant doctor. As it was he was much more useful than many men with formal medical qualifications. He had read widely and in an emergency was quite willing to undertake considerable feats of surgery or gynecological procedures. Nothing was too much trouble for him and he was liked and trusted by everyone. He saved several lives through his resourcefulness and willingness to accept responsibility.

Kia Hem carried out a very useful health survey and he was a most delightful traveling companion. Our other companions on this trip were two Police Constables, a young Lun Bawang called Kading and a middle-aged Dayak called Muli. One needed to be very selective in taking policemen on such trips. Kading, a chunky, solid man, was at that time the only Lun Bawang in the Force. Muli had been stationed in Lawas for a long time and was a very popular figure in the ulu. We could not have asked for more congenial companions.

The Lun Bawang were very keen to establish schools. At that time there was only one school in Long Semado which was in the charge of a lively Indonesian teacher who had come from Sulawesi. It was a very creditable little school with eighty-six pupils. But there had been friction between the teacher and the Penghulu which had to be smoothed over. Plans for future schools had to be discussed and some rather unfavorable comparisons with the educational position in Indonesia listened to. Requests for more equipment had to be dealt with. And not all the Lun Bawang were fully education conscious. In one village, which was soon to receive a school, I called in most of the older men and delivered myself of a moving address on the future and importance of the school. I anticipated an interesting discussion at its conclusion and waited for the Penghulu to start the discussion. But the Penghulu's mind was far away. "Tuan," he said, "what about a few more permits to purchase guns?"

I paid another call on my Indonesian colleague. He received me kindly. On my arrival he was busy cutting currency notes in two. There was a currency reform in progress at the time which involved an attempt to reduce the money supply by cutting all notes in half. Members of the public were to retain one half; the other half was held by the Government. Each half was only worth 50 percent of the original face value. The idea was that when inflation had been overcome you would get the other half back again. It was a novel idea but I do not think that it was very successful.

From the ulu, Kia Hem and Muli returned directly to Lawas, but Hedda and I and Kading returned via the Limbang. This meant crossing the Trusan and the watershed beyond to reach the Adang, a tributary of the Limbang, and following the hills on the left bank of that river until we reached settlements which could provide us with canoes to take us downriver. The Adang and the valleys above it used to support a large population, and it is this area which is described in that best of Sarawak travel books, *Life in the Forests of the Far East,* by Spenser St. John, who passed this way in 1858. The Adang was inhabited until just after the war when the

Hedda with the party of Lun Bawang who took us over from the Trusan to the Limbang
(photographed by the author)

Racha Umong, a hunter and notable Lun Bawang personality who led our party from the Trusan to the Limbang. He has since served as a member of Council Negri and as Chairman of the Evangelical Church of Borneo.

remaining Lun Bawang moved over to the Trusan. It was a group of these people who took us over under the leadership of a notable personality called Racha Umong. He was a prominent leader of the Sidang Injil Borneo, as the Borneo Evangelical Church is known, and was later to become a member of the State legislature. He was an excellent organizer and a fine shot, though the latter attribute sometimes worked to our disadvantage. There was a lot of game in the country we passed through and whenever Racha shot a pig, the unanimous decision of the party would be that where the pig had died was undoubtedly the best possible site for a camp, even though as far as Hedda and I could see, it was in the middle of a murky swamp.

It is remarkable to see a group of Borneans setting up camp. They drop their loads and, if they are not members of the Sidang Injil Borneo, light up one of the simple cigarettes which country people make. Some go off into the bush and others stroll around and look at the available small trees and saplings. The framework of a lean-to hut quickly goes up, lashed with creepers. Then other members of the party come back with thatch. One of the best is a circular kind of palm leaf which can be laid on with little more ado. More conventional palm leaves need to have the leaflets on one side bent over and interwoven with those on the other side. This makes a very durable thatch. Some very large leaves can be placed on individually. If only small leaves are available they have to be skewered on lengths of stick and this takes more time. With surprising ease and rapidity a rain-proof shelter is erected, and provided you have not pitched camp on a nest of fire ants, as happened to us on one occasion, you can expect to enjoy a good night's rest.

Our pathfinder was an elderly man with very poor eyesight. Despite this handicap he seemed to have an almost uncanny memory for the streams and mountains we passed. We never went astray except briefly on the last day. It took us eight days travel and we met no one except for a little party of Penan collecting petrified resins. First we passed some obscure signs of human presence which greatly excited our Lun Bawang party. Then we heard a distant dog bark, a very strange sound in that great expanse of forest. The Lun Bawang set out to locate the dogs' owners and eventually we met up with the Penan on a ridgetop, two men, three women, and six children. They had their shelters near a clump of wild sago, which provide the Penan with their basic source of sustenance. The Penan were known to some of the Lun Bawang from their days in the Adang and they all seemed very happy to see one another again.

The jungle is rather a silent place. At sunrise you hear the gibbons whooping for joy and at sunset there is a great cacophony of insects. But on the forest floor during the day it is generally quiet; the active life is in the canopy far above. Sometimes a pheasant or other bird will call loudly or a troop of monkeys go charging away through the branches. I always used to think that trudging through jungle until you grew tired was a wonderful opportunity for reflection and for drawing up those great plans which make life worthwhile, even though they so rarely come to fruition.

After the quiet of the forest it is a delight to come out on some clear, running mountain stream, but the delight is often short-lived because of the sand flies. These are unquestionably the main curse of Borneo—they are far more troublesome than the leeches and mosquitoes and all the other hostile invertebrates of the country. They seem to delight especially in frequenting the shingle banks lining a sun-dappled stream where the tired traveler wishes to eat and rest and bathe.

The first house we came to was a small Kelabit longhouse and it was they who conveyed us downriver to the area which has been settled by Dayaks. The contrast between the big, vigorous thirty-six door Iban longhouse, Rumah Kedu, to which we came and the small Lun Bawang and Kelabit houses we had been amongst was most striking. The Lun Bawang were obviously ill at ease though we were kindly treated. All this country was once populated by Lun Bawang but was depopulated by Kayan raids followed by illness (mostly cholera and smallpox before the First World War). Dayaks were allowed to move in during the twenties.

The Limbang is a splendid stream. The old Lun Bawang name is Fa Brunei but whether Brunei gave its name to the river or the river gave the state of Brunei its name is not clear to me. The very first Sultan of Brunei is thought by some to have been a Lun Bawang chief who was converted to Islam. In the eighteenth century the Limbang supported a large population, and it is said that there were even Chinese pepper planters to be found far upriver.

Our return to Lawas was accomplished uneventfully and it was not so very much later that we went on long leave. We were sorry to go. There is something about Lawas which delights those who have been fortunate enough to serve there. Curiously enough, it was regarded in the Rajah's day, together with Lundu, another delightful station at the western end of Sarawak, as a punishment station. Officers who were felt to have misbehaved or who had annoyed the Rajah (or the Ranee) were likely to be forthwith banished to one of these two stations. Lawas enchants even the most unexpected people. Some years after I had left, a hardboiled European land and rubber speculator applied for an area of land in the District which he had examined from the air. It lay in a little side valley near the Sabah border and when I asked him what it was like he said, "I tell you Mr. Morrison, it's a wonderful place—it's like a cross between a kind of Shangri-la and H.G. Wells' *Valley of the Blind*."

About the time we went on leave our wireless operator, Ali, also left on transfer. He was a very senior member of the Posts and Telegraphs Department and could more or less pick where he wanted to go. He had himself transferred to Lundu.

4

KANOWIT

We spent our leave in India. This was not what we had planned because I had obtained special permission to take leave in East Africa in order to fulfill a longstanding ambition to see Ruwenzori and the other great mountains of the area. I had to seek special permission because Colonial Service Officers were required to take their leaves in temperate climates. We planned to pass through India, seeing the cave temples of Ellora and Ajanta en route. Hedda had never been in India and found it so fascinating that we quietly abandoned the East African plan.

Towards the end of our stay I received in Darjeeling a letter from Barcroft saying that I was to be posted to Kanowit, in the Rejang, and that the Secretariat was anxiously awaiting news of my return. By this time I had learned to take statements from the Secretariat with a grain of salt and despite the anxiety expressed, we carried on with a pleasant visit to Kashmir. When we eventually returned to Sarawak, I found that not only was there no need for me to have hurried, but that the officer I replaced was most reluctant to take his leave so soon.

Kanowit District covered most of the extensive drainage area of the Kanowit tributary of the Rejang in the middle Rejang together with several smaller valleys. It was populated predominantly by Dayaks. It was the first center to be established by the Rajah's government in the Rejang and existed long before Sibu was founded. It was here, in 1859, that two of the Rajah's officers were murdered by the Kanowit, a local tribe related to the Kayan, of whom only a small remnant now remains. The murderers were harbored by the Kayan and this was one of the main reasons for the great Kayan expedition of 1863 which broke the power of that people. In those days there were very few Dayaks in the District, which, apart from the Kanowit, was only sparsely populated by people called Bukitan. The Iban gradually pushed over from the 2nd Division, took over the land and absorbed the Bukitan. There were a number of small Chinese bazaars at the mouths of the smaller rivers in the District and a strip of Chinese settlement on each bank of the Rejang.

The District has had a turbulent history and was the scene of the last Dayak rebellion against the Rajah's authority in the 1930s. The rebels were led by a disgruntled ex-Penghulu called Asun, but poor administration contributed to the flare-up. At the time, Kanowit was administered from Sibu, the District was not traveled as it should have been, and the lack of close contact between government officers and the people contributed to the unrest which developed. The Kanowit and its tributary, the Julau, and the smaller Rejang tributaries of the Poi and the Ngemah were all seriously affected. A line of blockhouses was built to impede rebel access downriver. Many of the longhouses in the rebel area were made to move downriver to the Igan below Sibu. Asun eventually surrendered and was banished to Lundu District. After the war he was allowed to spend his last years in his home area on the Entabai tributary of the Kanowit. He died shortly after I left the District. Even in his old age he struck me as being a formidable personality.

A minor uprising of a similar nature under the leadership of a man called Bakir was only narrowly averted after the war. Bakir was a truculent, would-be leader, but he lacked popular following and was persuaded to give up shortly before I arrived in the District. He too was sent to Lundu, where he was eventually murdered in a quarrel while on a trading venture over the border in Indonesia.

There was still trouble when I arrived. This centered on the personality of Penghulu Naga of the Ulu Kanowit, a loud-mouthed and argumentative man who would be regarded nowadays as something of a stirrer. He was reputed to have been involved in a headhunting raid against the Kanto Iban of Indonesia before the war. He was round-headed and short and looked like a baby walrus. His marriages had been unfruitful and it was only recently that his latest wife had borne him a son, a very attractive little boy to whom he was devoted. His differences with the

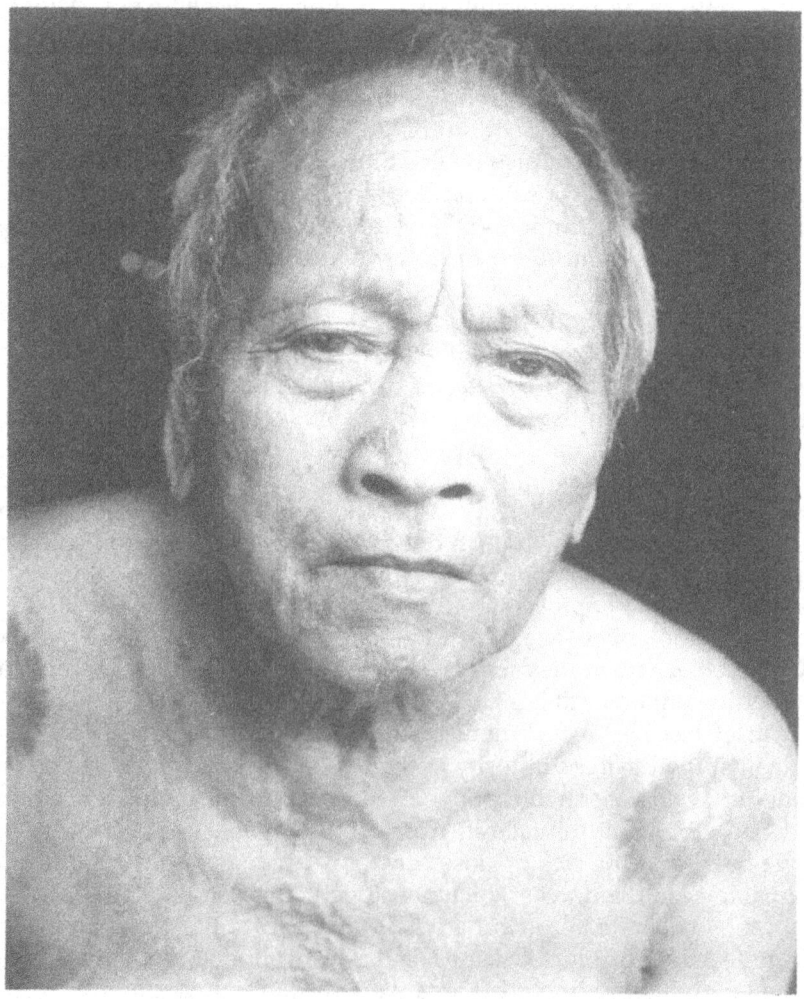

Asun, the last of the great rebels against Brooke authority

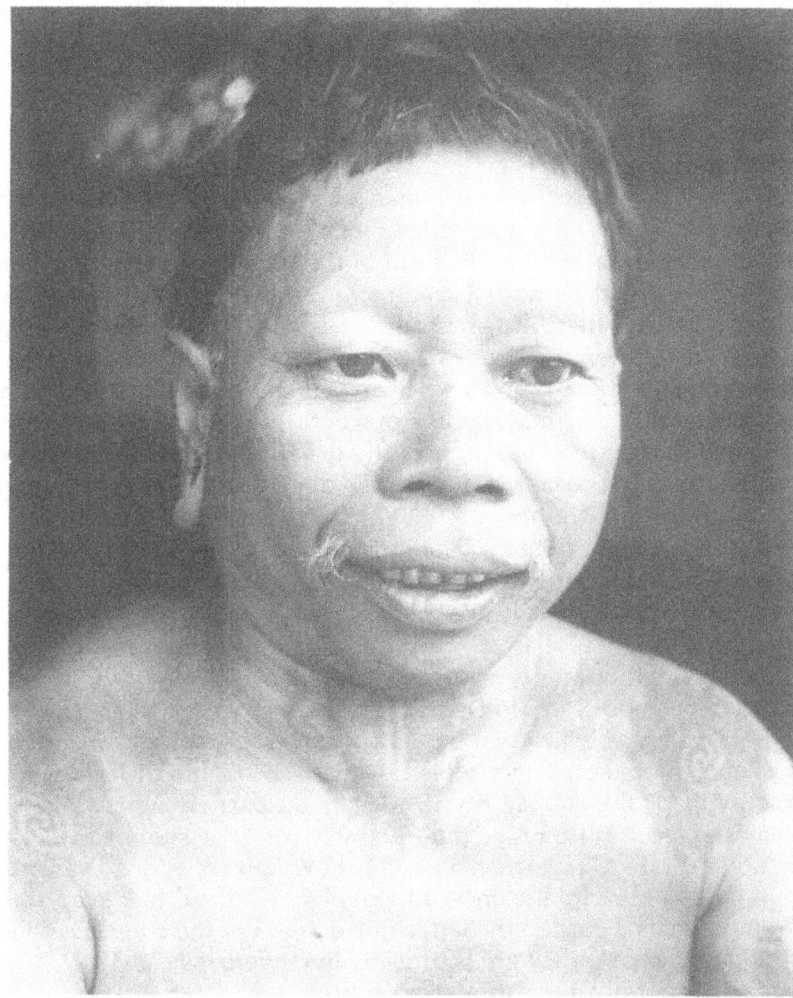

Ex-Penghulu Naga. I had to find his replacement.

Government came from his having brought over several longhouses from the 2nd Division to settle in the Ulu Kanowit. Even though it was done in the war years, he had no authority to do this, for Iban moves were controlled to prevent serious quarrels over land. He could not, or would not, get these houses to return from whence they had come after the war. He had, reportedly, had the effrontery to tell the people of these houses that it was their country and they could do as they pleased in it.

My introduction to Naga came shortly after I had taken over the District, when Naga was summoned to appear in Kanowit to meet the Governor, who was accompanied by the Secretary for Native Affairs, Dennis White, my Resident, Leonard Morse, and several leading Iban figures from Kapit District, including Temenggong Jugah, who was later to play a prominent role in the formation of Malaysia. The Governor dismissed Naga summarily in what was really a sensational end to a career in the government service. Naga was required to put up a large pledge for good behavior, and I was ordered to obtain the pledge money and Naga's shotgun, to find a successor Penghulu, and to evict the recalcitrant longhouses. While I went upriver to collect the pledge, Naga stayed at the house of an elderly Malay policeman who knew him well.

The pledge was quickly forthcoming and Naga never did cause serious trouble, but I had considerable difficulty in finding a successor Penghulu. Some potential replacements were afraid of Naga; others simply did not want the trouble and expense of being Penghulu. Together with the Senior Native Officer, a very experienced veteran called Abang Abu Seman, I carried out a most exhaustive tour of the area and eventually found a man called Siden to take over the post, although he lived in an inconvenient location at the head of the Mujok tributary. The longhouses which had moved without authority eventually returned to the 2nd Division. I felt rather sorry for them, but there are good administrative grounds for wanting to control such movements. When the Dayaks had unlimited forest land available to move into, it did not greatly matter. Nowadays there is no longer unlimited land available for their very extensive traditional farming practices and control is unavoidable.

Kanowit itself had a small bazaar and the usual government organization of a District Headquarters. The bazaar was being rebuilt; it had been burned down for the second time in a few years shortly before our arrival. The first time had been during the war when it had been burned by Dayaks. The District suffered considerably from Dayak depredations during the final months of the war. More than twenty Chinese gardeners were killed and their heads taken. It was much easier to take a Chinese head than that of a Japanese. Bad men in the Poi, from whence some of the Dayak ringleaders in the headhunting came, used to refer sometimes to these unfortunate Chinese as "Jipun pelandok" or Mousedeer Japanese.

The temporary bazaar which was built after the Iban attack was inadvertently set on fire by a Foochow baker. There were not many Foochow in Kanowit and they were disliked by the Hokkien majority, who were the earliest Chinese settlers in the District. When the second fire broke out, the man in whose shop it had started fled for his life and was taken downriver in a Foochow launch. When the launch came upriver again on its next trip, the enraged Hokkien, who had lost everything in the fire, sallied out in boats, boarded the launch, and attacked the crew. The police were fortunately able to break up the fight before any lives were lost.

The bazaar being built was an elaborate brick affair, far too elaborate for the available trade. Originally Kanowit had been the only bazaar in the area, but after the war proliferation of small bazaars was permitted; these were convenient for Dayaks wanting to do some shopping, but effectively cut Kanowit off from its trading hinterland. It did not prosper.

Except for one Malay shop, all the shops were owned by Chinese. I was instrumental in preventing one from being sold to a rich old Iban from upriver called Enteri, who made a lot of money during the rubber boom of the Korean war. Enteri came down to Kanowit with $10,000 and one of the Kanowit businessmen, or towkays, sold him an uncompleted shophouse. He would have had to find another $12,000. I told Enteri to go away and sleep on it and refused to register the transfer until the next day. The towkay was very angry and Enteri changed his mind. The money eventually returned to him only amounted to $9,500 but he prefered to let the matter rest. Later I was to call on Enteri at his home in the Entabai. He was the only man I ever knew who had a pet porcupine, a most amusing animal which rummaged round his bilek when let out of its cage. The thought occurred to me that in view of my great services to him, Enteri might like to present the porcupine to me, though I did not directly express such a wish. But sad to relate, Enteri proved himself to be nothing but an ingrate, for instead of presenting the porcupine to his friendly DO, he eventually sold it for $5 to a towkay in Julau bazaar who ate the wretched animal.

Both the District Office and my bungalow were situated on bluffs overlooking the Rejang, which here is a huge stream. The only other Europeans in the station were members of a long-established Roman Catholic Mission. Despite the long period dating back to the end of the nineteenth century during which the Mission had been at work in Kanowit, the impact it had made in the District was surprisingly limited. The missionaries were popular and respected, but the Christian portion of the Dayak population was quite small. The Dayaks have been a difficult field for missionary endeavor.

On the other side of the Rejang lived an Australian couple—the Bewshers—who ran an Education Department Rural Improvement School. The Bewshers were former Borneo Evangelical Missionaries who had worked in the Limbang among the Bisaya before the war. They had adopted two Bisaya boys, twins whose mother had died in childbirth and who in accordance with the pagan Bisaya custom, had been left exposed to die. They also had a son of their own. The school was an original idea. It catered for young Dayak married couples and set out to teach them improved agricultural practices, hygiene, and home economy. I thought it a very worthwhile effort though it obviously could not yield early results. But it appealed neither to the Education nor Agricultural Departments and some years later it was closed down. Its site was eventually taken over by a government secondary school which plays its part in turning out would-be white-collar workers with a rooted aversion to any thought of life on the land.

I had been told to spend as much time as possible traveling the District and this I proceeded to do. I dislike retracing my tracks when traveling, and in Kanowit it was easy to travel up one river and over the watershed to another one. One's reception tended to vary. Not unnaturally, houses which only twenty years earlier had been uprooted and in some cases burned down and moved forcibly downriver tended to have a rather different view about government authority than did communities which had known no such disruption. I myself was not the ideal officer for an Iban area. I was acquiring a useful knowledge of the language, but the ideal officer is one who loves talking and enjoys nothing more than a good argument, a man of immense stamina who can talk and sometimes drink all night and yet be ready to start on his rounds again early the next morning. As I was none of these things, some of my hosts must have thought me a rather poor specimen.

Kanowit is a fairly closely settled Dayak area and there were many land disputes to be listened to. The Iban were not at that time interested in education and apart from delivering exhortations there was little to do in that field. In fact, in one house I was asked by the Tuai Rumah to dispense with the exhortation. He put it rather bluntly and said that they did not want to listen to any nonsense about schools. Just in case I had not got the message, he explained that they did not want a school. I was usually accompanied by a Hospital Assistant whose visit was invariably popular. The great problem on these occasions is to weed out the malingerers who simply feel that taking medicine must always do one good. In one house a sick old man refused the administrations of the government man and just to show his independence paid a spirit medium $5 to cure him instead. The medium called on the evil spirit to leave the sick man. Part of the ceremony consisted of the medium lying underneath a blanket while his assistant held a blowpipe upright for the spirit to run up.

In pagan Iban areas belief in charms and spells was still strong. A man who owned powerful charms could be much feared. There was also much fear of poisons. A recurring topic of longhouse discussion was pest damage to the padi crops. There was little to be done in the way of preventing insect damage—hill padi does not lend itself to chemical spraying—but rats can be largely controlled by the use of zinc phosphide poison. We used to advise the people to use zinc phosphide but one Penghulu forbade its use in his area. He feared that it might be used against himself.

In most of the pagan longhouses were to be seen the blackened skulls of enemies killed long ago. Headhunting is something which most people associate with Borneo, though it is a practice to be found in various other parts of Asia. It has a misleading connotation of respectability, as if the killing of another human being and the taking of his or her head was hardly more than a practical joke. To some extent the practice was condoned by the Brookes. Iban who took part in punitive expeditions on the government side were allowed to keep their heads. So too were Iban who engaged in authorized tribal warfare. With so much approved head-taking, it is not surprising that there was much unauthorized head-taking as well. It was frowned on and sometimes punished, but much of it went undetected.

A most graphic account of what the old Brooke system could really mean is to be found in an early Report of the Catholic Mill Hill Mission. In 1885 there was a formal peace-making between Pieng Kayan from the Mahakam in the then Dutch territory and Dayaks in Kapit, which lies upriver from Kanowit. But on their way back the Pieng treacherously killed one of a party of four Rejang Dayaks, thereby setting the whole river aflame. Father Dunn reported from Kanowit:

> Our Dyaks immediately sent a message to the Rajah of Sarawak asking permission to retaliate, plainly hinting at the same time, that whether the permission were given or not, they would do so. The permission granted, nothing was then thought or talked of, but preparation for war. War boats were launched and got ready, provisions collected, and weapons furbished up and mended, and in a fortnight's time nearly all the able-bodied men of the country, our Catechumens included, were in their long boats, making for the enemies' country on their much loved war-path; and at this moment this whole army, to the number of 3,000, are carrying fire and sword into every corner of the Kyan country. The effect all this has upon our work I may leave you to guess.

Later the same year Father Dunn reported:

> The Dyaks have been successful in their late expedition. All last week the victorious "Bala" were returning from the war, bringing with them Kyan heads by the score, and making the banks of Rejang and Kanowit ring again with their shouts or rather their yells of triumph. I never understood as I do now how richly these people deserve their name of Head Hunters. I wonder how the Rajah would feel to see, as we have daily during the past week, his government flag flying over boats decorated with strings of the half-roasted heads of women and children, for most of the heads taken were of this kind. Of the many boats that stopped at our landing place, one contained a little girl about four years old, that had been taken alive. I had the curiosity to go down to the water and see the poor little captive, but what was my horror

when I saw hanging just in front of the child—it could have reached it with its little hands—a gaping head blackened and shrivelled by the action of fire. A dreadful suspicion crossed my mind—could that ghastly object have belonged to the slaughtered mother of the child. As though in answer to my thought, a middle-aged man who sat near the child pointing to the head, said, "That belongs to the child's mother," adding with savage delight, "and it was I that took it."

One would think after reading this, that no feeling of humanity or pity could find a place in the breast of such a people; however such is not the case. When the war boats containing captive children passed a village on the river-side, the women would crowd down to the bank to look and count the heads, and taking them in their hands would laugh again with delight, but on perceiving the little orphan captive, forgetting everything else, they would clasp it in their arms, caress it, and cry over it with pity for its forlorn condition. What a strange mixture of savagery and humanity. Most of these warriors, who would not hesitate to cut down the helpless mother flying with her child in her arms, would afterwards take the child and care for it as though it was his own, putting himself to great trouble to find fish and other things for its food. A trader here offered property to the amount of £8 to a Dyak for a captive child, who answered that even for twice that amount, he would not give up his little prize. But what about the Christian boat, you will ask? As you know a number of the men in this boat were not Christians. One of these Pagans before joining the boat killed a pig to propitiate his gods, in the bowels of which pig he read a prognostication of safety and success. His bunch of charms was twice the ordinary size. However in spite of pigs and charms he was struck dead by a spear, whilst in the act of decapitating a woman. This was the only mishap of the party, except that several were struck with poisoned arrows but they sucked the wounds as I had instructed them, and so escaped unhurt.

I am glad to say that they brought no women or children's heads back with them. They brought back a certain amount of spoil, a Kyan child, the heads of two Kyan warriors and twelve old heads, which they found hanging up in the Kyan houses. Now during the heat and excitement of successful war, I think it would not be wise to interfere much with this disgusting custom of keeping heads. Doubtless in course of time, as Christianity takes a firmer hold on the people, their Christian instinct will lead them to put away this custom spontaneously, whereas at present they would only do so under considerable pressure, and with this idea that they were required to give up their custom to satisfy the whim or squeamishness of the Missionary. "Was not David a man after God's own heart, and in the Bible History pictures supplied them from Europe, did they not see David returning in triumph from the fight, with Goliath's head swung over his shoulders?" Tell me, how shall I answer such an objection in a manner intelligible to their rough untutored minds. I contented myself with refusing their invitation to the festivities with which the bringing of enemies' heads into a Dyak village are always accompanied. I was much pleased with a message to me from the war party of one of our villages, saying that if it were sinful to keep their enemies' heads, they were willing to give them to other people, who are still pagans. By biding time, and allowing things to take their natural course, I shall manage to get these ugly trophies put into their proper place beneath the sod, which will be better than having them handed round the country from Christian to Pagan village.

You will see an account in the Gazette of the affair, with the number of killed on both sides. As far as report here gives, the Dyaks have lost seventy men, and the Kyans, including women and children, must be between 300 and 400. Seven villages were burnt. We are all very well here, and all join in the kindest regards to you and the Fathers at Kuching. It may reassure you to hear that our two servants brought nothing from the Kyans' country to hang over the kitchen fire.

The official *Sarawak Gazette* expressed itself with judicious moderation:

The party of Dyaks who went against the Pieng Kayans of Makam, to punish them for their late treachery, have returned. Although aware that the Dyaks were marching against them, the Piengs made no preparations, not believing that the Dyaks were bold enough to carry out their intentions, consequently they were worsted and suffered considerable losses.

There was little serious crime in Kanowit and court work was light. Security of life and limb was very high in Sarawak. There was the occasional murder—generally of a Chinese boat-hawker—though no boat-hawker was lost during my time in the District. Boat-hawkers were traders who ran little shops in boats tied up at the landing place of a large longhouse. It was a lonely, dangerous life but profits were high and overheads low. Almost every year in the Rejang one or two boat-hawkers were robbed and murdered. The perpetrators were rarely apprehended but it never discouraged the boat-hawkers. The dead man was quickly replaced. The boat-hawkers were like fat trout frequenting a favorite pool. No sooner does the fisherman catch one such trout than another quickly takes up his abode in the same place. The only serious incident I was called on to investigate was, however, a very gruesome one.

During the height of the rubber boom a Dayak man from the 4th Division—a solitary and introverted person—was tapping rubber on a share-cropping basis and living in a longhouse not far from Kanowit. The leadership in this house was not of the best. After the rubbertapper had been there for some time his considerable savings were stolen. Some of the people in the house sought to incriminate a Chinese rubbertapper who was also living there. They demanded that he undergo trial by ordeal. This involved grabbing a stone out of a caldron of boiling water. If unscalded he would be deemed innocent. The Chinese rubbertapper not unreasonably demurred, saying that if people really thought he was the thief the police should be called. Pretty obviously, the Dayak rubbertapper did not believe the charge against the Chinese but blamed the people of the house. And that night he set fire to the longhouse and in the confusion, as people rushed to put out the flames, he stabbed them indiscriminately with a spear, killing two men and two women (one of whom was pregnant) and wounding several others. One of the wounded men realized what was happening, jumped out of the house, secured a balk of timber, and returning to the scene, clubbed the assailant to death. It was a very horrible scene when I arrived the next morning—the ruai (communal room) strewn with bodies and the people of the house terribly distraught and upset.

It would be wrong to think that because a DO travels his District conscientiously that he knows everything that is going on in it. He certainly learns quite a lot and gets to know the people of his District. The interest shown by the Government is appreciated, even if in practice you cannot settle all the matters brought to your attention. But only a fool thinks he knows very much. The country people of Sarawak, and probably most other countries for that matter, long ago learned to operate on what the intelligence world calls the need-to-know principle. There are many, many matters which tact, self-interest, or the simple wish not to be bothered by authority decree need not be known.

Dayaks, like all Sarawak people, are very well-mannered. They are likely to laugh at your gaffes and follies after you have left. One of the few exceptions to this occurred when I was touring the houses of Penghulu Briak, whose area took in the Machan valley between Kanowit and Julau. I had to visit one house up a small side river after heavy rain, leaving Hedda at a house at the river mouth. Because of the high water, we had at one place to pull the canoe over a log spanning the river, and stepping into it again, I fell in the river and lost my spectacles. It was not a serious mishap, but the Dayaks with me were most solicitous. "Oh what a dreadful thing, to have the Tuan fall into the river and off our boat," they cried. "Oh the poor Tuan." This went on until we reached the longhouse where Hedda had remained. She was much amused at my bedraggled state and insisted on taking a photograph. At this the floodgates of mirth were finally loosened and my solicitous companions and the rest of the house dissolved into convulsions of laughter.

I believed they named the place where I fell in Lubok Chermin (Eyeglass Pool). An unsympathetic Secretariat refused to refund me the cost of my spectacles, which I had clearly lost in the course of duty. I thought this most unreasonable. Later when I worked in the Secretariat myself, I called for the file and found that the decision was the work of a man whom I had thought was my friend.

Civil claims for loss of goods when canoes sank were common in the District. They usually involved claims by Dayaks against Chinese launches, the Dayaks averring that they had been capsized through the excessive wash of the launch. Some such claims were well based. A large launch can throw up a disconcerting wash, and it was the practice of the launches to keep to the banks and to cut corners. They did a good deal of damage. A feature of such claims was that there was nearly always a large sum of money in what the Police Reports used to call "Wang Note Perentah" (bank notes) in an iron box in the boat which had sunk. Such boxes were never recovered. Some of the claims were very dishonest. Standing outside my bungalow I once saw a Dayak outboard capsize in the Rejang. It was an overloaded boat driven too fast through the swell set up by a launch which had passed by some time earlier. The people in the canoe were picked up by another launch which passed by shortly after. I found next morning that the capsized Dayaks had charged their rescuers with having sunk them.

Gambling and opium caused one a certain amount of work. In the Rajah's time, gambling was licensed and the local casino, or gambling farm as it was termed, provided the Government with useful revenue. The licensee made sure that there was no gambling anywhere else; it was orderly and if someone lost heavily you knew about it. When Sarawak became a Crown Colony the system was abolished. The result was that more gambling than ever went on and much of the gambling activity moved to cockfighting, to the great detriment of the Dayaks. Much the same sort of thing happened with opium. Under the old system, certified addicts could obtain a modest quantity of the drug. The opium was of good quality; it was provided openly and there was no corruption. Declared illegal, the practice simply spread underground and much of the opium was adulterated. Both gambling and opium rackets became the main source of corruption in the police force. Unless moral pressures strong enough to reform society in such fields can be brought to bear, it always seemed to me that intelligent regulation rather than ineffectual prohibition was better for everybody.

I had some personal experience of how corruption was nurtured by suppression. In one of the stations where I served, I knew that there was a lot of gambling going on in the bazaar and I could never get the bright young Police Sub-Inspector to do anything about it. He was a flashy dresser off duty and gave many parties. One night I decided to carry out an investigation myself, went to his house where I found him in a slightly fuddled state, and straight away took him with me to the bazaar. We found a gambling school without difficulty—in the back of a coffee shop—and striding in I found about thirty of my parishioners engrossed in a game known as Pai-kow. Entering the door, I held up my hand and said in a loud and solemn voice, "stop."

If I had thought about it at all, I suppose I would have expected the gamblers to cower with looks of alarm and meekly submit to the forces of law and order. But gamblers, I was to find out very quickly, are made of sterner stuff than this. They made a concerted rush for the door in front of which I was standing. And it takes more than a well-meaning DO and a befuddled Police Sub-Inspector to stop thirty sturdy Chinese from going through a door if they have set their minds on doing this. For a few short and hectic moments there was much pushing and shoving and some round English oaths. At the end of it the Sub-Inspector and I were in possession of many torn singlets and abandoned slippers, more than $100 on the table, and two of the gamblers. One was a small man who was last in the queue trying to get out; the other was an inexperienced lad who had hidden himself under the table. No one had struck me but someone had punched the Sub-Inspector in the eye.

I duly fined the coffee shop owner and the two captured gamblers, and then the whole story came out. The Sub-Inspector had been issuing his own personal permits to gamble with a scale of charges providing more than adequate remuneration for every policeman in the station. The incident brought to a premature end a career in the police force which had been marked by much early promise but perhaps a little too much initiative.

I used often to visit Julau where a government substation was located. After Kanowit it was the biggest bazaar in the District. The Julau Chinese were notable for the excellent relations they maintained with the local Dayaks. They were also extremely hospitable. Their hospitality was proffered in such a pleasant way that it seemed churlish not to accept. Whenever I arrived in Julau it just seemed to coincide with a dinner party being given by one of the leading Julau towkays. The local Penghulu, Banyang, a particularly intelligent and pleasant man, would be there too.

Banyang had himself been a rebel. His half brother Kendawang had been, I think unjustly, imprisoned during the Asun trouble for having failed to turn in his gun within a stipulated period of time. He had been on particularly close and friendly terms with several European officers and he was deeply hurt by the sentence. He broke out of jail, killed a man, and was joined by Banyang. They spent some time as

Keeping in step with the police. The author with Datuk Abang Haji Marzuki after the opening of the new Julau Chinese school.

outlaws but were eventually persuaded to give themselves up. When their surrender was being negotiated, they demanded that the Rajah should send them a gold-hilted sword as a token of good faith. They were sent one of the dress swords worn by senior service officers as part of their official uniform. Kendawang was sent to Lundu and Banyang to Marudi in the Baram. Here the DO, Donald Hudden, helped him to obtain some elementary education.

We held a regatta in Kanowit. In a river country such as Sarawak regattas are traditional events. The various longhouses enter racing boats of varying sizes; nowadays some of the emphasis has unfortunately been diverted to outboard-driven speedboats. Regattas are fun and bring together people from all over the District, but they are very exhausting for the organizers and they can be very exhausting for the judges. Many Borneans are excitable people, especially Dayaks, and in a close finish the losing boat is liable to question the decision of the judges, and the whole of the boat crew may come rushing up to argue their case heatedly with the judges. A feature of the Kanowit regatta was an event introduced by one of my predecessors which involved a short race by small boats in which there had to be one European. The race went to the first European to reach the top of the steep bluff overlooking the river where the judges had their box, a wild and slippery scramble by the Europeans, which greatly diverted the spectators lining the top of the bank.

There was a great meeting, or Aum, of all the Iban Penghulus to revise the Customary Law which applied in matters of family and farming and social behavior, except for marital matters between Christians. The 3rd Division Customary Law which was being revised was slightly different from that which applied in the 2nd Division. The work to be revised was largely a list of offenses and the fines which could be imposed under them. It also outlined the prohibited relationships between men and women. The concept of incest was very much more complicated than in the west. But the rules of conduct always seemed to me to be remarkably sensible. In particular, the position of women was an enlightened one. They enjoyed a far greater degree of equality with men than is the case in Muslim Law. Both man and wife had equal rights to discard the other. They each retained the property they had brought with them when they married, and property acquired since was equally divided. I only thought that seduced girls or divorced women received very inadequate compensation for the hard work of childbearing, but children are so adored in Dayak society that I do not think that they suffered much as a result. The young people enjoy a good deal of freedom in matters of sex though I doubt whether it is any freer than in western society.

The Aum was an interesting occasion. The leading figure was the venerable Temenggong Koh of Kapit District, though much of the revision was undertaken by Koh's eventual successor, Temenggong Jugah, with the District Officer Kapit,

Temenggong Koh, the paramount Dayak Chief in the Rejang,
addressing the 1952 Conference (Aum) on Customary Law

Anthony Richards, who was the most knowledgeable European officer on the subject, playing the main role on the government side. At the opening of the Aum, Koh lodged a formal, but tongue-in-cheek, request that the Iban trackers who were at that time active in the Malayan Emergency should be permitted to bring back heads with them.

One Penghulu achieved something of a legal tour de force. He was the Penghulu of the lower Poi in Kanowit District. I had earlier, and with some reluctance, found him not guilty of the offense of bigamy. The charge evidently rankled, and at the Aum he successfully persuaded his fellow Penghulus that the offense should be deleted from the Customary Law. He argued cogently that it was already covered under the law relating to adultery. The offense was therefore removed from the statute book. How many Queen's Counsel, I wonder, have ever achieved such a feat.

Another occasion which brought about a great gathering in Sibu was the visit of the Duchess of Kent on one of those showing-the-flag exercises which British royalty and their loyal subjects so patiently endure. Such visits are a mixed blessing for the people on the ground. They involve a lot of work but also enable you to get various things done which would not otherwise be done. The Duchess only flew in for lunch, but the Residency in Sibu was given a splendid face-lift and the Resident ordered one of the biggest refrigerators in Southeast Asia, a refrigerator which an unfeeling Secretariat later handed over to the Medical Department. If one has to put up with royal visits, there is everything to be said for having royalty like the Duchess of Kent, a singularly graceful and courteous woman who was easy going and relaxed in unfamiliar surroundings and who was much liked by the pressmen accompanying her.

The occasion was particularly complicated because the Sibu airfield was not at that time considered suitable for a VIP aircraft, and the Duchess came in by flying boat accompanied by another aircraft carrying a lifeboat that could in emergency be dropped by parachute. The rivers of Borneo are not ideal for flying boat use because there is so much floating debris in them. A fleet of launches and outboards had to scour the river looking for bits of floating wood which could hole a flying boat hull on impact. There was no trouble of this kind, but when the aircraft took off, the aircrew, who had been hospitably entertained at the Island Club, forgot to take down the little Royal Standard and flagpole which the RAF insist on pushing up through the cockpit roof while on the ground or water on such occasions. As the flying boat took off, the flagpole broke away and for one moment it looked as if the aircraft was falling apart. The royal visit was altogether a memorable occasion and the Resident named the new government speed boat "Marina."

The Resident was Dennis White. He and Barcroft were the outstanding senior officers in colonial Sarawak who had served in the Rajah's government. He was a very able man, deeply and sympathetically interested in Sarawak people. He was an excellent linguist and had a remarkable memory for people. He and Barcroft were at one time the principal figures in line for the post of Chief Secretary in Sarawak. The post went to Barcroft, and White went on to achieve considerable success as British High Commissioner in Brunei. His many good points were marred by pomposity, making him unpopular with his European colleagues. But he treated Hedda and myself with every consideration and having served in Kanowit before the war, he was a great support to a sometimes harrassed DO in the field.

We took one local leave in Kanowit. We had never been in the 2nd Division and so I asked whether, when I traveled up to the head of the Kanowit, I could carry on into the 2nd Division and cross it to Simanggang, commencing my leave the day I crossed the limits of my own District. This rather unusual proposal was approved, and so we made our way over the head of the Layar valley which runs down to Betong and so on to the Skrang River, which we descended to Simanggang. This was a most pleasant journey. Dayaks did not often see the DO from the next District but they seemed to take our journey very much for granted.

Our path led us over the shoulder of Sadok mountain, famous in Sarawak history because of its association with Rentap, the most famous of all the Iban leaders who opposed the Brooke government. During the 1850s, Rentap was a serious threat to the Rajah's authority. He had a stronghold on the top of Sadok and this was not reduced until the third attempt in 1861. The quick ascent which we made was in odd contrast to the difficulties encountered by its government besiegers. In order to take the stronghold they had to manhandle a cannon to the top of the mountain. Sadok is not so much a peak as a ridge top, at one end of which Rantap's fort was built, constructed of belian ironwood, thick planks of which in those days were impenetrable to small arms fire. No traces now remain of the fort. Level ground not far from the top of the ridge was planted up with rubber. After the destruction of the fort, Rentap retired to the Ulu Kanowit where he died a few years later. His influence was in decline when he met with final defeat, having lost some of the popular support that he had once enjoyed.

We came down to the hospitable house of Penghulu Bakar in the Skrang, a very pleasant old gentleman but rather deaf, and here we met Datu Zen, the Senior Native Officer in Simanggang who had kindly come up to meet us. He was a fine example of the old-style Malay leaders who had been the main prop of the Rajah's authority. He was a small, quiet, dignified man with a gentle air of natural authority. He knew no English and kept his travel notes in the Jawi script. He had lived all his life in Dayak Districts and he spoke their language and understood their customs perfectly. He was a much respected figure. When Hedda wanted to take his photograph, he insisted on dressing up in Iban finery.

It took us two days to reach Simanggang, stopping at the house of Penghulu Sait on the way. Sait was said to be the richest Dayak in the 2nd Division, a pioneer businessman who had prospered mightily during the Korean rubber boom. His house contained a great collection of valuable jars and brass cannon, and he had installed electricity which only operated when he was in residence. Sait had grown well-rounded with age. He wore many heavy gold rings. He came to an untimely end through failure to appreciate the ravages that time does to a man's agility. He fell out of a tree while picking fruit and sustained fatal injuries.

Simanggang was a pretty little station. In those days it could only be reached by launch from the capital. The government quarters were dotted over a little group of hills by the river. The old fort, Fort Alice, was built on a bluff commanding the river. It was originally built to discourage Iban forays out to sea. The river, the Batang Lupar, is very shallow and having an extensive estuary it suffers from a severe bore which hinders navigation. Somerset Maugham, who was here in 1922, was nearly drowned in the bore, and it is the setting for one of his rather uncharitable stories, "The Yellow Streak." Maugham did not endear himself to the European officers whose hospitality he enjoyed in Sarawak, but in his short stories and *A Writer's Notebook* he has left some of the most graphic of all word pictures of the Sarawak scene.

We stayed with the Resident, Alan Griffin, a prewar officer and one of the few survivors of the disastrous withdrawal by European officers from the 3rd Division to Dutch Borneo in 1942. He was a big, kind, argumentative man with an unjustified inferiority complex which sometimes made him prickly. He was a very conscientious traveling officer. Although a bachelor he had never entered into one of the de facto local marriages which, understandably, had been a common practice among European bachelors.

When the Japanese invaded Sarawak at the end of 1941 they contented themselves initially with occupying Kuching and the oil town of Miri. They did nothing to take over other areas. The Resident Sibu, Macpherson, decided to withdraw to Long Nawang in Dutch Borneo, taking government officials and some businessmen with him. Griffin was DO Kapit at the time. The party slowly made their way up the Balui and over to Long Nawang. Philip Jacks, the DO Kanowit, whose advice to take a much shorter route up the Katibas was overruled by Macpherson, was sent with another man to take news of the withdrawal to the outside world. They caught what was probably the last Dutch plane to leave Samarinda. Griffin grew uneasy and found Macpherson's autocratic ways hard to bear. He and a Lands officer called Baron went back to Sarawak with a party of Kanowit Dayaks returning home and were interned in Kuching. All the Europeans who remained in Long Nawang were captured by the Japanese and murdered. Had they remained in Sarawak, as did the missionaries, they would probably have come to no harm.

Despite the vast size of Borneo, not a single European, no matter how familiar with the country, was able to remain at liberty during the war. This contrasts with Malaya, where a number survived the war at liberty living with the Chinese resistance and many more would have survived given the mental stamina necessary to carry them through. The Resident Simanggang, Arundell, and the District Officer Baram, Hudden, two of the best and most popular officers in the Rajah's service, tried to remain at liberty in remote areas but were eventually murdered by killer squads sent out by the Japanese. A group of experienced Sarawak officers attached to the Punjabi battalion in Kuching, which withdrew into and eventually surrendered in Dutch Borneo, turned back to try and join up with other Europeans at liberty. They were all murdered by Dayaks on the Dutch side of the border. Only in the 5th Division did parties at liberty survive. One party was captured far up the Ulu Limbang but was not harmed. Another party in the Ulu Trusan gave themselves up and claimed miraculous guidance for the step derived from their study of the Book of Jeremiah which they were reading at the time.

Hedda and I carried on with our journey to Lubok Antu, a small upriver station on the Indonesian border. It was a singularly tiresome journey in one of the worst boats we ever traveled in. The outboard propeller projected below the hull and every time we went aground on a shingle bank we broke a shearpin. This should normally happen only if you hit a piece of floating debris. We were glad to arrive in Lubok Antu, where we planned to spend a few days and climb a neighboring hill called Bukit Besai, from which on a fine day you get a superb prospect of the lake system of the great Kapuas River on the Indonesian side.

Lubok Antu is a beautiful place. The fort was called Fort Arundell after the murdered Resident who served here for many years as a DO and married a local Dayak lady. He was an old-style English country gentleman who liked rural living. He used to call for dinner by blowing a hunting horn. It was found after the war in the remains of the farming hut where he and his family were murdered by a group of Poi Dayaks who had been sentenced to death for their part in the Asun rebellion. Arundell had successfully interceded with the Rajah to have their sentences commuted.

Within half an hour of our arrival we received a telegram and a telephone message ordering me to return to Kanowit immediately. We learned that there had been some disturbance in the 1st Division, but it was not until we reached Sarikei that we learned from Philip Jacks that there had been some trouble in Kanowit too. Philip had a somewhat solemn manner which belied a light-hearted nature. "Have you heard, old boy," he said in sepulchral tones, "that your bungalow has been attacked by masked and armed robbers?" No one, of course, had told us anything of the sort. It was not a very cheering thought with which to speed us on our way.

When we arrived back in Kanowit, I found that the situation was not quite as black as appeared might be the case. During our tour upriver and into the 2nd Division, the Rejang was undergoing one of its periodic penyamun scares. Penyamun means robber, and the rumors—Sarawak is a very rumor-prone place—concern vague but real fears of the presence of robbers, headhunters, and malign forces. Such scares crop up periodically and then die away again. In Kanowit there were rumors of demons called Antu Inong. One had even been seen in the longhouse of Penghulu Empam, a prominent local Catholic who had recently been decorated by the Pope.

Our house, which was an isolated one, was in the custody of the same elderly Malay policeman who had befriended Naga when Naga was dismissed. There was a great storm one night. The telephone broke down and on these occasions such rambling government houses respond with some creaks and groans. Doors and shutters bang and rattle. The policeman thought he heard someone knocking at the door, but when he called out no one replied. He called out again and still got no reply. He opened one of the windows and peering out saw several indistinct figures. He was a courageous man, and picking up his shotgun, he fired at the figures which then disappeared. When people did eventually come to the house in the morning, he was in a state of near shock and reported that the bungalow had been attacked. The poor man was very upset, as well he might be.

There had indeed been a disturbance in the 1st Division. A Police Corporal manning a practice road block had been shot by a small group of communists who had, quite coincidentally, been extorting money in a nearby bazaar. They killed the Corporal and escaped over the border into Indonesia.

From the communist point of view, this was a peculiarly short-sighted action. In the subsequent inquiry, the state of readiness of the police showed many weaknesses. Sarawak's modern police force dates back to this incident. The then Commissioner, Shannon, was replaced, and the force was modernized and expanded. Shannon may not have been the ideal man to build up a police force and some of his officers were of poor quality. Nevertheless, on occasions like these complete justice is rarely done. Shannon was held responsible for the state of the force, although his own requests for more staff and a greater allocation of funds had not been fully met by the Government.

It was not only Iban and Malays who were superstitious. The local Chinese in Kanowit were equally so. When I was trying to get them to move out of their old temporary shophouses into the newly completed brick shophouses, I met with much resistance. No one wanted to move into the brick shophouses and start paying rent. The towkays who owned new shophouses did not want to move into them either because they would have lost business to those remaining in temporary shophouses nearer the river. My pleas and objurgations went unheeded until one towkay announced that three peacocks had flown into his temporary shophouse. The intelligence was greeted with dismay as a most unfavorable omen by the other traders, though I myself concluded that the peacocks were actually Green-winged Doves, which have a curious habit of flying through buildings. The towkays vacated the old shophouses almost overnight.

About halfway through our tour in Kanowit, our good Bolhi decided to leave us. He was an excellent man to have with one in a Dayak District. He understood the life and spoke Iban as well as he spoke Malay. He had been less useful in a Lun Bawang District where he could not communicate so well. He was a keen sportsman and a good shot. But his family was growing and needed better education facilities than it could enjoy while he worked for me. And his wife wanted to be with her family in Sibu. We were sorry to lose Bolhi. He became a pillar of the Public Works Department in Sibu and gave his children an excellent education.

One of the problems of being a DO was that you were, in the earlier days of our service, expected to provide much hospitality for all and sundry who might wish to visit your District. This had been quite a good system before the war when there were few European officers. Visitors were welcome and they brought their own servants who helped yours. After the war there was far more movement of visitors. And many of them brought no servant with them. It became a tiresome system, but it was years before the Government at last built small local resthouses to accommodate such visitors.

You not only dispensed hospitality to visiting colleagues. In a Dayak area you had many local callers. You would hear a discreet cough outside and then a Dayak or party of Dayaks would come in. You welcomed them and gave them a drink and talked of current affairs. Sometimes it was possible to conduct very useful business in this way because people were more prepared to talk. You were, however, placed in something of a dilemma. You did not want your visitors to stay all night nor did you wish to appear mean in your provision of refreshment. If, however, you were too generous it might be difficult to bring the proceedings to an end.

Nevertheless, dropping in for a drink with the DO was a pleasing custom. You drank their liquor when you went to their longhouses and it was only right that you should respond. On one occasion in Kanowit, out of curiosity I sought to see how much arak (a quite potable Chinese distilled rice spirit) some visitors could consume. The quantity was prodigious and the proceedings uproarious. When my visitors eventually staggered off, they lost themselves and their Identity Cards. It was an embarrassing experiment, though no one seemed to hold it against me. I did not repeat it. Later on, as sophistication grew, your visitors were likely to expect you to provide brandy or gin and it became a costly operation.

Some of the most unusual visitors to pass through Kanowit were a small herd of elephants. The Borneo Company had a pioneer timber business in Sarawak. They extracted hardwood timber from a large concession upriver from Kapit on a tributary of the Balui River. Before the war they had imported an experimental batch of elephants from their timber concessions in Thailand, but the war came too soon for the experiment to have been fully evaluated and only one elephant survived. A second batch was brought upriver in a large barge while I was in Kanowit. The Company asked for my good offices in providing the elephants with a supply of banana stems which grew in profusion along the river banks near Kanowit. They thought to pay 15-20 cents per stem. I entrusted the task of finding the several hundred stems required to the station carpenter and odd job man, Inu, a man who seemed able to cope with unexpected requests quickly and efficiently. He once again responded quickly and efficiently, but after conferring with banana growers, informed me with regret that due to the Korean war boom there had been a sharp rise in the price of banana stems, which could not be provided for less than 60 cents a stem. The Company took a poor view of this example of commercial enterprise, but there was nothing I could do about it.

Neither the elephants nor the upriver timber business throve. The idea was to float logs downriver, but many were lost and many more stolen, while some of the Company's Dayak contractors swindled the Company unmercifully. I always liked the story told me by a friend who had been with the timber manager when he visited a house above Kapit occupied by some of these contractors. Not unnaturally, the visitors were royally entertained; the tuak flowed; the utmost jollity prevailed. The businessman surveyed the happy scene and beamed. "Nature's children, old boy," he said. The Company was paying Dayaks for logs allegedly felled and put in the river to float downstream. It was quite impossible to prove that they had done anything of the sort. Nor had they. Later, great fortunes were made in extracting timber from the readily accessible swamp forests, and nowadays with modern equipment the process continues in hill areas as well.

Particularly exhausting occasions in Kanowit were the visits by teams recruiting Iban trackers for service with the British Army in Malaya. There was tremendous enthusiasm on the part of young Dayaks for this, and the District Office was besieged by young men, all of whom wanted to tell me personally why they should be chosen. Those who were not accepted grew angry and those who were chosen sometimes balked at the last moment if, in their excitement, they had a bad dream. Dreams were regarded as messages from the spirit world. Nevertheless they gave good service and were popular with British troops. Similar respect had been voiced by Australian troops during the Pacific war. Referring to Dayaks as a number of interior peoples and not exclusively to Iban, the official Australian war history has this to say: "Of all the Asian and island peoples among whom the Australian soldier campaigned and trained in six years of war . . . none won more respect from him than did the Dyaks, with their courage, dignity, friendliness and generosity."

5

BARAM

We spent altogether about eighteen months in Kanowit, and I was then given a transfer to stand in for the DO Baram who was about to take a prolonged leave. Baram was a particularly popular and interesting District and I was lucky to get a posting there. I owed it largely to the help of Dennis White. Although in retrospect my Kanowit posting was a very rewarding one from the point of view of interest and experience, I had been a consistent grumbler. Looking back, I think this was unreasonable. But unbeknownst to me, Hedda, who had grown weary of the grumbling, went to see Dennis White and asked him to have me sent somewhere else.

We traveled to Marudi on a powered barge called the "Dido." Most of the government-owned vessels were named after ships connected with Sarawak's past and the "Dido" was named, not very appropriately, after the beautiful corvette commanded by Captain Henry Keppel in 1843-44. Keppel was ordered by the Royal Navy to support James Brooke in anti-piracy operations. He was one of the great sailors of the Victorian era, small and fiery, brave and generous. It was his book, *An Expedition to Borneo in H.M.S. Dido*, published in 1846, which made Sarawak and James Brooke famous in Britain. Most of the book consists of extracts from the Rajah's diaries. The two men became fast friends. Keppel was to outlive Brooke by more than thirty years.

My favorite story of Keppel, however, has little to do with Sarawak. In 1848 he commanded the frigate "Maeander," which brought James Brooke back to Borneo after he had been appointed Governor of Labuan and Consul-General for Borneo. The "Maeander" returned to Britain via Australia and the Pacific in 1850. It was Keppel's intention to call at Tahiti, which the French had established largely as a naval station. But not far from Tahiti, the "Maeander" fell in with an American whaler and Keppel invited the Captain, "a respectable looking old salt with gray hair," on board. He entertained the American to Manila cheroots and Jamaica rum. On parting, Keppel told the whaler captain that he had been six months without European news, whereupon the whaler captain "guessed" that he must be aware of the war between France and England. He added that the French Admiral was at sea looking for the English fleet. He then took his leave.

Keppel was thunderstruck. He seems only to have half believed the whaler captain, but he was a man who would take no chances. He was also a determined man who wanted to see Tahiti. When the "Maeander" arrived off Papeete, he sailed boldly in with every gun loaded with round shot, grape, and canister. It became immediately obvious that there was no war. The "Maeander" was greeted by an English pilot and a French officer, and Keppel was so entranced by the beauty of the scene that he entirely forgot about his loaded guns. He was reminded when he told the 1st Lieutenant to fire a salute to the French Admiral's flag. "You forget, Sir," said that officer with some asperity, "that we have round shot, grape, and canister in every gun. I have nothing but this scoop to draw them nor can we get outside against the sea-breeze to empty them. I could not fire a pistol here without hitting someone."

Keppel, however, had to call on the French Governor, who greeted him with every courtesy and took him to lunch with a number of French naval officers. After a while the Governor drew his chair near to Keppel's and spoke of their lack of news from Europe and the interest aroused by the visit of a British frigate. The Governor went on, "Every five minutes I am receiving reports of the withdrawal of round shot, grape, and canister from every gun in your frigate." There was nothing for it but for Keppel to give a frank explanation. "Whereupon," wrote Keppel in his autobiography, "everyone of the gallant French Captains rose without a moment's hesitation, shook me by the hand, expressing a hope that under similar circumstances their officers would have done the same." In due time the salutes were fired and returned, and "we mixed as one family. I have ever found French naval officers perfect gentlemen."

It was a far cry from Keppel's "Dido" to our barge, but it conveyed us safely and comfortably to Miri. We slept on deck under an awning and were fortunate to have fine weather for the voyage, though it was the end of the landas season. It then followed us up to Marudi, the Administration Centre for Baram District. Marudi lies some thirty-five miles from the mouth of the river in a straight line, though much further following the course of the river. In Marudi I took over from Francis Drake, another of the Rajah's officers, a large, quiet man with a computer-like brain. When checking accounts he had the uncanny ability to check all columns simultaneously.

The District covers the whole of the Baram valley and was established in 1883, before there was any government station at Miri. The Baram River is not as large as the Rejang, but it is nevertheless an extremely impressive stream and has a number of important tributaries. Marudi is situated on the first elevation to be found along the banks of the river, from where the fort commanded one of the narrower reaches of the river. The government quarters were nearby. Below lay the bazaar with the Malay kampong beyond. The DO's house was a fine old rambling ironwood building with a view over lawns to the Baram and beyond to blue mountains dominated in the distance by the spectacular peak of Mount Mulu. There were scorpions in the bathroom and the guttering was defective and some inspired plumber had built the septic tank above the well used in dry weather, but it was one of the most pleasant abodes in which we ever resided. Not all its history had been pleasant though. The Japanese had occupied it during the war and had beaten a wretched upriver Chinese trader to death in what was now the sitting room. The trader was suspected, quite unjustly, of having an illegal wireless set. The Japanese, as was their gentle custom, tied him to an ironwood pillar and beat him for hours. He died from his injuries.

Baram District is one of the most attractive in Sarawak for the officer who likes traveling, and we set out to see as much as we could during the time available to us. Our first trip took us to Long San, the longhouse of the paramount chief, Temenggong Oyong Lawai Jau, both to pay our respects and to discuss plans for a pioneer malaria eradication scheme. The Temenggong was a remarkable man. He was one of the last of the great old-style Bornean chiefs, who had nevertheless recognized the need for change and was the principal architect of the conversion of much of the

Baram to Christianity. The old customs which the people followed until after the war had little to commend them. They were so riddled with superstition and injunctions which had to be followed for the slightest of reasons, that life was very difficult for the Orang Ulu. Unpropitious omens were continually requiring them to stop work or to abandon journeys or other ventures. Nevertheless, the Orang Ulu were deeply conservative people and the old ways had a strong hold on them.

If there was to be change, an initiative was required and this was provided by the Temenggong. In an account that he gave later he said, "I don't want to say that my ancestors were or that they did evil by following the old custom but I began to understand that if we were to continue to follow the old custom we would be left far behind all the other people in Sarawak." He conferred with many of the other headmen and, with their consent, went down to Marudi in 1947 and told the venerable Father Jansen of their wish to abandon the old customs. Father Jansen had served in Miri and Marudi for some fifty years, though with little success in the Baram. He hastened upriver and brought the good word to Long San. Many of the Orang Ulu made the decision to become Christians. They disposed of their heads and, perhaps more unfortunately, of all their charms and amulets and figures, some of which would have been well worth preserving for posterity. Father Jansen died the next year from dysentery, contracted while bringing the first priest to take up residence in Long San. By the time we came to visit Long San there was a well-established mission station and school in existence.

Not all the Baram people became Catholics. Some adhered to the old custom and others became members of the Evangelical Church. While the great process of heart searching was in progress in the Long San area, Mr. Hudson Southwell of the Borneo Evangelical Mission was at work in the Kelabit country. He had hastened downriver, and quite a number of communities in the upper Baram and in the Apoh and Akah tributaries of the river accepted the evangelical teaching. For the outsider, it must seem that the more tolerant Catholic attitudes towards alcohol and tobacco are easier for the Orang Ulu to accept. Unlike among the Lun Bawang, drink had a largely social function among the Kayan and Kenyah and was not destroying them. But the differences, which persist, do cause some problems. As one Tua Kampong put it later to Hedda, "It is difficult for us. How are we to choose between the Fathers who drink and smoke but don't marry and those who marry but don't drink or smoke?"

In the Rajah's day, the spheres of influence of the two main missions were largely decreed by government—the Anglicans had the 2nd Division and the Catholics the 3rd Division. This practice had begun to be more loosely observed before the war and after the war it was given up entirely. This did not much matter when whole communities opted for one form of Christianity, but it could lead to bitter quarreling when a house became divided. Sarawak never suffered from anything like the great and squalid soul rush of New Guinea, but there were enough different churches at work to cause trouble and to make the purveyors of Christianity at times look rather unchristian.

The malaria eradication scheme which we went to Long San to discuss with the Temenggong was a very interesting project. Malaria was endemic in Sarawak and severely affected the health of rural communities, particularly in the long-settled upriver areas of the Rejang and Baram. Its debilitating effect was one of the main reasons for a great decline in the numbers of the Kayan and Kenyah. The disease was found all over Sarawak but its impact had been most severe among these peoples. Consequently, Baram District was the logical choice for a pilot scheme when the

Government put aside $4,000,000 during the Korean rubber boom for the eradication of malaria. This was an imaginative move. The Medical Department was given a block vote to be spent largely at its discretion since there was little previous experience as to how the campaign should be conducted. This was the right way to start, but I well remember how bitterly the Department later resented being called on to analyze its expenditure and to put it on a more regular and controllable basis once the scheme was well established. The World Health Organization provided the technical expertise under the leadership of a most hardworking Columbian called Julian de Zulueta.

Malaria is conveyed by mosquitoes of which there are a great abundance in Borneo. Most mosquitoes are, however, nonvectors of the disease. It was first necessary to establish the identity of the vector and the nature of its habits. The vector in Sarawak is, in fact, a little-seen species which emerges late at night and rests low down on the walls of houses. Once the nature of the vector had been clearly established, control consisted of spraying with DDT the underneath of all houses, including farming huts, and the lower few feet of all internal walls. This kills the infected vector and so interrupts the life cycle of the malarial parasite. It was a very successful scheme in Sarawak. Malaria was reduced to the point where outbreaks became extremely rare. The effect on the health of the ulu and on the population growth of the people who lived there was dramatic. The trouble is that malaria can always be reintroduced. There was no similar control of the disease in Indonesia and cross border movements provided continuing reinfection.

Ironically, although the anti-malaria scheme arrested and then sharply reversed the depopulation of the ulu, an even more intractable source of depopulation has now taken the place of malaria. So many of the younger people have obtained salaried employment—mostly in the government service—and moved to the towns, that nowadays there is a shortage of young people in many ulu houses. The old people remain, ever growing older, but without their children to help them in their old age.

Julian accompanied us to Long San to explain the scheme to the Temenggong and to negotiate terms of employment for antimalarial workers. The terms agreed upon were generous, based on the Government's understanding that while spraying was going on there would be no rest periods. I was incensed to find later that our Christian workers considered that the Sabbath took precedence over the needs of antimalaria work. They were seemingly unaware that there was divine approval for doing good on the Sabbath. Muslim workers did not insist on the same consideration in respect of the Muslim rest and prayer day, which falls on Friday.

The visit to Long San provided us with our introduction to Baram hospitality. In the house of a great chief such as Oyong Lawai Jau this was spectacular, though the pattern was generally the same in all Orang Ulu houses. After you had bathed and people had assembled in the house, you were first greeted with songs of welcome. One of your hosts—it could be a man or a woman—would sing a long extempore account of your alleged virtues, the people joining in a chorus at the end of each stanza. The song would end with a great crescendoing chant of "oo," and you were proffered and expected to gulp down a glass of borak, the rice beer of the Orang Ulu. All the guests in turn would be treated in this way.

You were then expected to respond. You attempted a song of praise to the person who had sung your praises, extolling the virtues of the people of the longhouse. You then proffered a drink of borak to the person you were addressing. You could continue and sing more songs of praise if you felt so inclined, and the exchange could continue for some time. Visitors like myself would sing in simple Malay, but it did not really matter. You could sing in your own language if you wanted to.

Then would come ceremonial war dances by men and a very pretty slow-moving dance of the flight of the hornbill by girls with hornbill feathers attached to their fingers. You too would be expected to perform clad in ceremonial war gear: a rattan cap with the long tail feathers of an Argus Pheasant protruding from it, a sort of poncho of goat skin over your shoulders, a shield in your hand, and an elaborate parang strapped to your waist. Your hosts were indulgent. It did not matter how poorly you performed as long as you made the effort.

These solo dances led on to a communal dance, a kind of conga performed up and down the length of the longhouse. It would be led by a man playing the Bornean guitar, or sape, and followed by all and sundry. Everyone sang, often in very good harmony, and the dancers would execute little side movements of the arms coupled with stamping of the feet. Later on there would be more drinking, and proceedings might grow a little boisterous, with those who had retired to rest being dragged back to the party by the girls. It was great fun, though your headache next morning was liable to be a severe one.

Borak is a bitter drink. In my opinion it does not compare with well-made Iban tuak. It is the staple indigenous drink over much of Borneo but Borneans are rarely alcoholics. They drink at parties and some of the drinking on these occasions can be gargantuan, but they are not normally compulsive everyday drinkers. Those who are have generally learned the habit from Europeans.

The Orang Ulu do not make use of the xylophonic gongs known as engkrumong as do the Iban. They use the sape and also a melodious flute called the keluri. Their tunes are somewhat repetitive but have great charm. Going outside an Orang Ulu longhouse to cool a fevered brow on a fine, still moonlit night with a great river flowing endlessly by, and hearing the sape playing gently, even the most philistine will think himself transported to fairyland.

When you finally leave the longhouse, the Orang Ulu have their own very special form of farewell. Sweet young girls come up to you and say goodbye and then they reach up with their little hands and stroke your face. But their hands are covered with soot from the underside of cooking pots. And when you go down to your boat they do their best to push you in the river and splash you if they do not succeed. You and the other guests take your departure with wet clothes adding to the discomfort of raging headaches and looking like Royal Marine Commandos returning from some desperate night affray. The meaning behind the horseplay is to demonstrate what good friends you now are, such good friends that even practical jokes are now in order.

The Baram provided fine opportunities for varied travel, up one valley and over into the next one. One of the first tours which we undertook was to the Bakong, a left bank tributary of the lower Baram. The valley adjoins Miri District. Here there was a small Muslim community of former Penan converted to Islam in the last century. They had an interesting burial place nearby, a small cave in a limestone outcrop full of bones and skulls and broken Chinese porcelain. There was a considerable trade in Chinese export ceramics to Borneo until at least the eighteenth century. These ceramics, especially various kinds of large brown jars, constituted some of the most valued possessions of Bornean peoples. Some of the broken pieces of celadon in the Bakong cave were of fine quality. The Penan and others used to inter some valuable objects with the dead for them to take with them, but they took the precaution of smashing the porcelain to forestall thieves, knowing that in the next world it would be miraculously put together again.

The Bakong had a number of Dayak houses which had moved there from the 2nd Division. They farmed swamp valleys which lay between low, sandy, podsol hills. The area had the worst sandflies of any place we ever visited in Sarawak. The people were well off but even here, in a comparatively recently settled area, there were many quarrels over land. The Bakong had been the scene of a good deal of disturbance during the last days of the war. A number of Japanese sought to get from Miri to the Ulu Rejang via the Bakong and Tinjar rivers. Some of these people were killed by the Iban. In one case seven were massacred in a longhouse where they had been generously entertained. When they were drunk, the Dayaks seized and bound them, threw them down to the ground below the longhouse, and killed them with their parangs. The Japanese retaliated and some houses were burned down. As we were going over the watershed to the Tinjar, we stopped on one hill and the Dayaks with us told us of how they had killed another solitary Japanese. They had given him every assistance, and when they reached the hill and stopped for a rest, they drew their parangs and slashed him to death. He was sitting, they told me in the most matter of fact way, "just about where you are sitting now."

Hedda had an unpleasant experience on this trip. Traveling ahead while I made a detour to visit a small house, she trod on a small snake which curled itself in alarm around her right ankle. The Dayaks were horrified and quickly cut it to pieces. Probably it was harmless, but there are some small vipers to be found in these areas which are dangerous. Hedda was luckier than a local Dayak official who accompanied us, a stout and convivial man. He did not impress me with his industry, but a horrid retribution was in store for him. A hornet insinuated itself into his underpants while he was bathing and stung him severely in a near vital part. Poor man, it was most painful, and the two stings, which were close together, looked as if they were the bite of a snake.

Our Dayak friends brought us over the watershed to the Tinjar where we were once again in Orang Ulu country. The Tinjar was one of the rivers which had suffered most severely from depopulation. Fifty years earlier it had supported a much larger population. The houses were comparatively small and very far apart. The old tradition of carving mythical dogs and grotesque figures with huge eyes out of wood was still maintained here. Large carved dogs served as the uprights for tables or platforms made of a single slab of tapang wood. Such slabs are not planks in the conventional sense but the buttresses which certain very large Southeast Asian trees throw out at their bases. They are delightful objects but too large for most houses. One of our friends who became DO Baram used to argue that he could not possibly be transferred elsewhere because his tapang table was too large to move.

Timber was a source of much trouble in the Tinjar at that time. It was in the years before the great timber booms and a European company was operating without much success in Marudi. Logs were being bought from Orang Ulu, and there were tiresome disputes over payments and arguments as to how much timber had actually been delivered. The operation eventually went bankrupt. Trying to sort out the extraordinary complexities of timber deals was a tiresome task for the DO. Timber was the richest natural resource in Sarawak, but private enterprise exploitation of this resource has in my view been an almost unmitigated curse for the state and its people. Great fortunes have been made out of timber by the few, but the people in general have gained little from the destruction of the forests. And most of the profits have gone elsewhere.

Our next tour was up the Baram again to cover the periodic bird's nest auctions and Penan trading meetings. The edible bird's nests are produced by a family of little cave-nesting swifts found widely in Southeast Asia. They make the nests largely or entirely from a salivary excretion. The amount of saliva used varies with the species. The most valuable nests consist entirely of saliva; those mixed with moss and fibres cost progressively less. The Chinese esteem bird's nest as a rare and precious food. It forms an ingredient in certain chicken-based soups. In point of actual fact, it is a dull, tasteless, and leathery ingredient but has considerable snob appeal. There were important bird's nest caves near Long Lama in the middle Baram. The rights to these caves were owned by Kayan families and the nests, in neat little cupped-together bundles, are auctioned publicly, a Sarawak Administrative Officer checking the weights and acting as the auctioneer. The auctions were instituted originally to protect the Kayan from being cheated and were continued long after the need for supervision had passed.

There was much more need for supervision of the Penan trading meetings, or tamus. The Penan, true jungle-living people, collected fossilized resin called damar and a jungle rubber called jangkar. Their staple diet was wild sago, supplemented with game which they secured with blowpipe-operated poison darts. The monkeys they killed often contained gallstones like shiny black pebbles, which were much in demand for Chinese medicine shops. Another sought-after ingredient for Chinese materia medica were the dried and blackened gall bladders of Honey Bears. The Penan are gifted craftsmen. They weave beautiful mats, probably the finest in the whole of Southeast Asia, and they are skilled blowpipe and parang makers.

They are timid, inoffensive people, lacking permanent abodes and, even more importantly, boats. They were dependent for supplies of salt, iron, cloth, matches, tobacco, and other essential goods on the settled Kayan and Kenyah. A Penan group would virtually belong to an Orang Ulu chief. The Orang Ulu gave them some measure of protection but exploited them. The trading meetings had been designed to ensure some measure of fair play to the proceedings. It was an unpleasant relationship—one of the few things I really disliked in Sarawak—but it was impossible to abolish the relationship because the Orang Ulu controlled the transport. The Penan were beginning to give up their jungle life and to settle in permanent houses. But even here the old links with the dominant Orang Ulu were likely to be reasserted. The Orang Ulu could ensure that much of the profit from Penan craftsmanship continued to be diverted to Orang Ulu pockets.

At the tamus the Penan would assemble at various points on prearranged dates to meet the various traders. Their goods would be exchanged with the Orang Ulu "owners" as the DO or SAO (Sarawak Administrative Officer, replacing the Chief Native Officer) did his best to ensure that the exchange was fair to the Penan. The Orang Ulu would then very often sell the produce they obtained to accompanying Chinese traders who were not permitted to deal with the Penan directly. The Penan were not simpletons and the traders had to look at their purchases carefully. It was not unknown for a slab of jangkar to contain a large stone. At the end of the meeting the next one was arranged. This was done by giving the Penan lengths of fine rattan knotted to correspond to the number of days which would elapse until the next meeting. They had to undo one knot each day until they knew it was time to assemble again.

This journey took us up to Lio Matu, a small government station at the limit of canoe navigation on the Baram. It was a wonderful experience to travel up this great and beautiful river running through forest-covered hills. Some were covered with primary forest, but many of the slopes adjoining the river had been farmed in days gone by. The houses were far apart, the welcome always a kind and generous one. Sometimes we had to pass through rapids. Where these were long and shallow it was often necessary to get out and pull the boat. On these occasions I felt I had to leap out too and lend a hand, though I knew I was often more a hindrance than a help.

Other rapids had to be surmounted on full power. The Baram outboard drivers and boatmen are the most skillful in Sarawak but rapids inevitably had their element of risk. With the engine running at full speed you would make your way slowly upstream against the rush of water and past projecting rocks, utterly dependent on the skill of the driver behind you and the pilot/guide in the bows and on the reliability of your Johnson outboard motor. If there was human error or if your engine faltered or broke a shear pin, you would be in serious trouble. The boat would be swept downstream and probably overturned. If you were lucky and did not hit your head on a rock, you would probably survive but everything in the boat would be lost. Most people who have traveled extensively in Sarawak have been in boating accidents, but Hedda and I were lucky. We were in many leaky boats but never in one that sank.

After I left Baram attempts were made to improve some of the rapids by blasting the more dangerous rock obstructions. The work was initially carried out by Royal Engineer parties. Some success was achieved, but one of the most interesting things was the reaction of Orang Ulu, whose help was needed. I had thought that this would be given generously and with little thought for sordid considerations of payment. I could not have been more mistaken. The demands were often extortionate and made without any apparent thought to the fact that the work was intended to benefit the Orang Ulu themselves. Sarawak country people have well-developed business instincts.

Our tour to Lio Matu took us about three weeks, but in former days, touring by the DO Baram often used to take up months of travel time. Donald Hudden, the best DO the District ever had and who held the post at the outbreak of war, would be away from Marudi for up to three months at a time. He would proceed leisurely up the Tinjar and then cross over to the Baram. His tours used to be a great progression for he used to take the leading figures from each longhouse he visited with him. He called them his fighting cocks for their presence helped to dilute the generous hospitality he encountered.

Hudden was in Marudi when war broke out. The Dutch Air Force, in a brave but forlorn effort, attacked the Japanese invasion ships off Miri, causing some damage. One Dutch aircraft—I think a Dornier flying boat—landed at Marudi with two dead Dutchmen on board. Hudden sent the rest of the aircrew up the Tinjar to join the ill-fated party of the Resident 3rd Division which was massacred at Long Nawang in then Dutch Borneo. Hudden himself went up the Tinjar and then over to the Baram. He spent New Year's Eve 1941 in the jungle, and one of the Tinjar men who was with him told me that he opened the brandy he had with him and shared it with his companions, telling them it was a special day which must be celebrated. He moved into the remote headwaters of the Bahau in Dutch Borneo and lived by himself in an isolated farming hut. He would not live in a longhouse, fearing that this would invite reprisals on the people. Here he was eventually murdered by a mixed group of Dayaks and Penan. The only European in Marudi to survive was a Catholic priest, the late Father O'Brien, who went up into the Kelabit country with the idea of escaping into Dutch Borneo. He eventually turned back, and after a remarkable journey was captured by the Japanese in the Ulu Limbang.

It is easy after the event to see that the Europeans should have stayed where they were, which in fact is what they were told to do. But they faced a terrible dilemma, and few people in those days expected the war against Japan to last for nearly four years. One particularly brave and quixotic story concerned a party from the Lower Rejang, led by the DO Sarikei, which withdrew to Lubok Antu and Pontianak and made good their escape to Java. But in Lubok Antu two members of the party, the Assistant District Officer Sarikei, Bill Morison, and the DO Saratok, Anthony Richards, discovered that the DO Sarikei had no instructions to withdraw. And so they turned back and returned to their stations. Local men had now taken over and adapted to the departure of the European officers and the people to whom they felt they owed a duty no longer wanted them back. They stayed at the Catholic Mission in Sibu until they were picked up by the Japanese and sent to Kuching.

We were to make two other fine journeys while we remained in the Baram. One took us to the Tutoh and Apoh on the right bank of the Baram, and then over into a formerly populous river called the Patah, and so back to the Baram and over to the Tinjar. The other journey took us to the Kelabit country. We never enjoyed anything more than these two journeys on which we had the company of two outstanding local officers, Wan Hashim bin Datu Tuanku Taha and Tingang Malang. Wan Hashim was the son of a distinguished officer of the Rajah's service. He was thin and wiry and possessed of inexhaustible energy. He was very much a Baram man who knew and understood the Orang Ulu intimately. Tingang was a quiet and gentle person, a Kenyah Chief in his own right. He exercised a quiet authority. It was simply inconceivable that any Baram man would not do whatever Tingang wanted him to do. The poor man was to die prematurely from an incurable thyroid condition.

The Tutoh is a big river. From here you can reach the Limbang over a low watershed across which Kayan war parties used to drag their boats. The population was very small, the timber resources extensive and valuable. The Chiefs of this area have since become vastly rich. In the Tutoh I had an encounter with an elderly Chinese whom I suspected of running an illegal shop. I demanded that he produce his Trading License and the honest fellow promptly handed me a Prison Discharge Certificate. He had once been given four months for assault and battery, almost certainly a miscarriage of justice. Poor fellow, he could no more read English than I could read Chinese, and matters were eventually settled to everyone's satisfaction. Even if the shop was illegal, he deserved to have it legalized for sheer originality in dealing with his District Officer.

The Apoh was a rich agricultural area and a stronghold of the Borneo Evangelical Mission. Hospitality was as warm as ever but largely non-alcoholic. The Patah was now almost empty, although formerly it had a large Kenyah population and was the home of the Temenggong and his ancestor, the great Tama Bulan, who is featured extensively in the writings of Hose, who spent most of his service in the Baram. Hose retired at a comparatively early age in 1907 after twenty-three years service and lived comfortably for many years thereafter, having interested the Shell Company in taking up a lease in Sarawak for which he obtained some useful payment of royalties from the Company. He was well known, the Harrisson of his day, but his books are of mediocre quality. A much better book of the period dealing with the Baram was written by an American, W.H. Furness, *The Home Life of Borneo Headhunters.*

The Baram peoples have moved about a great deal. Although their houses are elaborate, they are not of permanent construction. Bad omens, bad luck, ill health, bad dreams, or the search for better farming land has until recently kept them on the move. The moves were often very extensive. The main disadvantage of the Patah was that it has very bad rapids.

We were very hospitably entertained in the longhouse here. My traveling diary records: "Quite a good party in the evening. Performers not outstanding but bags of enthusiasm. One incontinent old tosspot was sick over the tin which Hedda had her flash bulbs in. Fortunately it was closed."

One of my predecessors lost his false teeth in the Apoh in a somewhat similar kind of incident. In a small house he was plied with much borak and being notably conscientious, he consumed far more than was strictly desirable. Eventually he was sick over the side of the house but parted with his false teeth in the process. The false teeth were then seized by one of the voracious pigs which live under the houses and were seen no more. My colleague was not deterred but went firmly on his toothless way to the Kelabit country and back— on foot. I was told that he came back looking rather emaciated.

The journey over to the Tinjar went smoothly. We were met by a welcoming party on the watershed and conveyed down to the longhouse at night. It was a remarkable experience to be thus conveyed down a rushing stream in pitch darkness by the superb boatmen of the area. We had no engine—they paddled us down—and their shouts and yells added to the scene. It was wonderfully well-ordered confusion, but we all arrived safely at the house where a party awaited us. These people are called Lirong. Once they were a large community of several hundred doors, but their numbers declined through disease. They had been particularly badly affected by an outbreak of smallpox or measles about thirty years earlier.

It is a curious fact that although the social relationship between European officers and local people was much closer in Sarawak than in Dutch Borneo, the Orang Ulu communities were much better preserved in Dutch territory. Talking once to a Kenyah headman from the Long Nawang area who had come over to Sarawak with a party of his people to work, I asked him if his house in Kalimantan was a large one. "No, not very large," he said. "How many doors?" I asked. "Oh, only about 200," he said. This would have been about three times as large as the largest Orang Ulu longhouse or group of longhouses in Sarawak and about ten times the average size.

At the head of the Tinjar are several long-settled communities of Penan who have succeeded in adapting to agricultural life quite successfully. The Catholic Mission was active in these parts and we met the local Catechist, a Chinese whom the irrepressible Wan Hashim addressed as Tuan Imam, the title given a senior Mosque official. I was a little disconcerted on one occasion when we reached a small government office after a rather hearty send-off from a longhouse which had left me with a blackened face and wet to the skin. I had removed my shirt in the boat, only to arrive shirtless and sooty-faced to a formal greeting by the schoolchildren all immaculately attired.

Moving among these charming and highly intelligent people, it was sometimes hard to believe that within quite recent times some of their customs were barbarous, their lives centered round a preoccupation with warfare and the taking of heads, their activities governed by oppressive superstition. Furness, who was in the Tinjar at the turn of the century, recorded this account of how a Kayan Chief called Aban Avit, was blooded by his father when he was a little boy.

> Said Aban:
> My father, a very great warrior and known and feared by the people of many, many rivers, wanted his sons to be as brave and fearless as he was himself. So one day he dragged out into the jungle old Ballo Lahing (widow of Lahing), and tied her fast to a tree by rattans on her wrists and ankles. She was a slave-woman, captured when she was a young girl by his grandfather over in the Batang Kayan country, and at the time I speak of she was very old, and weak, and very thin and couldn't do any work because she was nearly blind. My father told my brother yonder and me, and one or two other boys, all of us little fellows then (I remember my ears were still sore from having these holes for tiger-cat teeth cut in them) well, he told us we must go out with spears and learn to stick them in something alive, and not be afraid to see blood, nor to hear screams—then I felt just as you do. Besides, I was really very fond of old Ballo Lahing; she it was who tied on my first loin cloth for me. I remembered it well, for she laughed a great deal at me and then I saw how few teeth she had, and she often used to sing me to sleep. I couldn't bear the thought of hurting her and sending her away off to Long Julan, so I flatly refused to take a spear with me. But my father said I must; there was no harm in it; that it was right and I must take one; he pulled me by the arm and I had to follow. Then I was afraid she might see me and so I sneaked round behind the tree and just pierced her with the point of the iron, then she guessed what my father had tied her there for, and screamed as loud as she could, "Oh don't, oh don't, oh don't" over and over again, and very fast. I pricked her a little harder the next time to hear what she would say, but she only kept on shrieking the same words. Then one of the other boys, smaller even than I, ran his spear right through her thigh, and the old people laughed and said that was good; and the blood ran down all over the wrinkles on her knees; and then I wanted to make it run the same way, so I pushed and pushed my spear hard into her; and after that I never thought whether it was Ballo Lahing or not, I just watched the blood; and we all ran round her piercing here and piercing her there until she sank right down on the ground with her hands in the rattan loops above her head, which tumbled over to one side, and no more blood came out of her. Then my father praised us all loudly, and me in particular, and said we had been good boys and had done well!

One of the activities of our tours was to look for airstrip sites. Air travel was the obvious solution to the travel problems of the Baram, and airstrips had already been built by those communities in the ulu which supported the BEM. The Mission light aircraft used to fly into them regularly. I never did find an airstrip site in the Ulu Tinjar and none has ever been built there. In Marudi I sought to establish that a small airstrip could be built just behind the government quarters. The Shell Company offered to take a series of levels if I would have some clearing undertaken. I had no money for this and asked for volunteers from the government staff. The staff very willingly turned out and we cleared a track early one morning. But some of the staff were badly stung by wasps, and I spiked my ankle on a rotten log and was in hospital for some time. It was not one of my happier or more popular initiatives. Since that time a very fine airfield has been built in Marudi.

We celebrated the coronation in Marudi. Every second year there is a splendid regatta in Marudi and the alternate years, on one of which the coronation fell, had a program of land sports. We therefore combined the two. We were honored by the presence of Bishop Vos, the Catholic Bishop. He should really have been in Kuching, but I inferred that he did not wish to be embarrassed by the unwillingness of the Catholic Church to take part in joint religious services. It was quite normal for the Anglicans to participate with Muslim dignitaries at celebrations and prayers on such occasions as Remembrance Day, but the Catholics were not permitted to do this.

We had all sorts of sports and competitions, mostly in the space in front of the new bazaar. But this was a very muddy area and one of my particular recollections was that of the tug-of-war final between two strong teams of powerful Orang Ulu. As they pulled, they dug themselves deeper and deeper into the ground until the rope itself was dragging along the ground. The marks on the rope became obscured and the umpire, the Kapitan China, awarded the pull to the wrong side. Hard feelings were averted by the prompt action of the Australian manager of the local timber company, who presented a case of beer as consolation prize to the losers, i.e. to the winners.

Even more eventful was an evening lantern procession through the bazaar by schoolchildren, an event which nearly brought my career in Sarawak to a premature end. The old Chinese custom is to throw firecrackers in front of a procession. Unfortunately, on this occasion, I was accompanying the children from the Catholic Mission School at the head of the procession, and many firecrackers were thrown among the children. This was an unpleasant and dangerous thing to do and after it had happened several times my temper reached boiling point. The next time I saw a man throw a firecracker among the children, I seized him and sought to punch him on the nose. Fortunately, he broke free and disappeared into the darkness. Had I been successful in my endeavor I would probably have been dismissed from the service. Sir Charles Arden Clarke once told a Resident of mine that in his view every DO should be allowed four free assaults a year, but the Colonial Office had never embodied this sound principle in Colonial Regulations. It was altogether an exhausting occasion, and for the good of her subjects, I hope that Her Majesty Queen Elizabeth may reign longer than Queen Victoria.

We made the long journey up to the Kelabit country at the head of the Baram in July. The area is often referred to as the Kelabit plateau but this is a misnomer. It is simply the high country where the Baram has its source. It contains a number of beautiful and fertile valleys. It is the most remote area in Sarawak and it was here that the Australian SRD landed at the end of the war. Its Kelabit inhabitants are a particularly vigorous and energetic people related to the Lun Bawang of the Trusan.

I had paid a quick visit to the area when I was DO Lawas, but it was a new area for Hedda. Our journey took us up the Akah River as far as navigation was possible and then on an extensive walking tour round to Lio Matu on the Baram. In some ways this was a pleasant trip. The country is beautiful and the Kelabit the best agriculturists in Sarawak. They produced so much padi that they could even feed it to the pigs, which were correspondingly fat and healthy. But the number of disputes which were brought up was exceptionally large, and hearing them, even with the help of Tingang Malang, consumed much time.

The entertainment was also heavy. One system of drinking was new to me. It consists of drinking out of a large jar in which the borak has been brewed. You drink through a bamboo tube. In another tube there is a float which has to be lowered by a certain amount. This arrangement is capable of manipulation so that the intake required to lower the float is gargantuan. In some houses, pigs or a buffalo had been killed in our honor and were served up at the party. It was a generous gesture but hardly cordon bleu cooking. The animal was hacked up and everything—skin, bones, the lot—cooked in great caldrons. This mass of food would be dumped on a mat and pieces passed around by hand. Great hunks of meat or pig fat would be pressed on one by kind but inebriated hosts. It was a little difficult to coordinate the requirements of good manners, the need to save your stomach from disaster, and the desire not to hurt the feelings of your hosts.

There were all sorts of complicated personal problems to be settled. Many of these related to gun deals of staggering complexity, but the worst concerned the marital problems of a young trained teacher. His marriage had run into difficulties. Under one of the old pagan customs of the Kelabit, both he and his wife had been allowed to take temporary lovers, but the husband wanted to make the temporary arrangement permanent. The wife was consumed with jealousy, and then the valuable bead hat of the second girl disappeared. This created uproar in the village. The wife had denied that she had taken it.

When I eventually met the wife, who had returned to her own village, she again denied that she had taken it, but it turned out that she had admitted the theft to the Penghulu. She was then rather more frank with me but still refused to say where she had put the beads. She told me she had thought of killing the other girl, but thought that God would not approve, so took the beads instead. Such action by a jealous wife was a fairly well-known custom in the past. It was all settled eventually. The wife was fined, the beads were returned, and the teacher married the other girl, but unraveling the story took many hours. The teacher in question was not the only one whose performance as a teacher was somewhat affected by his love life. I find that one volume of my traveling notes contains the following: "Could DMHS (Director of Medical and Health Services) provide some element in the Training College diet calculated to reduce sexual potential by not less than 30% for 5 years after graduation?"

One important event while we were at Bareo, the center of the Kelabit area, was the first landing of a BEM plane. An airstrip had been built under the supervision of Harrisson shortly before, but the first flight—by a Shell light aircraft—ended disastrously. It had landed safely, but taking off with Harrisson on board, crashed at the end of the runway. Bruce Morton had asked me to signal him in when he tried to fly in during our tour. It was my task, which I did not greatly relish, to show from the ground whether the strip was fit to land on. Fortunately I advised him correctly. He made a perfect landing, but I refused to allow him to take Hedda for a flight round Bareo. He was a marvellous and extremely careful pilot, but it was not until our farewell visit to the 4th and 5th Divisions thirteen years later that we eventually flew with him. Bruce, who had told me that I was only a layman in Lawas, rebuked me once again in Bareo. When I asked him whether the Mission insured their aircraft, he looked at me pityingly and said, "We prefer to trust in the Lord."

Walking back to Lio Matu involved some jungle travel. It passed uneventfully. Hedda walks slowly because of childhood polio and we used to send her on with two of the party at first light and catch up with her later. Walking thus early, with a light early-morning mist on the track, she and her companions one morning met a bear snuffling through the herbage. Her companions were alarmed, for the Honey Bear is a very brave little animal. Its eyesight is not good and when alarmed, it is liable to charge at the source of disturbance. Fortunately, the men with Hedda had no guns. They kept quiet and the bear ambled peacefully off into the forest.

There was a very good though only semi-trained local Hospital Assistant in the Kelabit area. It was difficult to provide him with all he needed because so many people from the adjoining areas of Indonesia came in for treatment. I took a rather unsympathetic line—which I am glad to say was reversed by the Medical Department later—and said that people from the Indonesian side must go for treatment to the Indonesian centers. I told this to one elderly headman from the Indonesian side and was embarrassed to find that he and his people had for years believed that they were on the Sarawak side of the border and had regularly paid Sarawak Head Tax.

I had no Hospital Assistant with me and did what I could, when necessary, to act in this capacity myself. We had been provided with a fine assortment of drugs by the Shell Company, whose hospital in Miri in those days provided services for the public. The drugs included a box of snakebite remedies. I did not take it along because, although most comprehensive, it required you first of all to identify the family of snake which had bitten the patient. Acting as Hospital Assistant is often tiresome because for every genuinely sick person there are many others who claim to be suffering from various maladies in the belief that medicine is a good thing and should be taken at every opportunity. To one man who seemed to be suffering from pneumonia I had given some Sulfamezathine tablets. Without my knowledge, the same man went to Tingang, who prescribed Sulfaguanidine, which is used in cases of dysentery. The patient took the lot and despite his unethical conduct towards his medical advisers, survived the treatment.

One of the Kelabit houses had a very good school. The teacher was from Indonesia and had taught the children to play bamboo pipes called soleng. I had seen the same thing in the Trusan. Each child carries a bamboo pipe of varying size and the effect is rather that of a dissected organ, one player to each pipe. Unfortunately, he had impressed on the children that the time to serenade the visiting DO was at first light and while the DO was shaving.

It was shortly after our return from the Kelabit tour that I had differences with the Secretariat in Kuching. Working in outstations, you quickly became very prickly about those exercising authority from afar. I used to call it outstationitis. There is nothing unusual about this. Those far from the seat of authority inevitably regard those in the seat of authority as selfish and incompetent clowns obsessed with their own importance and unmindful of the problems of those elsewhere who actually do some work.

My time in Baram was coming to an end, but I wanted to remain in Sarawak until 1954 to enable us to spend our long leave in Europe during the northern summer. And I knew that the post of DO Betong in the 2nd Division, where I had never served, would become vacant shortly. The obvious thing was to transfer me to Betong. But I suddenly received a telegram saying that it was intended to transfer me temporarily to act as Information Officer in Brunei while the permanent Brunei Information Officer, Pengiran Yusof, was on a course. This infuriated me because I did not want to serve in Brunei, and I knew that the Acting Resident Kuala Belait would be available to take up the information post. Unbeknownst to me, however, there were some personality differences between the Resident Brunei and the Acting Resident Kuala Belait, and it had been decided to send the latter to Betong. In my just indignation I sent off one of those telegrams which, in retrospect, might have better been slept on for twenty-four hours. The result was that I was told I would have to proceed on leave instead. This was to bring us to Australia for the first time, but I was very angry, the more so since I had, when in Lawas, turned down an offer of immediate transfer to Hong Kong as Information Officer.

It was under these rather trying circumstances that I had to undertake my last tour in the Baram to escort the Governor on a visit to the Tinjar. This called for considerable organization, but with the excellent team of local administrative officers available in Marudi, it presented few real difficulties. The Resident, Alan Griffin, had also spent several years in the Baram so that we were well-equipped to deal with the gubernatorial progression.

The Governor enjoyed traveling and kept the pomp and circumstance of his office to a minimum. He was the despair of the Constabulary because he was adept at losing his bodyguards. If a policeman accompanied him, his main task was to act as the Governor's gillie when he took a rest from his official duties and went fishing.

He was accompanied on this tour by his friend Loke Wan Tho, the head of the immense Cathay Organisation of Singapore. Wan Tho was a slight, bespectacled Chinese. He had inherited immense wealth and had been educated in Switzerland and Cambridge. He showed himself to be a most capable businessman, but he was also a gifted photographer who was deeply interested in birds and art. He was a most pleasant traveling companion and later we were often to stay with him and his wife, Chris Loke, in Singapore. The friendship of the very rich can be a little hard to manage, but Wan Tho's was so graceful and unassuming that it was a pleasure to enjoy it. Sad to relate, the marriage eventually fell apart, a rift which was embarrassing for us since we had been treated with every courtesy and consideration by Chris. They both married again and this time Wan Tho was to find marvellous and blissful happiness. But he and his new wife were not to enjoy their happiness for long. They were both, shortly afterwards, killed in a plane crash in Taiwan.

The Governor was, of course, treated with the utmost hospitality in the Tinjar. We had, first of all, to run the gauntlet of the house of Penghulu Lawai which was situated at the entrance to a curious lake, one of the only lakes in Sarawak, called Loagan Bunut. It swarmed with fish and Penghulu Lawai's people controlled the lucrative fishing rights. The fish were conveyed live to Marudi in large bamboo cages. Lawai was a quiet man, but his wife Kasi was the most powerful hostess in the Baram. She loved a party and she liked her guests to enjoy it, too, even if it killed them. The drinking was always heavy and the proceedings boisterous.

We survived a night at Lawai's place and then pushed on upriver. At the next stop there were some very pretty girls and we plotted to have the Governor, after he had retired, photographed while being dragged from his bed by girls and brought back to the party. I played some part in originating this proposal. It had in fact occurred to me, though I kept the idea to myself, that in a photograph it would not be entirely clear who was doing the dragging. The proposal, or such parts of it as were considered suitable, were explained to the Governor and the girls. All were willing. When the time came for the Governor to retire, I tactfully adjourned to the other end of the longhouse. But, alas, Wan Tho confided in the Resident what was about to happen and the Resident reacted in a somewhat blimpish way. "Not while I'm Resident," he said firmly, and that was that.

Kasi, the powerful hostess of Long Teru, sings a song of welcome to my Resident, Alan Griffin. Between them is Kasi's husband, the Penghulu Lawai.

Despite his rather unbending behavior on this occasion, Alan Griffin was an outstandingly good administrative officer and Resident. He was kind and sociable, he liked his fellow men of all races, and he loved an argument. He could not bear the idea of working in the Secretariat and never did. Alas, like all too many Sarawak officers, he did not long survive retirement. He died in 1965, after a very valuable final spell during Confrontation as Resident Sibu. He was survived by his young wife and small son.

Sometimes I heard it argued that the Governor on tour should keep more distance from the people. I think this was wrong. He showed interest and met the people and enjoyed their kind of hospitality. The treatment he received was that which they would have extended to a great Chief of their own people. I never had the slightest reason to think that such touring detracted from the dignity of office or respect for the personalities and institutions of government.

By the time we had finished the Tinjar tour we were all very tired. But Kasi was lying in wait when we returned to Lawai's house where the launches were to meet us. Stern measures were called for. After the proper greetings had been completed and when my turn came to be regaled by our indefatigable hostess with a song of welcome, I made haste to respond and presented her with half a tumbler full of neat whisky. Kasi drank the whisky as she was bound to do according to the local rules of polite conduct, rose somewhat unsteadily to her feet, and retired to her quarters in a dignified and ladylike manner. She never reappeared that evening and we all had a good night's rest.

6

The Secretariat

Our abruptly ordained leave took us to Australia, the Pacific, and New Zealand. Being unplanned it was in many ways unsatisfactory. In Australia we met kind relatives and toured by bus and learned how to do better the next time. The Pacific tour took us in a dignified Solent flying boat, surely the most civilized aircraft that ever flew, to Fiji, Samoa, and Tahiti, spending a fortnight in each place. Samoa and Tahiti provided an object lessen for the visiting colonial official. In Samoa, the New Zealand government had done a superb job under the League of Nations mandate in preserving the health, institutions, and lands of the Samoans. In particular they had held the ex-German lands in trust for the Samoans, in stark contrast to the Australian government which sold off German holdings in New Guinea to the highest bidders and bought themselves a great deal of future trouble in the process. But despite their exemplary record, New Zealanders were disliked.

In Tahiti, the French had consistently failed to do any of the things which the New Zealanders had done. They had not protected the health of the people—alcoholism was acute—they had not protected the Tahitians' lands, and they had allowed in a large immigrant Chinese population. The French too were disliked. And so to New Zealand to meet more kind relatives and to have our travel arrangements regimented as only the New Zealand Tourist Bureau knows how.

Return to Kuching involved some rancorous and costly disagreement with the Secretariat over travel expenses. It was also clear that no one had given much thought as to what I was to do, although I had been recalled by air. I was put to work for a time as Acting Chief Registrar of the Supreme Court, a post for which I was little qualified. "We are giving you a house across river," said the Acting Chief Secretary, Hugh Ellis, "because we don't expect that you will be here for more than six months and this way you won't need to buy a car." Thirteen years later I finally left Kuching on retirement.

Most of Kuching was built on the right bank of the Sarawak River. The left bank was lined with Malay kampongs and had the Astana (Government House) and the old Police Headquarters in Fort Margherita, which was built after the Chinese insurrection of 1857. Some Senior Service quarters had been built on the left bank, which was always known as across river, but it meant crossing the river by boat every time you went to town. This added a distinctive and rural flavor to life and appealed to a small but select group of Europeans including ourselves. It had its disadvantages. When it rained you were liable to get very wet going or coming. This was tiresome if you were going to a party on the right bank but funny if it meant that guests coming to you got wet. Then you would rig them out in your spare shirts and sarongs, and they often looked all the better for it. Beyond the European houses, residential lots had been provided for Dayaks who had moved to Kuching and they were very pleasant neighbors. We had a comfortable, rather isolated house looking out towards Santubong. We were looked after uncommonly well by Malay girls who lived nearby in the kampong. It became quite a family relationship. At Hari Raya, the Muslim New Year, we would be invited to have lunch with the family of our employees where we would enjoy the finest curry lunch in all Sarawak.

After a couple of months as Chief Registrar, where I had enjoyed the company but where my lack of legal knowledge had pained the Chief Justice, I was moved to the post of Principal Assistant Secretary (Defence). And so I became a member of the Secretariat, the institution which I had so loathed as an outstation officer. In those days, thoughts about defense centered largely on gloomy forebodings as to the likelihood of hostile action by the People's Republic of China. I remember one exercise I was engaged in which consisted of planning the evacuation of Sarawak civilians from Miri and Seria if the oilfields should come under air attack by China. The plan involved mobilizing a great armada of Chinese launches for the evacuation.

There was not much thought given to internal subversion in those days. The process was only just beginning to make itself felt in Sarawak and to affect the Chinese schools. Young teachers and students in the Chinese-medium schools had been affected by a curious combination of pride in the achievements of the new China coupled with ideological guidance contained in printed matter which was allowed to come in freely. It was a purely Chinese phenomenon, which was stimu-

Looking westward over Kuching town and the Mosque

lated to a considerable extent by a strong measure of Chinese racial chauvinism. The Chinese schools were vulnerable, having been left to operate very much as little worlds of their own. Their managements were especially weak. Originally, Chinese schools had been established by small groups of education-conscious Chinese, often at great personal sacrifice. Over the years they had become well established and the school management boards had become socially important bodies. A successful businessman would automatically gravitate towards membership of a school board, both because his financial support was important for the school and because membership of the board gave him status in the community. But they were often men of little education themselves. They exerted little effective control and left the running of the schools to the teachers. The younger and politically conscious teachers generally left the older teachers alone so long as they did not interfere. Much of the communist indoctrination took place outside normal school hours at study sessions and picnics.

The first communist group to be formed in Sarawak was known as the Sarawak Overseas Chinese Democratic Youth League and was formed in 1951. In the same year there were school disturbances in the main Chinese secondary school in Kuching directed against conservative school teachers who had opposed communist activities in the school. The Youth League was disrupted in 1952 when a state of emergency was declared in the 1st Division after the murder of a policeman. It was succeeded in 1954 by a body calling itself the Sarawak Liberation League, which two years later was succeeded by another body calling itself the Sarawak Advanced Youths' Association. This body came to be termed by the Government the CCO (Chinese Communist Organisation) or SCO (Sarawak Communist Organisation). Its activities spread from the student field to work among the unions and farmers. With the development of politics it sought to penetrate a political party. Its activities were peaceful until the period of Confrontation when it moved into armed struggle activities. The aim of the SCO was to build a communist state in Sarawak. Its organization, development, and training were in accordance with communist precepts and without any outside aid, apart from communist writings and broadcasts. It was successful in building up a remarkably strong and efficient organization. In 1954, shortly after I reached Kuching, there was trouble at a Chinese school at Mile 17 on the Simanggang Road. A Chinese Education Officer brought in from outside Sarawak—local Chinese officers tended to turn a blind eye to such things—called attention to a highly inflammatory wall poster in the school. Efforts by the Government to eradicate communist influence in the school had little success. The 17th Mile remained a problem area for years to come.

It is an extraordinary experience to observe at first hand the growth and development of a communist organization. Although I had, at the end of the war, served with Force 136 with the Malayan People's Anti-Japanese Army in Malaya and had some awareness of what communist organization could achieve, I was initially very sceptical about the seriousness of the communist problem in Sarawak. I sympathized—and still do—with the frustrations of educated Chinese. The avenues of advance open to them were limited. A young Chinese school leaver might become an assistant in a business or work as a laborer. He might go back to the family farm, but opportunities for agricultural expansion were restricted because Chinese land holdings were limited to certain areas. Without a good knowledge of English, opportunities in the government service were almost non-existent. The young people with intellectual ability could become school teachers or work on one of the many small Chinese newspapers which proliferated in Sarawak. They suffered from genuine frustrations. And it was hard to believe that there was any harm or anything very surprising in the development of radical thought among the young. I did not attach much importance to the warnings of the Education Department or the police. I subscribed to a school of thought which held that the trouble with the police was that they saw a communist behind every bush.

It was only with the passage of years that I came to realize that those personable youngsters were building up a movement which was later to engage in armed insurrection at a cost of many hundreds of lives and in the most vicious and ruthless elimination or intimidation of those who did not agree with them.

One of the problems of the Secretariat office in those early days in Kuching lay in a shortage of accommodation. There was no good hotel in Kuching. The government resthouse was always overcrowded. There was a constant shortage of government quarters. These shortages were particularly tiresome when you had official visitors who had to be billeted out on understandably reluctant hosts. Solution of the problem was to come partly from another shortage, that of space in the Anglican cathedral. The latter was a fine old building constructed entirely out of ironwood, but it had become far too small for the congregation. To raise much of the money needed to build a new cathedral, the Anglicans sold a valuable corner property in central Kuching to an Indonesian Chinese businessman who built a modern hotel. The balance of the money needed was raised through public subscription. In this they received help from an unexpected quarter and in a rather unusual manner. Tom Harrisson, who was hardly a regular church goer, objected to the removal of the old cathedral. In one of the early broadcasts of Radio Sarawak, which opened in 1954, he broadcast a remarkable appeal in reverse, beseeching listeners not to give so much as a single, solitary cent to the building appeal. The result, however, was to stimulate subscriptions, not to reduce them. The Anglicans were left to reflect that God at times does indeed work in a mysterious way.

In the outside world, Harrisson was probably the best known man in Sarawak. He was an extraordinarily gifted, imaginative, wayward egocentric who seemed to take perverse pleasure in misusing or failing to use to the full his great endowment of talent. His life seemed to be devoted very largely to flouting the elementary disciplines and restraints which form the basis of civilized life and good scholarship.

He had an English upper-class upbringing—Harrow and Pembroke College Cambridge. He early acquired distinction as an ornithologist, especially for his part in the Great Crested Grebe inquiry, the report on which was published in 1932.

His versatility was borne in on me when a year or so later I read his scurrilous Letter to Oxford. I knew his brother Bill Harrisson at Cambridge and I first met Tom Harrisson in my last year there. He was briefly both at Oxford and Cambridge but never took a degree. While at Oxford he led an expedition to Sarawak in 1932 which visited the Baram. He and his fellow expeditionaries must have been a thoroughly tiresome lot of opinionated and clever young men made the more tiresome by there being several of them together. The expedition laid the foundation for Harrisson's future interest in Sarawak.

Later he was with another Oxford expedition in the New Hebrides and stayed on there by himself when his colleagues had left. The result was an interesting book called *Savage Civilisation*, perhaps his best work. The war found him working with an

Tom Harrisson pays a Hari Raya call on Datuk Taib Mahmud
and his Australian born wife, Datin Leila

original form of sociological inquiry organization, which he had helped to found, called Mass Observation.

He eventually joined the Australian SRD, and it was his knowledge and imagination that led to the operation into the Kelabit areas at the head of the Baram. It was brilliantly conceived and sparked a successful uprising against the Japanese in sparsely populated and lightly held areas of inland Borneo. As mentioned elsewhere in this book, its main and least recognized achievement, in which Harrisson played no part, was to prevent serious loss of Chinese life at the hands of Dayaks in the 3rd Division. After the war Harrisson became Curator of the Sarawak Museum and held the post until 1966.

The Museum was already a good one—the Brookes had shown commendable interest in Museum work—and Harrisson developed it into an institution of world standing. In particular he developed the *Sarawak Museum Journal* into a very wide-ranging and unique publication.

Harrison wrote extensively, particularly about Kelabit, the coastal Malays, and archaeology. His writing was not confined to the museum journal. He contributed articles to numbers of other learned and not-so-learned journals in other countries. Their quality is often uneven. About the only thing they have in common is an almost invariable reference to the fact that the author had been parachuted into Borneo. He was a brilliant publicist, and since he liked Borneo and Borneo people, he did a great deal to make them better known and better understood. But Borneo was also the sounding board for his own ego and the SRD operation was, I think, the emotional climax of his career.

Harrisson did enough that was good for him to deserve appreciation, but at the same time, he had a vicious temper and an unbridled tongue and by nature he was intensely jealous. I never knew a man with such a capacity for quarrelling. His relations with others, especially a string of unwary visiting academics, were characterized by a long series of incredibly squalid and unpleasant rows. He bullied his subordinates and sought to dominate and crush their personalities. He set a very bad example to his successors.

Harrisson had a strong money sense and was largely amoral in financial and business matters. He was lax in his curatorial responsibilities. The standards of administration of the Museum while he was Curator would never have been tolerated in any other Department. But in Sarawak he was a big fish in a small pool; he was a formidable personality and was well known—at least by name—to important people in Britain. Governor Abell both recognized his talents and found him amusing. No senior colonial civil servant was going to try and apply the same standards to Harrisson as he would have done to any other Departmental Head, nor would the Colonial Office have thanked anyone who tried. Harrisson and his career went unscathed. He was aided in this by his great respect for the establishment. He was obsequious towards high authority and most courteous and obliging to those who could promote his interests. He could be very stimulating in small doses and extremely entertaining with an often startling (though rarely kind) gift of self-expression. He was extraordinarily quick in debate and repartee but argued much less effectively in writing.

I often wondered what made Harrisson the way he was. He was on bad terms with his father, who made a fortune building railways in South America and committed the unforgivable sin of leaving all his money to brother Bill. Given a sympathetic and understanding father, he might presumably have been different, though some who knew him claim that he was essentially a psychopath. It seemed to me that to some extent, his was a case of partially-arrested development. One side of him never grew out of a stage of uncouth adolescent rebellion.

It is hard to say how much of his work will stand the test of time. On the anthropological side he was a quick and perceptive observer. The spread of his interests, however, was limited—he concentrated on the Orang Ulu and avoided contact with Dayaks—and I think that much of his writing was too hasty and careless to endure. His voluminous notes—if they survive—would probably be unintelligible to anyone else. His handwriting was extraordinarily shapeless, unformed, and illegible. He never learned a local language well. He communicated with Borneans in bazaar Malay. His archaeological discoveries were probably far more important, especially those at Niah. Other archaeologists had written off the area after concluding that the caves were archaeologically barren, but Harrisson persevered and discovered a very large and important repository of the remains of early man. I personally do not think that this was just good luck. He undoubtedly had high gifts of flair and intuition.

Harrisson made Sarawak a very much better known place than it otherwise would have been, but he lacked much in the way of social and political awareness and played no part in Sarawak's political development. I am afraid that he will be remembered in Sarawak, not with the affection which one side of his nature craved, but rather for many ugly misdeeds which another side of his complex character clearly recognized for what they were. The respect in which he was held by the outside world was quite different from the picture the local observer gained of him at ground level.

I did not like Harrisson. I knew him well but kept my distance. Not all his deeds, however, were evil. He did some good in his own way and despite the many unpleasant episodes with which he was associated, Sarawak would have been a duller and poorer place without him. When the news of his death in a road accident in Thailand in early 1976 was received as I was writing this book, I felt to my surprise some sense of personal loss.

At the end of 1954 I was moved from the post of Principal Assistant Secretary (Defence) to the equivalent position in Finance. This meant that I became the Assistant of the then Financial Secretary, John Barcroft. This in many ways was an important post, though often a very unpopular one. The incumbent had to act as the filter for requests for funds from the Departments, and this often meant turning down requests. The key to success in such a post is never to tell a Departmental Head that what he wants is unnecessary. The correct course is to express both interest and lively sympathy and, if you have to turn it down, to say that at present it may not be possible to find the funds.

The other important principle, in my view, is never to work methodically through your files. If you do you can quickly become bogged down in considering at great length matters which are both tedious and unimportant and so delay much more important matters. The thing to do is to look quickly at all files and pick out those which are both interesting and important. I gave a very high priority to the problems of outstation officers who sustained mishaps while traveling. You also had the opportunity to get your own back on colleagues guilty of reprehensible conduct, such as failing to send you their travel allowance or failing to tip your servant generously when they had accepted your outstation hospitality, by appointing them to some of the more tiresome annual boards of survey, jobs of extreme boredom and uselessness. I could see some point in having surprise Boards of Survey conducted without warning to see whether the goods and chattels and monies of the Government were in good shape and correctly accounted for, but the annual boards struck me as being a total waste of time—though ideal for ensuring that reprehensible conduct was justly rewarded.

I arrived in the Financial Branch just in time to be an unwilling participant in a singularly inept financial exercise. In preparing the annual estimates for 1955, it had been found necessary to raise some additional revenue. The decision had been taken to achieve this by a very steep increase in the cost of Trade Licenses, which would mainly affect Chinese businesses which did not pay company tax. Trade Licenses were required of all businesses in order to operate, and the fees were flat rate fees which bore no relationship to business turnover. Purely as license fees they were acceptable, but the increases to be imposed were very steep, amounting in some cases to 1,000 percent. This had been agreed to by the Finance Committee and by the Supreme Council. The Finance Committee at that time consisted of Barcroft, the Accountant-General (who in my view should never have been there at all), a British businessman, a prominent Malay personality, the Datu Bandar, and two Chinese businessmen. The increases were the brainchild of the Accountant-General and of my predecessor and appealed to Barcroft's considerable sense of "schadenfreude." They had been supinely agreed to by the unofficials.

Even to my inexperienced eye, the plan was asking for trouble. The new rates were unfair and unreasonable, especially for the smaller businesses. There was nothing to be done about it except await the inevitable uproar. This was rather slow in coming—the trading community took a little time to realize what had happened, though one respected Chinese banker in Sibu fainted on receiving the news. Sarawak-wide protests quickly followed, leading eventually to the only hartal, total business closure, that Sarawak has ever known. This in turn brought about all the unpleasant things which happen if goods, especially rice, suddenly become unavailable. The Government had to climb down and, in consultation with a number of business representatives, work out a somewhat complicated system of sliding scale fees based on import and export turnovers. I was the Secretary of the Committee. The Chinese businessmen showed a real willingness to work out a fair system, and they would certainly have been willing to do this if they had been consulted in the first place. The only stonewaller on the Committee was the solitary Indian representative. The Trade License controversy stands out in my mind as the most stupid example of misgovernment that I encountered during my time in Sarawak.

Apart from the hartal, 1955 was a quiet year for me. I was not directly concerned in the most important events of the year, which concerned the introduction of a new system for financing schools. It involved the Government taking over responsibility for the operating costs of all schools (less the cost of approved fees) and half of the cost of capital expenditure. This brought to an end some of the undesirable features of Chinese school finance, although the cleavage between the Chinese and English education systems remained unchanged. It also provided teachers with far greater security. Looking back, it seems to be a modest move, but at the time it was a big step forward. The new system came into effect in 1956 and thereafter the Government's role in education grew steadily.

Early in 1956 I was appointed to act as Development Secretary, a particularly desirable post. Development plans had been in existence almost ever since the cession of Sarawak to the Crown, but the process was greatly accelerated as a result of the commodity booms of the Korean war and the consequent expansion of revenues, which had led to the accumulation of substantial surplus balances. A proportion of these were set aside to cover the cost of development over and above the annually recurrent budget for expenditure. The allocations of surpluses were augmented by further grants from annual revenues and by grants for specific schemes from the British Colonial Development and Welfare Fund. I was fortunate to have the support of several excellent Sarawak officers. Those to whom I am particularly indebted were Mr. Chin Shin Sen, a very senior local officer, who later moved from Development to establish a very efficient training branch; Mr. T'en Kuen Foh, who unraveled all the many financial tangles which were beyond my comprehension and went on to become Sarawak's first local Financial Secretary; and Mr. Chang Ngok Chong. Chang came to the Development Branch after several years service in a small outstation, Song, in Kapit District. During this time he had continued his education with Secretarial and Accountancy Studies and he could speak Iban. I thought his case was a most deserving one and was astonished to find the extent of prejudice against the outstation officer on the part of Kuching-based Asian officers. I had no cause to regret my choice.

The problems of development had always interested me, and I had been critical of some aspects of the plans for Sarawak. They seemed to me to devote too great a share of the available finance to urban development. When I was DO Kanowit I had written an article for the long-established government monthly publication, the *Sarawak Gazette*, entitled "Urban Interest Paramount." It had not been accepted for publication, and it was therefore salutary to be placed in a position where I could exercise some influence on the development pattern. I was to find, however, that it is easier to criticize urban expenditure than to find ways of reorienting expenditure towards the countryside.

The Development Plan for 1955-60 had already been published by the time I became associated with the work, and one of the first major tasks in which I became involved was education. Primary education was by now making good progress and was beginning to turn out an increasing number of students qualified and anxious to continue with their secondary education. The 1955-60 Plan had been drawn up on the assumption that most secondary schooling would continue to be provided by Mission and Chinese schools. It was proposed to build only three small government junior secondary schools during the period of the plan. This was a totally inadequate provision. The Missions did not have the finance to expand their school system to cater for all the English-medium school leavers. They could only have done so with large-scale government aid, hardly a desirable course in a multiracial, multireligious country. The Chinese-medium schools could have been expanded, but this would have accentuated the separateness of Chinese education and would not have catered for English-medium school leavers. The answer, obviously, was to expand the government secondary school program.

The new Director of Education, Murray Dickson, and I successfully argued the case for expansion, and this laid the foundation for the extensive network of government secondary schools which now exists in Sarawak. Building and establishing these schools, however, presented numerous problems. I thought that we should concentrate primarily on getting good teachers for the new schools and that the accommodation should be of the simplest possible kind. But the Supreme Council decreed that the new schools should be built to a worthy standard of permanent construction. Consequently, the first two schools built were disproportionately expensive and took a long time to complete. When we sought to lower the standards, the architects and engineers produced weighty arguments that in the long run this would be more expensive than building to a permanent standard of construction.

Having embarked on an expensive building program, the Government sought to economize on the cost of hiring teachers. It was decided to try, through the Colombo Plan, to obtain teams of teachers to staff the schools from the Governments of Australia, New Zealand, and Canada. The economies effected by this course were in fact very limited. The Commonwealth Governments did provide teachers as experts under their technical assistance programs, but they had to be housed and partly maintained at Sarawak's expense. Their quality was generally high and the best were first class, though there was a proportion of what we used to call two-year tourists. Those being classified by their own governments as experts sometimes found it difficult to adjust to the role they were expected to play by the Sarawak Government.

The Commonwealth Governments were remarkably generous to Sarawak in providing experts and in training Sarawak students. Such assistance had commenced before I became Development Secretary but I played some part in building it up. One idea I had which involved some arduous work was to bring to

Sarawak the Commonwealth officers who were dealing with Colombo Plan matters in the High Commissions in Singapore. These were usually officers who had little opportunity to learn about Sarawak on the ground. I persuaded the Government to invite these officers, the Australian and New Zealand First Secretaries and the Canadian Trade Commissioner, to visit Sarawak as government guests. All arrangements were made, though the Canadian had to drop out at the last moment. The appropriate officers came from the Australian and New Zealand High Commissions. The plan was to show them as much as we could of Sarawak in the time available and in particular to emphasize the need for secondary school teachers.

Our guests—Alex Borthwick (Australia) and Jack Shepherd (New Zealand)—were interested and able men. Both have had distinguished careers in their respective foreign services and they clearly liked what they saw of Sarawak. Their visit was not, however, all plain sailing.

I impressed on the Acting Chief Secretary, John Barcroft, that he must have our visitors to dinner. This presented no problems, for Barcroft was a hospitable man, but unfortunately he was in one of his silly moods. He had too much to drink, his other guests were turf club cronies, and he could talk about little else except the need to import some good bloodstock under the Colombo Plan to improve the local race horses. Alex and Jack were not amused or impressed.

Murray Dickson and I then took them to Saratok in the 2nd Division to see something of rural educational problems. The voyage was pleasant, and the visit to Saratok began well with a visit to a Local Authority school for Dayak children where we lunched. In the afternoon we were to walk over to the longhouse of a Penghulu where we were to spend the night. A feckless Education Officer had, however, misled us into believing that this was a short and easy walk. Actually it was a long, hard walk along shadeless paths which wound their way up and down steep little hills. It was also a hot afternoon. Our guests, accustomed to the easier lifestyle of Singapore, found the going fairly hard, especially Jack Shepherd, who was wearing a new pair of tennis shoes. Murray led the way and being a very fit man was soon far ahead; I brought up the rear. Towards the latter part of the afternoon I caught up with Jack sitting on top of a hill nursing his blisters and in a far from benign mood. "I've had it," he said, and then added with more than a touch of venom, "and Dickson's had his bloody schoolteachers, too." We eventually hobbled in to the longhouse where the people gave us a most warm and friendly welcome and the good-natured Jack's ire was abated.

The next day we went to Sarikei where our visitors were the guests of the DO while Dickson and I slept on the launch. The DO was a hospitable man, but at dinner Alex made some remark which gave him offense and Jack had to use considerable diplomatic skill to smooth things over. There was a certain frostiness still apparent the next morning, but then the DO took us to visit Chinese schools and when the host and guests came to realize the extent of their mutual interest in the problems before them, goodwill was once again established.

Sarawak benefitted very greatly from Colombo Plan aid. I believe that in relation to its size and population, Sarawak received more such aid than any other territory in Asia. This was due, I am sure, partly to Commonwealth goodwill and the attractiveness of Sarawak and its people and partly to the fact that the Sarawak government set up an efficient training and liaison organization, run largely by capable local officers, and looked after the experts sent us better than elsewhere. The Sarawak students sent overseas made themselves liked and fitted in readily, and the

Commonwealth experts reported favorably and sympathetically to their own governments about the needs of Sarawak and the treatment they received.

Although I played some part in establishing the system of government secondary schools, I came later to doubt whether the kind of western-style education that it represented was ideal. Those who emerged from it had a good modern education, but it also filled them with a desire to become civil servants or professional men or schoolteachers who wanted above all to live in the big towns. It filled students who had come from the countryside with a contempt for the way of life of their families and forefathers. They became alienated from their own family background.

Until a special Training Branch was established under the aegis of Mr. Chin Shin Sen, student training overseas also formed part of the responsibilities of the Development Branch. The main problem here was that initially most of the best qualified applicants for further training were Chinese, and it was the policy of the Government to try and maintain a fair racial balance in those being trained for the higher posts in the Government. With the development of education this problem was eventually corrected.

One regrettable aspect of the training program was a lack of dedication to public service on the part of some who were given training in potentially lucrative professional fields. This particularly applied to doctors. The object of the Government was to train men to take over from Europeans, or expatriates as they came to be known. In medicine, however, many of the students regarded their overseas training as the next best thing to winning a large lottery. It was the key to wealth. Some have given and continue to give fine service to the public in the government medical service, but by far the majority quickly went into private practice, their families having readily repaid their bonds. It was a depressing spectacle. One of the earliest students sent overseas to train in medicine had great difficulty with his exams in Australia—he really lacked the talent. An indulgent Sarawak Government interceded with the Australian authorities to allow him to repeat his failed courses, but when he eventually qualified he immediately went into private practice in Singapore. Only draconian measures, which could never have been contemplated by a colonial government, would have prevented the practice. As it is, the Sarawak Medical Department today is largely staffed by other expatriates, Indians, who find government terms of service in Sarawak more attractive than the employment open to them in their own country.

Replacement of expatriates by local men moved more quickly in the administrative field than any other. Apart from the transfers of some senior officials, no British administrative officers were recruited after 1956. The needs of the senior service were met by promoting from the junior service, the Sarawak Administrative Service, and by appointing young university graduates as they became available. The older men were good in the field but, through no fault of their own, were sometimes less equipped to deal with the mounting volume of paperwork. The young university men had no problems with the paperwork, but sometimes lacked interest in the field work, the traveling that forms the basis of rural administration. Their attitudes and responses were very different from those of the young expatriate officers whose places they took. They were also much more sensitive and much less amenable to criticism. The relationship with their Residents was a delicate one, but it was, on the whole, handled well on both sides. Most of the problems which occurred came from the pace of change. There was no time to have a young Asian university graduate work as a cadet for a year or so under an experienced DO, nor would the Asian officer readily accept such a role or the minor duties which went with it while he was learning about administration. It led to some odd situations. One Resident visiting a District to tour some of the substations found that the young Chinese DO was genuinely astonished to find that he was expected to accompany his Resident on tour in his District.

Overseas training produced a crop of readjustment problems. Young Asians were always well treated overseas and sometimes, because they were sociable and charming young people, they were thoroughly spoiled. New Zealand was the worst training area in this respect and Scotland the best. The trainees would return to Sarawak expecting to go right to the top of the ladder. The official view was that they had to make their way up the ladder just like anyone else with their qualifications and experience. To do otherwise would have wrecked the cohesion of the public service, which could not be localized overnight and needed to retain its share of contented expatriate officers if it was to operate efficiently. The time of very rapid promotions was bound to come fairly quickly, but in the meantime the newly qualified were expected to operate in the same way as their expatriate colleagues. In most cases they did so. Some, unfortunately, will always claim that they were unfairly discriminated against, though I can see no justification for such claims in the cases known to me. No such program of replacing expatriates with local men can ever run entirely smoothly, but I think it is fair to say that the transition in Sarawak took place without serious stress.

One of the attractive features of being Development Secretary was that you could follow up matters which had interested you in outstations. One of my special interests was in the provision of airstrips for interior travel, and we were able to make some progress in this direction. The Government even went ahead and placed orders for a short take off and landing aircraft, the Twin Pioneer, as the local airline was not at that time prepared to commit itself to the purchase. At one time we had four of these quite large aircraft on order, though it was later reduced to two. Sarawak was lucky to have a very keen and energetic Assistant Director of Civil Aviation, the late John Seal, who carried out many surveys. He was also a botanist and loved to go off on these trips of investigation. The only trouble was that it sometimes took a long time to get him back again.

For the demonstration flight of the Twin Pioneer we filled the aircraft to capacity with leading Sarawak personalities. Some of them were later a little alarmed when the pilot, without telling us what he was going to do, gave a demonstration of single-engine flight. The Managing Director of the firm manufacturing the aircraft, Group Captain McIntyre, who carried out the first flight over Mount Everest in the 1930s, asked Barcroft solicitously if there was anything he especially wanted demonstrated, and Barcroft replied that as far as he was concerned he would like to see how much of the runway the aircraft could use before it had to take off. Poor McIntyre and the pilot who demonstrated the plane to us were both killed later during tropical trials in Africa when one of the wing supports collapsed. These were strengthened before we took delivery. But despite its early promise, the Twin Pioneer did not provide the perfect aerial bus for interior Borneo, mainly because it was an unexpectedly expensive aircraft to service and operate.

One of the more time-consuming duties wished on the Development Secretary was attendance at the meetings of the United Nations Economic Committee for Asia and the Far East (ECAFE). Sarawak had no real part to play at these meetings and nothing to say but felt bound to send representatives. Accompanied by Hedda, I attended the meetings in Bangalore in 1957 and in Kuala Lumpur in 1959. The activities of ECAFE produced much paper, much talk, and virtually no action, and although it was interesting to see an international conference at work, a little went a long way. To be fair, ECAFE never had any funds to dispose of and its quite capable staff of international civil servants were not in a position to achieve anything. In many ways, a colonial territory was in a much happier position than some of the newly independent territories of Asia. If expert advice was needed, the Colonial Office had the capacity to provide first-class experts quickly and at no cost to the colony; the colony did not have to spend a large proportion of its revenues on armed services; and economic assistance was made available on a substantial if not overwhelmingly generous scale.

Nevertheless, it was very agreeable to visit India again and in Kuala Lumpur we enjoyed the company of a Bornean who has since achieved considerable fame. For that meeting, Sarawak provided an official and North Borneo an unofficial. I was the official and the unofficial was Datu Mustapha, who in later years was to dominate the political scene in Sabah, as North Borneo was later officially renamed (Sabah was in fact the old name for the territory). We all stayed in the rambling old Station Hotel in Kuala Lumpur, and we found the Datu to be a charming and considerate companion. He was unknown in Malaya in those days and took the opportunity to pay a call

Tun Mustapha, later Chief Minister of Sabah, calls on the Tunku for the first time in 1959

on the Malayan Prime Minister, Tunku Abdul Rahman. This was in fact the first time they had met. The Datu took Hedda along to photograph the occasion. Another well-remembered ECAFE guest in the Station Hotel was an IMF representative, a bird-like, beady-eyed little American banker called Henry Murphy. He held that work was the curse of the drinking man, and when he received an invitation to lunch from the Governor of Malacca which stipulated that gentlemen should wear long trousers, he said, "Not that I intended to wear short pants, but now that I have received the invitation I feel kind of restricted."

I became Development Secretary at a time when the building of roads in Sarawak was in its infancy. There were roads running out from Kuching to two neighboring Districts and small road networks around Sibu, Sarikei, and Miri, but none of the Divisions were connected. Whether this seriously impeded economic development is open to question. Sarawak's extensive river system provided a network of communications which were cheap though slow. There was little to prevent country people bringing their goods to market. But the demand for roads was strong, both for convenience and because it was argued that good roads would stimulate economic development. The first major road planned was the Simanggang road, intended to link the 1st and 2nd Divisions.

The Public Works Department at the time was a weak one and incapable, so it said, of building the road itself. It was intended to do this by contract. There are many disadvantages in this. Over and above the cost of the road, the contractor has to make a profit, and the Government has to hire its own men to see that the work is done properly and to ensure that it is not swindled in those parts of the work which cannot be precisely estimated when the contract is let. The work was put out to tender, but when the tenders were received they were far in excess of the amount provided in the Development Plan. The PWD then executed an abrupt volte face and said they could build it themselves for less.

With a weak Department I found myself dealing with all sorts of matters which should not have come my way, such as negotiating the purchase of earth-moving equipment and the salaries of engineers. The work went ahead quite well, but it was to receive a tremendous impetus with the appointment of a dynamic Pole, Jan Wardzala, as Director in 1958. I used to think that Poles were an easy-going and not particularly industrious people. In fact our Polish officers—men who had fought with the Polish forces during the war but who were out of sympathy with the communist regime—were the most energetic and hard-working men you could hope to meet. Wardzala was a man of enormous industry and a brilliant organizer. His only weaknesses were his authoritarianism, which led to some unnecessary conflict with his officers, and an almost total inability ever to offer a word of praise.

With a much stronger Department able to do the work, it was possible to plan a comprehensive program of road building. I took part in a meeting of Divisional Residents to decide on the program and rarely have I known such a diffuse and imprecise discussion. I therefore committed to paper what I thought they should have agreed to and had the gratification of being told that this was precisely what they had intended.

Wardzala was a man who never took no for a final answer. He just went away and put up the same proposal again with slightly different arguments. In at least one of these cases in which he eventually had his way against much opposition, the extension of the Kuching airfield, Sarawak owed him a particular debt of gratitude. This was an expensive operation and most of the officials concerned—I was no longer Development Secretary but would have supported the majority—considered that it should be built for the immediate needs of air transport. But Wardzala was determined to build something much bigger and with a much greater bearing strength than could be reasonably regarded as necessary. Eventually he had his way and the airfield was completed just in time to become the indispensable gateway to Sarawak during Confrontation.

Wardzala would only work to a high standard. One example I particularly remember was the provision of bazaar water supplies. Most bazaars wanted to have water pumped up into a simple untreated reticulation system to save the trouble of carting water up from the river during droughts. Wardzala would have none of this. It had to be a properly treated system or nothing. Many Chinese traders found this a little hard to understand. When I explained on a visit to Baram that this was essential in the interests of health, Kapitan China Ah Ba appeared nonplussed. "I've lived in Baram for 40 years," he said, "and in that time I have known men die from drinking too much borak and too much beer and too much brandy but never, never have I known anyone to die from drinking Baram water."

Another outstanding Head of Department was James Cook, who came to Sarawak in 1956 after service in the Malayan Agricultural Service. He did for the Agricultural Department very much what Wardzala did for Public Works. He was not only an efficient and widely experienced agriculturist, but he also had a much rarer attribute, a broad sociological view of his responsibilities.

Sarawak has a smallholder economy and the skills of its farmers are uneven. The Chinese and Kelabit are expert agriculturists, but the Chinese have land problems and the Kelabit are a tiny minority living in a remote area. Some Malay communities are excellent padi planters. Most of the inland Natives were efficient swidden agriculturists, but this is a wasteful system and quickly impoverishes the soil. The coastal Melanau worked sago, but prices for sago, except for one brief boom at the end of the war, have always been low. Many Chinese practice an intensive cultivation of pepper. Rubber was the main cash crop, but the standards of cultivation and productivity were low. Little basic research had been done and there were few research facilities.

Cook laid particular emphasis on the latter, and one of the first projects which he initiated was the establishment of a Soils Laboratory and the recruitment of research staff. Rubber replanting with high-yielding material was stepped up, but poor soils and indifferent or poor agricultural skills made the going hard. Cook used to shake his head gloomily at the difference in the knowledge of rubber cultivation which existed between Sarawak and Malaya. Still, progress was made in a wide variety of fields.

What I particularly appreciated about Cook was his interest in Agricultural Extension, an interest which was unfortunately not shared by all his staff. In the circumstances of Sarawak, the improvement of agricultural practices is a long, slow, uphill struggle. You cannot move everyone onto fresh and productive land and start from scratch. You cannot overcome innate conservatism or lack of interest in new things overnight. Improvement must be gained largely by patient work at the village level trying to improve individual efficiency and teach farmers how to make better use of the resources already available to them. This sort of work tends not to appeal to the professional agriculturist who likes to see fine laboratories and big impressive schemes for the cultivation of large and tidy crops and who looks down on patient work at the village level teaching Dayaks to grow vegetables and cook them properly. There is in fact an equal need for both types of scheme.

Agriculture was the Achilles' heel of several community development schemes which were attempted in Sarawak. The most ambitious were inaugurated in Saratok and Kanowit Districts by an educationist and former Principal of the Teacher Training Centre in Kuching called John Wilson. Wilson was a lean, rawboned Scot, a dedicated teacher with a distinguished wartime flying record in Bomber Command. He was not a religious man, but no man was ever more devoted to the service of his fellows.

His work as Principal of the Teacher Training Centre involved visiting teachers at work after they had graduated. He was shocked by the problems which they encountered in those early schools where the teacher had to contend with apathy, ignorance, and neglect in the community he served. Such conditions did not apply everywhere but were particularly common in many Dayak areas. After several years as Principal of the Training Centre, he resigned and set out to try and help Dayaks improve their own way of life. His idea was to find communities which contained progressive individuals and help them organize themselves to achieve their rightful social and economic position in Sarawak society. He started his work in Saratok District in the 2nd Division at a place called Budu. Here he obtained permission to open a primary school for which he was paid at the rate applicable to a local teacher. He formed a Committee of Progress to support the school and went on to organize a Cooperative and to provide simple health services.

The work quickly grew into an attempt to develop the community rather than the school alone, although education remained the centerpiece on which effort was focused. He selected a number of promising young Dayaks for higher education, and without any help from the Government, succeeded in getting them sent for their secondary education to Scotland where they entered Nairn Academy. The Budu community paid for this themselves. Wilson's idea was that these young men would come back as the leaders of the future, and the selection of Scotland reflected his low opinion of secondary education in Sarawak. His assessment here was probably correct. There was a possibility that educated overseas, these young people would want to return to their own communities. There was no likelihood of this if they were educated locally. This would ensure that they would never want to live in the countryside.

Wilson brought in two European assistants, McBride and Thwaites. Thwaites was a Trained Nurse and it was typical of Wilson's drive that at a time when the Colonial Office, offering generous terms of employment, found it hard to recruit people, Wilson's advertisement stressing the fact that life would be hard and pay low, drew several hundred applications. He had not even obtained approval to recruit the two men, and there was some uproar in the Secretariat when they arrived in Sarawak in 1954. The uproar eventually subsided and both newcomers were engaged on local salaries.

Wilson had friends in the Colonial Government even though he could at times be extremely difficult. He was not a man to have much sympathy with any view other than his own. But the Governor and the Medical Department supported him. I myself did not always agree with him—his outlook was rather a narrow one and he tended to reflect Dayak prejudices much magnified through his strong will and personality. The Education Department did not approve of his emphasis on overseas secondary education; the Cooperative Department was pained by the manner in

John Wilson talking to a group of Dayaks in Budu

which the Cooperatives in the Scheme were run; and there was conflict with local government, which did not approve of the creation of these schemes largely outside the ambit of the District Council. But even among his critics there was a considerable degree of grudging admiration behind the recurring discovery that the bloody fellow had pulled a fast one again. Personally I gave his schemes my support because I admired his courage; no one did more and no one suggested anything better.

Once Budu was firmly established, Wilson repeated the process in the Entabai and Ulu Kanowit. This struck me as being a difficult area to work in, for there were long memories here of the Asun rebellion, but the schemes worked successfully. One episode in the area perhaps illustrates the sort of man Wilson was. He walked over from Budu by himself to investigate the possibilities, staying with the people just as any visiting Dayak from another river would have done. At one big longhouse he outlined his proposals and then sat quietly by while the people discussed them. The discussion centered largely on the question of what they would get out of it and whether the possible gains were great enough to warrant accepting him and his scheme. The style of discussion incensed Wilson, who spoke Iban fluently, and finally he could contain himself no longer. In a towering rage he leapt to his feet and told the people that it was not a question of their accepting him, but whether he would accept them, and he could tell them there and then that the answer was no. There was considerable commotion—Dayaks are outspoken people but never had they been addressed like this by a European—but no violence was done to him and the people of another house took him away upriver. His relations with the longhouse where the argument occurred were later very friendly.

Wilson laid particular emphasis on the need for Dayaks to move away from their economic dependence on Chinese traders and their Dayak front-men operating ostensibly Dayak shops with Chinese assistance and capital. He was able to show that the Dayaks could successfully establish their own economic organization if they loyally supported it and that they could dispense with the Chinese presence. Government-sponsored cooperatives tried to do the same thing but were hampered by complex regulations. Wilson sought to provide the Dayaks with an economic organization which could be run profitably and pay for the social services which they needed as well as providing marketing and shopping facilities. But the idea depended for its success on the loyal support of the entire community. This was not always forthcoming.

From the point of view of health facilities, economic organization, and education, the Budu and Entabai schemes enjoyed a very promising measure of success. Wilson also had original plans for rural secondary education. Normal secondary schools have to be situated in or near town areas to provide support for large staffs and extensive buildings. Wilson's idea was to disperse classes between the various schemes so that it was unnecessary to provide for more than thirty or so students at any one place. He thought that given good and versatile teachers, such dispersed schools would be as capable as conventional schools of turning out qualified students without the need for costly capital expenditure. Such schools, argued Wilson, could produce students who took pride in their own home environment instead of being estranged from it as was the invariable case with students sent to the conventional schools in towns or near bazaars. The schemes were beginning to feel their way in this direction when they were terminated.

The weakness of the schemes lay in agriculture. They had help from the Agricultural Department, but their participation in the rubber-planting schemes did not go well. Dayaks are rough-and-ready agriculturists. They are excellent when it comes to cutting down jungle for shifting cultivation, but they have little aptitude for the careful and methodical work required for planting high-yielding rubber. They might have been more successful if more agricultural help could have been given.

But the general results were impressive and this was very marked in the Entabai during Confrontation. The schemes had brought a surprising measure of stability and contentment to a potentially most unstable area. To my surprise it was never a problem area, although I would have expected it to be easily set aflame by Indonesian infiltration and propaganda.

The end of the schemes was a sad one. After the formation of Malaysia and the end of the period of Confrontation, the schemes remained in being and Wilson himself stayed on. McBride and Thwaites worked for a time in government development schemes. But in 1968 Wilson was peremptorily expelled from Sarawak. No reasons were ever given. The then State Government said it was the decision of the Federal Government though it is very unlikely that the Federal authorities would have expelled Wilson if the State Government wanted him to stay. There can be little doubt, I think, that the true reasons were to be found in Sarawak itself. The Kanowit schemes in particular were disliked by the Kanowit District Council. They meant that people upriver were beginning to think and argue for themselves. Some of Wilson's outspoken observations were probably recounted downriver, much embellished by the Dayak propensity for exaggeration. Wilson was probably too angular a character to have a long-term role to play in an independent Sarawak, but the manner of his mittimus was shabby.

The schemes struggled on for a time, but they were not strong enough or sufficiently deeply rooted to withstand the departure of Wilson and the curtailment of government support. The staff have been absorbed into the government service. The schemes themselves have collapsed. Perhaps such an external initiative was doomed to failure from the start, but it was a brave and honorable effort.

We had to spend a good deal of time and money in building offices. This is a straightforward matter except for one major pitfall. There is an invariable law that no matter how big an office you build, it will be found, within one year of its completion, to be too small. I used to argue for building offices as small as possible because I thought such expenditure largely unproductive. But whenever I was overridden, as I generally was, I had little cause for regret and the law still applied. One building that I was reluctant to have built was a new Information Office. I was in disagreement with the way the Information Office was run by its incumbent, Philip Jones. He was a large and good natured man, a pillar of the Church of England—he later entered Holy Orders—and I thought he was far too preoccupied with protocol and the presentation of Sarawak to the outside world. He acted as the government receptionist for all but the most important visitors. Perhaps unfairly, I showed no alacrity in pushing the interests of the Information Office until I was spoken to sharply and in a quite unparliamentary manner by the Chief Secretary, Ellis. It was the only time he ever upbraided me. And so the new Information Office was built and completed in 1959.

I enjoyed my tenure of office as Development Secretary. I acted in the post for nearly four years and I had high hopes that I would be confirmed in it. But I was to find that, although I was regarded as useful in some ways, interested, and able to get things moving, I was also held to be extravagant and not given to such matters beloved of developers as Long Term Projections. At the end of 1959, just when I thought I was about to be confirmed as Development Secretary, I was informed that I would shortly be appointed Information Officer. It was a great blow to my self-esteem. Nothing like it had happened to me since my school days at Malvern, when, after many vicissitudes I achieved the high station of College Prefect and was then allocated the altogether demeaning portfolio of Prefect of Choir.

I sometimes wondered whether this was not a time bomb which Ellis might have left behind him. He had a rather subtle and devious sense of humor. He was a lively Welshman, lively sometimes to the point of rashness. The immediate cause of his departure in 1958 was that while acting as Governor, during his wife's absence in England with the children he had a beautiful blonde lady, the wife of a Naval officer, to stay with him at the Astana. This did not upset local opinion—Ellis was a helpful and popular officer—but it certainly upset some of the European wives. They brought Ellis's little foible to the notice of the Colonial Office and he had to retire. He had a very warm send-off, particularly from the local Sarawak officers whose interests he had done much to promote.

7

THE INFORMATION OFFICE

Work as Information Officer turned out to be more interesting than I had anticipated, and I found that the predecessor I had criticized had assembled a capable and willing staff. My Deputy was the same good Morshidi who had taken me under his wing when I first went travelling in Sarikei. The Assistant Information Officer was Chih Chia-Kwei, a Foochow from the 3rd Division who had been educated in Shanghai. He had been one of the Chinese liaison officers attached to the Marshall Mission in the course of which he had visited Yenan. The Press Officer was a Singapore man, Ivor Kraal, an experienced journalist with a fund of ideas. Indeed I never met a man who sparked ideas with such rapidity. His ideas were not all good but a very respectable number were first class. I learned a great deal from him. He was later to have a successful career in the Information Division of the Malaysian Ministry of Foreign Affairs. A Chinese Press Officer, Chang Chih-kang, looked after the Chinese side of our press work. He was a Shanghai man and one of the few bachelors in the office. I was to give him some fatherly advice on the desirability of settling down and getting married, though I did not foresee that he would shortly afterwards marry my secretary. We had Malay and Iban sections which were producing good little newspapers in those languages. There was a Reading Room for the public, photographic and art units, and several film units.

The Information Office had a small staff and growing responsibilities. A particularly pleasant feature of work in the Office was to see how much resource and initiative men of modest formal attainments could achieve if given responsibility. The office boy, Asun, operated the solitary duplicator which existed when I took up my appointment. In the course of expansion we came to acquire a whole battery of duplicators, two small offsets, and a block-making capacity. With a little training by Gestetners, the suppliers of the excellent equipment which we used, Asun took up most of the additional responsibilities. He proved himself to be a most efficient printer and a natural mechanic. So did his assistant. The artists and photographers similarly showed talent of a high order. They could hold their own with Europeans doing such work and possessing far more elaborate formal qualifications.

For the multitude of distributional and organizational problems which always beset an Information Office, I was able to turn in particular to three men I used to call the Three Musketeers: a Malay, a Dayak, and a Melanau. Adeng, the Malay, was a former schoolteacher and Probationary Native Officer. Arnold Linang, the Dayak, and Nawawi, the Melanau, had both started work with the Information Office. They were a most resourceful trio, and I knew that if some unexpected problem arose they would individually or jointly find an answer. In common with most other branches of the Sarawak government service, there was no payment for overtime in the Information Office, but much overtime was willingly and loyally worked whenever the need arose.

I was able to have Hedda work part-time to give some on-the-job training to the photographers. They showed great aptitude. They were, however, involved in a sensational episode when one of the photographers, Razaleigh, was in midmorning given a lunchtime assignment. Hedda told him to go out and get something to eat, and Razaleigh brought back a large ripe durian. This is certainly nutritious food but not quite what Hedda had in mind. However, Razaleigh and Hedda and another photographer set to and ate the durian.

About this time I had a visit from the Singapore manager of Gestetners, an amiable and helpful man not long out from England. When he had completed his business, I told him that he must come downstairs and see our new darkroom. Now the durian, which is a delicious fruit, has a strong fragrance and eaten in even the most air-conditioned darkroom, the effects in a small space are somewhat overpowering. I took him below and, announcing that this was the new darkroom, threw open the door and propelled him inside. He reeled back, and even I who had come to love durians had to admit that the aroma was strong. We beat an embarrassed retreat. The manager had not yet acquired a taste for durians and I doubt whether he ever did.

The good Morshidi, who introduced me to rural Sarawak and was later my Deputy in the Information Office, at his farewell party

Poor Razaleigh was to be taken from us prematurely. He was a young man of exceptional charm, happily married, and beloved by all who knew him. Unfortunately he was an epileptic, and when we sent him to undertake a photographic course in England, where he did very well despite limited formal education, he died in a sudden seizure. I never knew a death that caused so many to feel as if they had lost a favorite son.

There were no very clear terms of reference for the Information Office and I largely wrote my own. The main object of our work was to publicize and explain the work and policies of the Government, especially through the press and the local broadcasting service. The press section used to put out a steady stream of well-produced releases which were translated into Chinese for the Chinese press. There was only one English newspaper to begin with, but there were never less than seven or eight Chinese papers.

My initial efforts were devoted largely to moving away from the former emphasis on external publicity. We had to produce the Annual Report for the colony and I

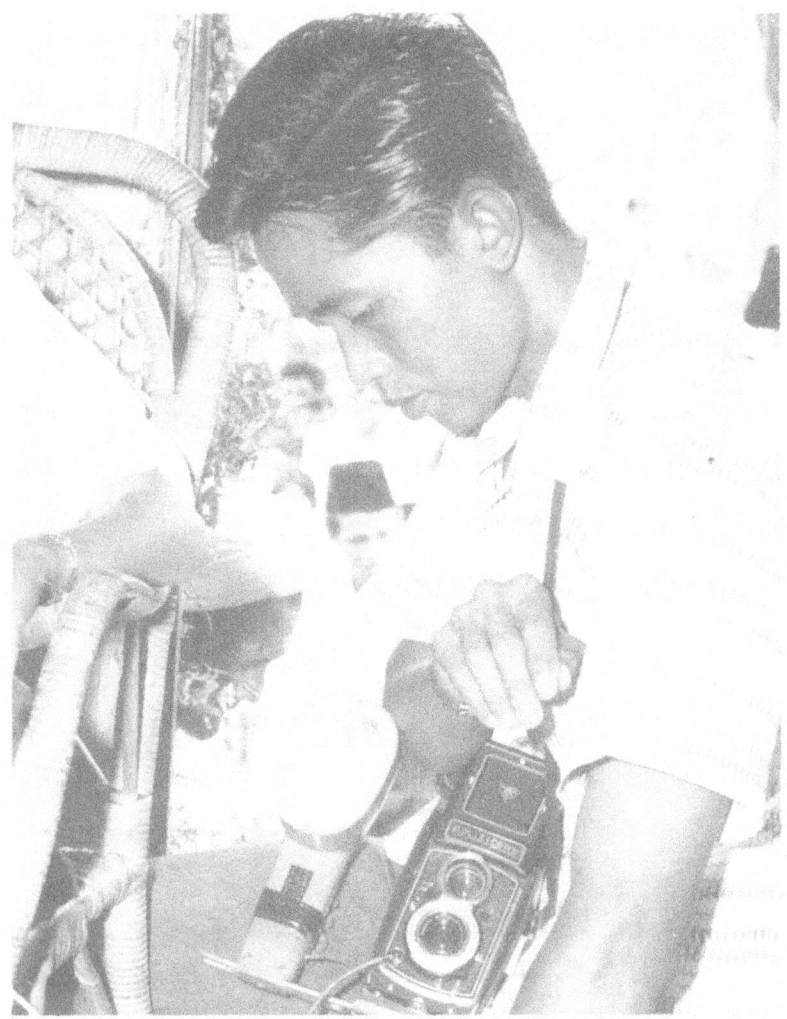

Abang Razaleigh bin Abang Haji Jaya

wrote a little handbook for Sarawak. I thought that this was about all that we needed to produce for the outside world, and I refused to meet visitors unless they were journalists or genuine seekers after information. I stopped the laborious conferences which used to take place regularly with our North Borneo and Brunei colleagues and, more surprisingly, with the Shell Company public relations organization. It seemed to me that, within reason, it did not greatly matter what the outside world thought of Sarawak and its government. The real public relations problems lay within Sarawak itself.

The Information Office worked in parallel but close concert with Radio Sarawak, the local broadcasting service. This had been established in 1954, fortunately as an entirely independent organization. It had become a well-established department in time to take advantage of the great transistor revolution of the late 1950s, which brought radio within the reach of everyone. Its head was Peter Ratcliffe, a lively, ebullient, dynamic personality and an excellent organizer. He had been with the

Ivor Kraal, who taught me about the press

British forces in Java at the end of the war, and his strong pro-Indonesian sympathies had won him many friends there. He came to hold strong views on the performance of the Dutch, especially after he had personally witnessed Dutch fighters shoot down an RAF Dakota engaged on a relief mission. He broadcast an eyewitness account of the event over the Indonesian radio, an initiative which did not endear him to the Dutch. He knew many leading Indonesian personalities and had access to President Soekarno whenever he visited Jakarta.

Radio Sarawak had been developed as a prestige institution and was far more lavishly equipped than the Information Office. It had good engineering staff and was technically excellent. It was multilingual, broadcasting in English, Malay, Iban, and Chinese. I did not always agree with Radio Sarawak, largely because I thought that too much effort was directed at Sarawak's small educated elite and that it was too closely modeled on western ideas of broadcasting. The standards which it sought to emulate were those of the BBC and ABC, and although such an ambition was in itself

Typesetter in a Chinese newspaper

a commendable one, I did not think it was necessarily well suited to an underdeveloped Asian country such as Sarawak. Our broadcasters abhorred repetition, while I thought that it was the key to being understood by a mass audience in Asia. These differences of outlook, however, did not prevent me from enjoying a very close and stimulating relationship with Peter and his staff, and they were a great help to me.

By the time I became Information Officer in 1960, politics had begun to play a significant part in the local scene. The first political party, the Sarawak United People's Party (SUPP), had been formed a year earlier. There was basic agreement between the Government and local leaders that the people of Sarawak should manage their own affairs as soon as possible. Government efforts in political development had been devoted mainly to developing education and laying the foundations for political progress through the establishment of local government authorities. It was hoped that healthy and workable political progress could be made from these twin foundations, though the development of education was inevitably a slow process.

The long-term objective of both the Government and emerging local politicians was independence within the British Commonwealth. The idea largely sold itself. There was already a strong sense of Sarawak identity, and few Sarawakians disagreed with the idea of a benevolent relationship with a protective Britain. The great flaw in the objective was that it assumed the continued existence of a strong British presence in the region. The idea that this might not be so never occurred to me at the time, and I very much doubt whether it occurred to anyone else in Sarawak.

The founders of SUPP sought to form a multiracial party. Its principal leaders were Ong Kee Hui and Stephen Yong. Ong was a Hokkien and a descendant of one of the earliest Chinese families to settle in Sarawak, a family which had long been prominent in Sarawak affairs. His grandfather was Ong Tiang Swee, who achieved great prominence under the Brookes. Stephen Yong was a lawyer and a Hakka. At the end of the war, he and three other Chinese—Danny Kok, Chan Siaw Hee, and Sim Kheng Hong—formed a successful salvage business. With his share of the proceeds, Stephen Yong went to England and read law; Danny Kok went to America and became a doctor; Chan Siaw Hee went into the transport business; and Sim Kheng Hong became a contractor. With the exception of Danny Kok, all the partners were to become prominent in SUPP.

The founders of the party had been given considerable encouragement by government officials, particularly by Ellis and Barcroft. What eventually emerged, however, was different from the genteel politicization of the status quo which was, in my view, about all that these officials had envisaged. Even before the party was formed, the growing communist movement in Sarawak had decided to work towards the formation of a political party, and it infiltrated SUPP from the start. The Governor expressed misgivings about the impact of political parties on the unity of Sarawak, and when SUPP was formed it failed to secure the support of prominent Natives. It did receive some support from Dayaks and other Natives, but mostly from individuals and communities which had been in conflict with authority or with their neighbors.

The party always overstated the extent of its Native support. Its leaders have claimed that government discouragement caused some leading Native personalities to go back on promises to take part in the formation of SUPP. Government attitudes may well have made Native leaders cautious, but I doubt whether it made much difference. In Sarawak, yes very often meant no, the affirmative more often a matter of wanting to be polite than a considered decision made in the full understanding of what was involved. I am sure that some of the early assurances of support by Native personalities for SUPP fell into this category.

Multiracialism in politics is a desirable ideal. Unfortunately, once politics become active, differences, jealousies, and underlying rivalries, awakened by the competition for power and influence between communities, quickly override similarities in outlook. Sarawak under the Brookes and as a British Crown Colony enjoyed a notable degree of communal harmony. The underlying harmony remained after the inception of party politics, but in practice, if not in theory, the parties themselves became largely communal. Real multiracialism calls for a strongly developed and common ideological base, and this was lacking in Sarawak as political development gathered momentum.

Sarawak politics became very complicated. An exceptionally detailed and comprehensive account has been written by a well-informed Australian political scientist, Michael Leigh, in his book, *The Rising Moon*. The details fall outside the scope of these memoirs. By 1962 there were six Parties: SUPP (multiracial in concept but with a Chinese mass base); Party Negara or PANAS (multiracial but mainly conservative 1st Division Malay plus some Land Dayak support); Sarawak National Party or SNAP (multiracial but predominantly 2nd Division Dayak); Barisan Ra'ayat Jati Sarawak or BARJASA (entirely Native, mostly the younger, better-educated Malays and Melanau); the Sarawak Chinese Association (conservative Chinese); and Party Pesaka (mainly 3rd Division Dayak). With this proliferation, a slightly bewildered, politically inexperienced, and largely expatriate senior government service did its best to hold the ring and to ensure that politics developed in as constructive a way as possible.

It has always seemed to me that the expatriates have been credited by local politicians and by academic political scientists with a degree of political expertise which simply did not exist. Both they and the emerging politicians were inexperienced. They had to find answers to the problems facing them to the best of their ability using common sense and an honest desire to promote the best interest of Sarawak. There was no Colonial Office master plan.

In the elections of 1959 SUPP had the field to itself, as the next party to come into existence—PANAS—was not formed until the following year. SUPP, therefore, enjoyed a considerable amount of success in these Local Authority elections designed simultaneously to elect members to the legislature. This was achieved through a three-tier system. The elected District and Municipal Councils elected members of Divisional Advisory Councils which in turn acted as electoral colleges for Council Negri. It was a cumbersome system, but it had always been official policy to build up the democratic process from the grassroots ward level.

The better organized and more politically conscious Chinese community made the running in SUPP. By early 1960 the Government was concerned about the increasingly Chinese nature of the party and the effect this was having on race relations. This led to the issuing of a directive to administrative officers on political guidance, especially for rural areas. Government officers were to do what they could to promote political education at a simple level. This was not directed specifically against SUPP, but the official attitude towards the party was outlined as follows: "SUPP, in spite of the repeated assurances of its leaders, and probably against their genuine wishes, remains a predominantly Chinese party with little native support. The successes so far achieved have exacerbated the underlying mistrust between the natives of Sarawak on the one hand and the Chinese on the other, which have always been recognised as existing below the surface."

The party spoke with two voices. On the one hand, there was a highly regarded and moderate leadership putting a persuasive case for a multiracial party and claiming to be one. On the other hand, there were inflammatory and purely Chinese utterances in the left-wing press. The moderate leadership claimed that the party provided a channel of expression for the angry young men of the community, but it did not visibly moderate what the angry young men were saying.

The most prominent of the left-wing journalists, Wen Ming-chuan, played an important organizational role in SUPP. He is now the Chairman of the Communist Party of North Kalimantan and lives in Peking. He was the son of a poor vegetable seller and had been involved as a student in disturbances in the Kuching Chinese schools in 1951. Our relations with him in the Information Office were cordial. He had a gentle manner and an almost soft appearance. Hedda and I attended his wedding, a splendidly bourgeois occasion organized by his friends in SUPP, at which the best brandy flowed like water and the Central Committee was nearly blown up by the most enormous firecracker I ever saw in Sarawak. It was suspended from a verandah just behind where the Committee was standing. Wen and his bride seemed to find the proceedings rather hilarious.

Although Chinese-educated, Wen had quite a good knowledge of English, and I suggested that this homegrown and frustrated intellectual deserved to be given an opportunity to further his education and to broaden his outlook. The Scholarship Committee was prepared to consider his case, so I made some inquiries as to whether he might be accepted for a period of study at Ruskin College, Oxford. It was an unusual proposition, but I was told that it would at least be considered. Armed with this knowledge, I made a formal submission to the Scholarship Committee and appeared before it to argue the case for sending Wen overseas.

I found that the expatriate members of the Committee were sympathetic and saw no reason why Wen's radicalism should be a bar to his further study. But one of the two Chinese unofficials on the Committee had very different views. He said that he had known Wen since he was a lad and that he was a real troublemaker. And how could the Government possibly send such a man overseas when there were lots of nice, well-brought up and well-behaved boys from St. Thomas's and St. Joseph's who wanted to go overseas, not all of whom could be sent. The non-Chinese unofficials backed up this viewpoint and the second Chinese representative, Stephen Yong, who could have been expected to support Wen's candidature, had forgotten to come to the meeting. And so poor Wen never did enjoy the mental stimulus of Oxford. He remained in Sarawak until, after a period of restricted residence, he left voluntarily for China in 1963. Perhaps it was just as well for Oxford.

Combating communism in the liberal environment of a British colony was a difficult task. Communism or a belief in communism was not illegal in Sarawak. There was nothing to stop the importation of communist propaganda or to prevent people from listening to broadcast communist propaganda; newspapers could expound communist ideology provided they kept within the limits set by the laws of defamation, libel, and incitement to commit illegal acts. Societies and organizations were regulated by law and the Government had power to refuse to register a society, but the communist organization was a secret one.

In those early days in Sarawak, the Government was becoming increasingly well-informed about communism because it had established a well-staffed Police

Special Branch and it sought to bring to public attention what was happening. The communist movement shuns publicity. In the Information Office, towards the end of 1960 we started to produce extracts translated from the Chinese and Malay press. This ensured that a fair proportion of the communist writings and poems in the three communist papers which were eventually established—one each in Kuching, Sibu, and Miri—were made available to readers who were not conversant with written Chinese. The demand for these extracts was quite surprising and they were widely read.

In 1960 the Government published a White Paper on Subversion, the contents receiving supporting coverage in broadcasts and the press. This was followed up the next year by another White Paper on Communism and the Farmers, which elaborated on the reasons for refusing to register a proposed Farmers Association because it was a communist front organization. Refusal to register did the movement little direct harm because the Association went underground and it remained active for years. In 1963 the Information Office published a comprehensive account of the communist movement entitled *Danger Within*. Although published by my department, it was in fact written by a Special Branch officer, Tim Hardy, and written so well that it needed the minimum of editing to provide a valuable and readable account of the movement. I wanted to call it *Cancer Within*, but the police demurred, pointing out with undeniable logic that cancer is often fatal.

Tougher legislation was also introduced. This started off with a gentle and, in fact, disastrous measure, called the Restricted Residence Ordinance, which was promulgated in 1961. The idea was that individuals considered a menace might have their movements curtailed or be confined to places away from their center of operations. When it was applied it resulted in the spread of communist ideology. Devoted communist cadres confined to some outstation hitherto unaffected by communism became an immediate center of interest and sympathy for the young Chinese of the area, and those restricted had a receptive audience to win over to their way of thinking. This was notably the case in Betong. The Restricted Residence Ordinance was quickly followed by the strengthening of various other ordinances dealing with societies, trade unions, and the press and finally by Public Order and Preservation of Public Order Ordinances.

By the end of 1962 the Government had a whole armory of restrictive legislation at its disposal. It was regrettable but unavoidable. Communism cannot be opposed successfully by the mouthing of platitudes and the earnest application of the best principles of western democratic thought, because the communists do not play by the same rules. They observe them only with a view to overthrowing them when the opportunity occurs. What is required is a combination of honest government, well-informed public opinion, tough sanctions vigorously applied, and a good Special Branch. And by good Special Branch I mean a body of dedicated and intelligent policemen who have a thorough understanding of Marxism and possess as much patience and tenacity as the communists do themselves. Brutal and stupid policemen are of direct benefit to the communist movement.

It never ceased to amaze me to see the communist documents and underground papers which we sometimes exhibited. They were generally handwritten in tiny but legible characters on sheets of airmail paper folded together to form very small and easily concealed booklets. These would be turned out by young Chinese working in the attic of a farming hut or shophouse. Not very many could be produced in this way, but they would be passed from hand to hand and read by many or used by study groups. The writing was tautological in the extreme and for the non-communist reader extraordinarily dull. The volume of such material was immense. Communists have a curious weakness for committing their ideas to paper. The communist system in Sarawak was very strong and well attuned to Chinese standards of industry but was too hard and too austere to be readily mastered by non-Chinese. Communists had difficulty adapting their beliefs and ideology to suit the different thought processes of Dayaks and Malays.

An interesting example of rigidity of thought arose from communist attitudes on education. As education developed from the dreadful situation of 1947 when, for instance, ninety-seven percent of the Iban population was illiterate and only one Native in the whole of Sarawak held the Cambridge School Certificate, the separate status of the Chinese-medium schools became steadily more embarrassing. English was already the medium of the Mission schools which were attended by many Chinese, and it was also adopted as the medium in government secondary schools. English was generally accepted as the channel for advancement and higher education and was equally acceptable as the medium of instruction to both Dayaks and Malays.

There grew up, then, two separate streams of education, and apart from some movement by Chinese-medium students to the English stream, there was virtually no mixing of the two. The Government aim was to bring the children of all races together, and this meant that the Chinese secondary schools would have to convert to the English-language medium though a high standard of Chinese could continue to be taught. This idea gained a good deal of acceptance in the Chinese community but was strongly opposed by many, especially by the communist papers. Their reasoning was that differences between the races arose from the deliberate policies of the colonialists. Get rid of the colonialists and differences would disappear. Differences in the medium of instruction would then play no part in people's thinking. Therefore let each community use its own language as the medium of instruction. This sort of argument appealed to Chinese racial pride. Many Chinese genuinely wanted to continue to run their own schools in the way to which they had been accustomed. But the argument aroused acute suspicion on the part of Native opinion, which thought it meant keeping the Chinese separate and the Natives backward. It would have been much more effective from the communist point of view if they had embraced the proposal for unifying the medium of instruction. It would have brought them into much closer contact with the other peoples of Sarawak.

By the time I reached the Information Office, Sarawak had come under substantially new management. When Ellis was forced to retire early in 1958, he was succeeded briefly by Barcroft, who died of a massive heart attack while on a visit to Lawas a few months later. Early in 1959 Barcroft was succeeded by Derek Jakeway, an officer of quite exceptional experience. He had served in Nigeria, the Seychelles (during a difficult time when the Governor and Chief Justice quarrelled bitterly), British Guiana (during another difficult period), and in the Colonial Office. He was a most accomplished colonial administrator and very skilled in negotiation and discussion. From the point of view of his subordinates, he had the tiresome knack of putting his finger on the weakest point in your submission or argument where you had not fully done your homework.

In 1959, Sir Anthony Abell departed after some ten years as the Crown representative. Few Colonial Governors ever did a better job. He was not a great innovator and he made no attempt to engage in the details of administration. He left this to his staff, but he brought to bear on their work a shrewd and experienced mind. Because of his extensive travels he was widely known and his hospitality was generous and informal. Any prominent personality visiting Kuching, such as Temenggong Oyong Lawai Jau, would normally be accompanied by a number of followers and you would meet them all at the Astana receptions. These were prominent people in their own communities and they were perfectly at their ease in the Astana even if they did not wear lounge suits. When John Wilson was in town once from Budu, he had with him a young Dayak trainee. Wilson was invited to stay at the Astana but declined because he thought he should keep company with his companion. He was forthwith instructed to bring the young Dayak with him too.

Abell was replaced by Sir Alexander Waddell, who had started his career in the Solomon Islands and had distinguished himself there as a coastwatcher during the Pacific War. Waddell was a large, rather military figure with a clipped manner of speech. It was not an easy task to succeed Abell, but he proved to be a good Governor and did his best to maintain the traditions established by his predecessor. He tended, however, to concern himself unnecessarily with executive detail, something which Abell never did. Waddell was married, and succeeding a popular bachelor

The Governor, Sir Anthony Abell, and the Chief Secretary, Derek Jakeway, confer in the Chief Secretary's office, below a bust of James Brooke

also poses problems for a Governor's wife. Lady Waddell proved to be a kind and tactful English lady and was very much liked.

An example of Waddell's executive urges occurred in the early stage of negotiations over Malaysia. *The London Times* carried a long anonymous article which was mischievous and ill-informed. I was bidden to draft a letter to the editor to correct the record. This I did with some fervor—the identity of the author, a member of the Commonwealth Relations Office, was perfectly clear—but my draft was considered too outspoken by the Governor and I was told to try again. This I did but it still failed to meet with the Governor's approval. He then drafted a letter himself—handwritten and in gubernatorial red—and told me to send it to the editor under my signature. I did not altogether agree with the Governor's draft but did as I was told. The reply from *The Times* was pompous in tone but had the merit of some unintended humor. It said that in matters such as this, it was not the practice of *The Times* to publish letters from Public Relations Officers, Press Attaches, and Information Officers. *The Times* preferred instead to publish letters from Ambassadors, High Commissioners, and Governors.

Sir Alexander Waddell talking to Penghulus at the opening
of the Batang Lupar District Council offices

A long period of service in Kuching can tend to isolate one from the problems of the countryside, but both as Development Secretary and Information Officer I was able to undertake a certain amount of traveling and to continue to improve my knowledge of Sarawak. I rarely noticed any reluctance on the part of my colleagues to see me out of the capital for a time. With a little ingenuity one could always find some circuitous and interesting route to reach the place one intended to visit. One particularly interesting tour took us to Baram via the Medalam tributary of the Limbang River and down the Tutoh tributary of the Baram. The watershed is a low one, so low that the Kayan used to drag their warboats across it in their attacks on the Limbang.

A special objective of our visit was to see a place called Batu Rikan at the base of Mount Mulu where a fair-sized stream comes welling up from the base of a limestone cliff. There is a somewhat fanciful illustration of this in that classic of early travel in Sarawak, St. John's *Life in the Forests of the Far East*. We reached Batu Rikan, but the visit was marred by a heavy downfall of rain and I subsided slowly into the river down a slippery reef face taking my camera with me.

When we reached the Tutoh we found a cheerful welcoming party of eight Kenyah and three small boys awaiting us. They had been there a week, fishing the rich waters of this little-visited area. This seemed a pleasant idea, but I found that they expected to draw full salary for both adults and small boys for the entire period. This was despite the fact that the welcoming party was unnecessarily large, we had reached the Tutoh on exactly the day we had said we would, and there had been no reason for them come early, as no one in Borneo ever arrives ahead of time. I thought this an extortionate imposition and said so. The Kenyah looked pained. "But Tuan," said their leader, "how embarrassing it would have been if you *had* arrived earlier." I refused to accept their bill as presented, but once I had left Marudi the DO paid it. He was a popular and sociable officer and was rarely given to saying no. Once, as Development Secretary, I sent him some funds for airfield investigation and found later that they had been spent on building a basketball pitch for the young people of Marudi Bazaar.

Hedda did a considerable amount of traveling on her own. This never caused me any uneasiness. Of course it is possible to capsize in a rapid in Borneo and get drowned, but it is no more likely than the prospect of getting run over by a bus in Piccadilly Circus. I knew that she would enjoy complete personal security and that she would be kindly and hospitably treated wherever she went. It was, however, a rather odd reversal of the normal practice whereby the husband travels and the wife stays at home.

In Kuching she was able to pay many visits to the coast. There was a generous arrangement designed to help both European and Asian officers to visit the coast for holidays, whereby people hiring government launches were charged only half the cost of the fuel used. This amounted to very little in the case of diesel-engined launches. The concession was little used but Hedda availed herself of it frequently. The launch crews seemed to enjoy those photographic jaunts down to the coast as much as she did.

A particularly memorable event took place when she once accompanied Sir Anthony Abell, who was taking some houseguests on a visit to the seaside in the Governor's yacht. Well out at sea, the Governor sighted a small head bobbing about in the water. On investigation this turned out to be the head of a large male Proboscis Monkey swimming strongly in the direction of Singapore.

The Proboscis Monkey is a curious, inoffensive animal confined to the swamplands of Borneo where it lives on the shoots of mangrove trees. The male weighs up to 55 pounds and has a huge belly to house its specialized digestive tract and an extraordinary long and bulbous nose. Its alarm call is a loud belch. The Iban call it Rasong, but its more common name is Blanda (Dutchman). It is not unusual for them to be swept out to sea while swimming across the mouths of rivers.

The Governor ordered a boat to be lowered and sent his somewhat reluctant Special Branch bodyguard to mount a rescue operation. The monkey climbed into the boat and sat in the stern sheets belching heartily at his rescuers. They towed him, looking like some gouty old sailor, to within reach of land when, with a parting belch, he plunged overboard and swam ashore. For some reason the Governor christened him Carruthers.

Carruthers

There was never any lack of work in the Information Office and in Sarawak we followed the quaint old British custom of working a five-and-a-half day week. On Sundays we would drive out into the countryside and go for a walk, and we never accepted invitations to that baleful Malaysian institution, the curry lunch. Curry lunch on a Sunday involves assembling at midday with people you see too much of anyway and drinking beer, pink gin, and brandy ginger ale until well into the afternoon. You probably do not have lunch until after 3 p.m. It is immediately preceded—for the hardened toper—by slugs of neat gin with particles of white pepper floating in it, washed down with more beer. You eventually return home in a semi-comatose state late in the afternoon and feel dreadful on Monday morning.

I became interested in a mild way in orchid culture. They are fascinating plants of extraordinary beauty and diversity, easy to grow and with very long lasting blooms. There were some very attractive species native to Borneo and a wide variety of hybrids produced by artificial cross-pollenization. It was particularly interesting to obtain the wild plants brought in from the jungle, straggly and unimpressive from the struggle for survival in the wild, and to see how quickly they responded to care and manuring and produced masses of blooms as they never do in the jungle.

Orchid growing is the passion of many and also a minor industry in Malaysia and Singapore. The competition is cutthroat and does not bring out the gentler virtues even among the most gentle of people. While we were in Kuching there was a sudden influx of what were known as Rats-tail Orchids. These were tree-growing plants with curious cylindrical leaves found in the jungles of Indonesian Borneo adjoining Sarawak's 2nd Division. There are three species, of which two are rare and much sought after. It is difficult to distinguish the species outside the flowering season. There was a great rush to obtain more of these orchids from the Indonesian Dayaks who collected them, and a number of orchid enthusiasts went over the border illegally in quest of the plants. The border crossers included one very energetic and determined Chinese lady, and it was said that her competitors offered substantial rewards to the Dayaks to take her far into the jungle and to lose her there. The plot failed.

One enterprise I helped establish as Development Secretary grew very greatly while I was Information Officer. This was the Borneo Literature Bureau, a small government publishing house established by Sarawak and North Borneo—largely at the initiative of Sir Anthony Abell—to promote local literature and to make books more readily available throughout the territories. The work of the Bureau was not confined to the production of written work in local languages. Much of its work was devoted to ensuring that the book trade was developed so as to ensure that in every little settlement books were available. Previously it was possible to buy books only in the larger centers.

One of the most striking aspects of the Bureau's work was the volume of writing produced in the Iban language. The Iban have always possessed a great body of oral legend—every community had its bards. When it became possible to publish work, a surprising number of books, mostly on legendary themes, were produced by educated Iban and more were recorded from illiterate informants. There was a much greater literary urge on the part of the Iban than any other Bornean community.

In addition to the Colombo Plan experts who came to Sarawak in various helpful capacities, we also had numbers of volunteer workers who came out to Sarawak under several voluntary schemes of aid, such as the British Overseas Voluntary Service and another organization sponsored by Canadian Universities. Much larger was the American Peace Corps, which brought a considerable number of well-scrubbed young Americans to Sarawak. All these schemes did useful work, particularly in providing highly educated, if not fully trained, teachers for the growing number of secondary schools. A peculiarity of the Peace Corps volunteers was the thoroughness of their training before they came out and the extraordinary amount of psychiatric examination which they had undergone. The idea, I think, was to weed out non-conformists who might bring embarrassment to the United States. But all our experience showed that it was precisely the individualist who was best fitted for dealing with unexpected problems in a new environment. Not all the Peace Corps members were conformists by any means. Quite a number of stout individualists had assessed the situation and learned how to give the right answers to the psychiatrists and so to beat the system. Most of the volunteers did well and they helped Sarawak over a difficult period of teacher shortage, but I doubt whether the psychiatrists did much good. It was noticeable that many of the Americans were less mature than often much younger Commonwealth volunteers.

When the Peace Corps was first announced, we had a visit from the head of the organization, Mr. Shriver himself. He came with a considerable retinue, and the Information Office had to arrange a press conference. But most unfortunately, none of the local journalists, with the exception of the *Straits Times* correspondent, bothered to attend. This was not due to hostility but simply because the papers knew that we would give them a release in both English and Chinese. It was an embarrassing moment, but the problem was overcome by mobilizing the entire multiracial staff of the press section of my department plus one or two others. Mr. Shriver was faced with a fine array of sympathetic, smiling faces. Some questions of a most friendly nature were asked and the conference went off very well.

One event which we particularly enjoyed was the annual "graduation" ceremony at the Brooke Memorial Hospital for lepers. There was enough leprosy in Sarawak to constitute a minor problem. Nowadays its treatment presents no great difficulty but the disease was feared. You sometimes came across country people who had been driven out of their longhouses because of skin conditions. Many were not even suffering from leprosy. The biggest problem lay in getting lepers reaccepted by their communities after they had been treated and cured.

The Medical Department hit on the idea of having an annual "graduation" ceremony in which those to be discharged were presented by the Governor with a scroll certifying that they had been cured of the disease. The certificates provided the proof that the discharged needed to gain reacceptance in their communities. The presentation ceremonies were exceptionally cheerful and pleasant occasions.

The marvellous kindness one enjoyed in Sarawak was not confined to rural areas. Personal relations in Kuching were very happy. One of the Sarawak traditions which contributed to this was the custom that on Hari Raya, at the end of the Muslim fasting month, you called on your Malay staff and other Malay friends, and you did the same with your Chinese staff and friends at Chinese New Year. A Dayak Day was also established to extend the tradition to that community. You would call at the house and wish the whole family the compliments of the season and partake of some light refreshment while you talked. It was not necessary or expected that you should eat or drink a lot, though this was sometimes difficult to refuse in the case of especially close friends. Particularly in staff relations it was a very good custom, because it meant that at least once a year you visited your staff in their homes and met their families and did so in a framework of established custom. At

The Governor distributing discharge scrolls at the
Brooke Memorial Settlement for lepers

New Year we used to invite the Information Office Staff to call on us. This cycle of visits is among the most pleasant recollections which we brought away from Sarawak.

One occasion of very special courtesy occurred when I received an invitation to dinner at the Chinese Chamber of Commerce. I did not read it carefully and told Hedda that she was invited too. We made our way to the Chamber of Commerce, many members of which were known to us, and arrived in good time. But slowly it began to dawn on Hedda that she was the only woman in the hall. She drew Ong Kee Hui, a leading figure in the Chamber, aside and asked if she had really been asked. "Of course we asked you, Hedda," Kee Hui replied, "you speak such wonderful Chinese." This was gilding the lily somewhat, but clearly Hedda had to stay and enjoyed a convivial dinner. When we went home we consulted the invitation card and found, of course, that Hedda had not been asked. Our apologies were gracefully accepted.

8

Establishment of Malaysia

Most of my period in the Information Office was dominated by the formation of Malaysia. When the Prime Minister of Malaya, Tunku Abdul Rahman, enunciated the proposal in Singapore on May 27, 1961, Hedda and I were driving round Australia in a Volkswagen van. We heard the news over the radio when we were near a little place called Turkey Creek in the Kimberley region of northwest Australia.

The idea of Sarawak becoming part of a larger federation was not entirely new. The concept had been toyed with in Britain, Singapore, and Malaya on several occasions since the war. The first definite proposal, however, was only put forward in 1958 and was limited to a closer association between Sarawak, Sabah, and Brunei. It had been favorably received in Sarawak and Sabah but quickly foundered on the opposition of Brunei. At the time Brunei was by far the most prosperous of the three territories, and its leaders saw no good reason to share their abundant oil revenue with their less prosperous neighbors.

The more elaborate and realistic proposals for Malaysia stemmed from two compatible considerations. One was the need to provide the British Borneo territories with a stable environment for future independence. Even though most of us in Sarawak were happily proceeding on the assumption that the goal for Sarawak was independence as an individual state within the British Commonwealth, at a higher level there were some misgivings. These were reinforced by the special problems of Singapore. Before the war Singapore had been part of the Straits Settlements. The other Settlements were Penang and Malacca. Singapore was thus politically detached from the greater part of mainland Malaya, which consisted of the Federated and Unfederated Malay States. After the war Singapore became a Crown Colony on its own, while Penang and Malacca became part of the Malay Federation. It was a curious situation. Singapore, with a predominantly Chinese population, was by far the biggest port and business center for the Malay Peninsula. The postwar aim of most leading Singaporeans was eventual merger with Malaya.

Singapore was little affected by the communist rebellion in Malaya, but the communist movement became strongly established on the island, and the colony had a somewhat stormy political history as it moved towards the management of its own affairs. By 1959, when Singapore achieved internal self-government, the dominant political force on the island was the People's Action Party (PAP). In the 1959 elections the PAP won forty-three out of the fifty-one seats in the legislature, but the party was in reality an alliance between communists and non-communists. One section of the party, including the leadership, a group of exceptionally able and largely English-educated men, was headed by Lee Kuan Yew and was non-communist. In order to achieve power, however, it had accepted a marriage of convenience with the radical left and this division was not long in causing a split. The radical left hived off to form the Barisan Socialist Party, and Lee was only able to govern with the support of his former opponents in the People's Alliance. The Government's position was shaky and it sustained some severe setbacks in by-elections.

The deteriorating situation in Singapore caused concern in Malaya. The Federation had a majority on Singapore's Internal Security Council but this was not a satisfactory long-term arrangement. The incorporation of Singapore in Malaya would provide a more stable arrangement and was in line with Singapore's aspirations. But Singapore's large Chinese population would upset the racial balance in the Federation. It was thought that balance could be preserved if the Borneo territories were incorporated as well in an enlarged federation. There were discussions between the Singaporean, Malayan, and British governments, and the proposal seems to have been finalized at the time of the Commonwealth Prime Ministers' Conference in London in 1961.

The Malaysia proposal meant a sudden and unexpected change of course for Sarawak. It took a little time for people to adjust their thinking, and the government service was set a major task in both explaining and promoting the idea. It represented the policy of the British government and the service was expected to see that the policy was successfully translated into fact.

We had the task of explaining not only the Malaysia proposal to Sarawakians but also the facts about Sarawak to Malayans. This was sometimes a difficult and delicate task. Malayans knew very little about the Borneo territories and they entertained many misconceptions, particularly about the nature of the non-Malay indigenous peoples and their often complex relationships with Malays. Problems and difficulties which did not fit Malayan misconceptions were liable to give rise to resentment and to be written off as mere colonial inventions. Malayans tended to regard Dayaks, Kadazan, and other Bornean peoples as primitive Malays kept backward and separate by the colonialists. Trying to bring about a better and more realistic understanding called for considerable care and tact. On the whole I think we were reasonably successful, and by the time Malaysia came into being many of the misconceptions had evaporated.

Eventually, the idea of forming Malaysia gained a large measure of acceptance in Sarawak. It was readily acceptable to most Malays and gained the acceptance of non-Muslims largely because of the confidence reposed in Britain and the advice given by British officers, as well as the favorable impression gained by Sarawak leaders in their contacts with the Tunku and other leading Malayans. The Tunku had a very winning personality and quickly gained the trust and confidence of those who met him.

The only dissenting voice came from the SUPP, which adopted the line that while Malaysia was a desirable objective, Sarawak should first achieve independence before negotiating entry into the new Federation. On the face of it this was a reasonable standpoint, but it was not acceptable to Malaya and in practice, if it had been persevered with, there would have been no Malaysia. With the benefit of hindsight, one can see now that this would have been totally disastrous for Sarawak. The real alternatives for Sarawak are not incorporation in Malaysia or independence, but incorporation in Malaysia or incorporation in Indonesia. An independent Sarawak dominated by its large Chinese population, even if the government took the form of a Chinese/Native Alliance, would be regarded as a threat to the national interests of all but a communist government of Indonesia. It could only be maintained by the continuing protective presence of a major power. With the irreversible decline in British power and influence in Asia, there was no possibility of this. Looking back some fifteen years later, I have no doubt that the advice we gave the people of Sarawak was in their best interests, even though some of the factors at work were not clearly apparent to us at the time.

Consultation between representatives of the territories involved presented problems because of their dissimilar status. A way round the difficulty was found, at the suggestion of Singapore, by having the problem discussed by a Committee formed from local members of the Commonwealth Parliamentary Association. This committee, which was called the Malaysia Solidarity Consultative Committee, met four times between August 1961 and February 1962 and drew up a memorandum which largely set out the principles later adopted in the formation of Malaysia. The effectiveness of the Consultative Committee owed a great deal to the resource and

Ong Kee Hui, pioneer politician and member of a family with a great record of public service, at a meeting of the Malaysia Solidarity Consultative Committee

persuasiveness of Lee Kuan Yew, who led the Singapore delegation. No man, when he wants to be, can be more exquisitely patient, courteous, and understanding in getting his own way. There was never any doubt in those formative days of Malaysia that much of the energy and impetus for the formation of the new Federation came from Singapore. Brunei sent observers to the Consultative Committee but was already showing extreme caution in approaching the proposal.

The Consultative Committee Memorandum was one of the documents submitted to the Cobbold Commission, which visited Sarawak and Sabah between February and April 1962. This was a joint commission set up by the British and Malayan governments. It had somewhat general terms of reference, to the effect that, given the agreement of the British and Malayan governments that the inclusion of Sarawak and Sabah in the proposed Malaysian Federation was a desirable aim, it should ascertain the views of the Bornean peoples and in light of that assessment make recommendations. The task of the Commission was in reality not so much assessment, as negotiation of acceptable plans for the two Bornean territories to join the new Federation.

The Chairman of the Commission was, rather surprisingly, a former Governor of the Bank of England, Lord Cobbold. The Malayan government did not want a Chairman with previous experience of the area and Lord Cobbold met this condition. He was a commanding personality and a courteous and patient Chairman. He fulfilled the task given him with distinction. The Malayan representatives were Dato Wong Pow Nee, the Chief Minister of Penang—a former schoolmaster and experienced state politician—and Ghazali Shafie, the Permanent Secretary of the Malayan Ministry of Foreign Affairs. Ghazali played a key role in the Commission. He was one of the outstanding Malay personalities, a first-class intellect, and a man of ideas and some fire. The two other British representatives were Sir Anthony Abell, Sarawak's former Governor, and Sir David Watherston, the last British Chief Secretary of Malaya. The five members worked harmoniously together.

They traveled widely, considered every submission sent to them, and received personal representations from anyone and everyone who wanted to see them personally. The work of the Commission has been the subject of some criticism, but I doubt whether it could have done more.

The Commission worked very hard and seriously but had some lighter moments. These included a truly Sarawakian introduction to the problems of travel in Borneo when they visited the Baram. Their itinerary included a visit to Long Akah to confer with a gathering of Orang Ulu in the house of Temenggong Oyong Lawai Jau. They traveled by air and landed at the newly constructed airfield at Long Akah.

After their deliberations and some traditional hospitality, they left the longhouse to make their way to the airfield, which lies on the other bank of the Baram. Their farewell included some blacking of faces, though the Orang Ulu did not consider it appropriate that such important visitors should be splashed by the young girls. But when the Twin Pioneer tried to take off, one of its wheels sank in the not fully compacted airfield surface and could not be lifted out again, despite the united efforts of a great throng of some of the strongest men in Borneo. The aircraft was stuck.

Lord Cobbold's patrician calm for once deserted him. He was very annoyed. He demanded that an immediate telegram be sent to the Prime Minister demanding that a rescue operation be mounted forthwith, and he did not mean Tunku Abdul Rahman either. It was a pleasing thought that the Governor of the Bank of England,

The Cobbold Commission. From left to right: Sir Anthony Abell, Sir David Watherston, Lord Cobbold, Dato Wong Pow Nee, Tan Sri Ghazali Shafie. Standing next to Ghazali are three Sarawak officers, Michael Sadin, Yao Peng Hua, and Siaw Jun Chin.

stuck fast in the middle of Borneo, should want to send a message to Mr. Macmillan saying, in effect, "get me out of here."

Lord Cobbold was a gentleman and when he calmed down he apologized handsomely for his outburst. The party returned to the Temenggong's house to spend the night while arrangements were made to take them downriver by boat the next day.

But this was not the end of their troubles. It was intended to leave at first light and to eat breakfast in the boats. But in the hurry of departure the District Officer left the breakfast parcels in the longhouse, and the omission was only noticed when they were already far downstream. It was a hungry party which reached Long Lama for a late lunch. Hedda was going upriver that day and met them in midstream. The boats available for the Commissioners' journey were small and the party looked very cramped.

The DO who forgot the breakfasts was a popular and debonair bachelor called Malcolm MacSporran. He would have been known in the eighteenth century as a jolly dog. It was he who was responsible for a curious episode which involved the Royal Air Force parachuting a consignment of cats into Bareo.

The DO was very fond of the Kelabit and the Kelabit area and spent much time there. The establishment of a good airstrip in Bareo made this much easier than previously. During one of his visits, some time after the Cobbold Commission, he reported that Bareo was overrun by rats and that a supply of cats was urgently needed. It was assumed in Kuching that this meant that the padi harvest was in danger. The Assistant Director of Civil Aviation in Kuching, John Seal, was also very fond of the Kelabit area and being a most energetic man, he decided that something must be done immediately. He approached the Royal Air Force to see whether, on their next training flight with a suitable aircraft, they would undertake to parachute some cats into Bareo. The RAF, always keen to do good deeds, readily agreed to the proposal. Seal, for his part, made an appeal for cats. A large array of cats was quickly assembled and suitably boxed for transmission.

The RAF sent over a great, lumbering, four-engined Beverley transport aircraft and set off with the cats for the interior of Borneo. Unfortunately, there was cloud over Bareo and the Beverley had to be diverted to Jesselton in North Borneo where it spent the night. Here the kind-hearted aircrew decided that the cats should be let out of their boxes for a run in a secure shed. The cats were no doubt grateful but strongly resisted efforts to put them back in the boxes the next morning. The Beverley took off for Bareo again and once again there was cloud cover and they had to be diverted to Brunei. Fortunately, the weather cleared that afternoon and a much-scratched and by now somewhat testy aircrew safely dropped their load.

It was not until later that I came to learn the true background to the cat drop. There had been an unusual number of rats in Bareo when the DO sent his message, but they had not reached anything like plague proportions. What had actually sparked off the appeal for cats was the fact that a rat had eaten a hole in the DO's pillow while he slept and removed some of the contents for nest lining.

The Cobbold Commission returned to England to compile its report. This took some time because, although the British representatives were free agents, the Malayan representatives had to confer with Kuala Lumpur on many points of detail. This was understandable—while Britain was divesting itself of responsibilities, the Malayan government was taking them on. Kuala Lumpur had to consider what was politically acceptable in Malaya, which would be the biggest partner by far in Malaysia.

The Commission's report contained a wide measure of agreement but unanimity was not reached. It was agreed that Malaysia was an attractive and workable project and would be advantageous to the parties. It was concluded that about one-third of the Bornean population was strongly in favor of Malaysia. Another third, many of them favorable, asked for various conditions and safeguards. Of the balance, some wanted a continuation of British rule but would probably support the proposal if various conditions were met. And a hard core, perhaps amounting to twenty percent of the total in Sarawak and less in North Borneo, were opposed to Malaysia on any terms unless independence was first achieved. It was probably an accurate assessment and as good as could have been made in the time available to the Commission.

The British and Malayan representatives reported separately on a number of matters. The main differences concerned the pace at which the new Federation should be formed, the British representatives urging a more gradual approach than their Malayan colleagues. On the British side there was some uneasiness, not fully brought out in the report, on what they felt was Malayan reluctance to make concessions in favor of non-Muslim susceptibilities and on such matters as national religion, national language, and the eligibility of Borneans to become Head of the Federation. Nevertheless, the Commission's Report opened the way for further detailed consideration of these problems by an Inter-Governmental Committee (IGC). The Chairman was Lord Lansdowne, the Secretary of State for the Colonies, and the Deputy Chairman was Tun Abdul Razak, the Malayan Deputy Prime Minister. Both Sarawak and North Borneo were well represented.

The IGC took the Cobbold Commission recommendations much further and modified a number of the matters on which the Commission had not reached full agreement. In effect, it was agreed that there should be a ten-year period of adjustment for the Borneo territories, particularly in matters relating to the national language and the medium of instruction in schools. It was agreed that Malay would be the national language of Malaysia, but English could remain an official language in Sarawak for ten years or more as decided by Council Negri. The state could retain its educational system as long as it wanted to. A generous financial agreement was reached which was subject to revision after five and ten years. The Borneo states were given control of Immigration and generous representation in the Federal Parliament—forty seats as compared with 104 for Malaya. From the Sarawak point of view it was a liberal and indeed generous agreement. About the only subject where local views were not met concerned the eligibility of Borneans to become Head of State. But this was never a realistic demand—it would have involved fundamental change to the Malayan constitutional system—nor was it of much practical importance. The Report was accepted without dissent by Council Negri in March 1963.

My most vivid recollection of the debate was the astonishment on the face of the President (Jakeway) when the member for Serian proposed that the name of the new Federation should be not Malaysia but Borbrusima. Jakeway was a generally imperturbable man and I never saw him look so surprised. It turned out that Borbrusima was an acronym designed to get away from the emphasis on Malay in Malaysia. It was made up of the first syllables from Borneo, Brunei, Singapore, and Malaya. Despite its undoubted originality the name was not adopted.

One of the subjects of most pressing public concern in Sarawak concerned religion. Islam was to be the national religion but complete religious tolerance was guaranteed. The Muslim population of Sarawak, however, amounted to less than one quarter of the total population in 1960. There were misgivings on the part of the Christian churches and missions that their work in Sarawak might be restricted. Missions in independent Malaya were no longer able to work among the pagan aborigines of the peninsula, because the Malayan State Governments consider the aborigines as fellow Malays who have not received enlightenment.

The restrictions in Malaya had been imposed by State Governments, not by the Federal Government, and there was no reason to suppose that anything of the kind could take place in Sarawak. It fell to my lot to explain matters to a gathering of mission representatives. It was the most ecumenical occasion ever seen in Sarawak and the only occasion known to me when all the warring factions of Christendom—Anglicans, Catholics, Methodists, Seventh Day Adventists, and the Borneo Evangelical Mission—came together under the same roof. I felt a little like Daniel in the Lion's Den. However, the local priests and missionaries who attended seemed to be reasonably satisfied with my assurances, and I like to think that they have had no cause to think differently. There is a great measure of tolerance in Islam and on the part of most of those who profess that faith. Historically, Islam has had a better record of tolerance towards Jews and Christians than has Christianity towards Muslims and Jews.

Since the establishment of Malaysia, the churches in Sarawak have been able to carry on as before. Working permits for missionaries are controlled but seem to be issued in a reasonably liberal way. The Catholic Church faces the biggest problem because the rule of celibacy effectively prevents much local entry into the priesthood, leaving that church the most heavily dependent on expatriate missionaries. The other churches are now comparatively well provided with local priests and pastors, though they still need the services of some expatriate missionaries. The question of religion has not proved to be a problem in Sarawak.

In North Borneo, or Sabah as it has been known officially since Malaysia Day, the situation was, for a time, less happy. The missions came under considerable pressure, but this was a local aberration and in no way typical of Malaysia as a whole. It made the work of the churches difficult, but I doubt whether it has done any real harm to Christianity in the State. It has weeded out some of the weaker brethren but has probably reinforced the faith of the truly faithful.

Shortly after the tabling of the IGC Report in Council Negri, elections were held. They were conducted on a basis of universal suffrage for those over the age of twenty-one and were carried out on the three-tier system. I personally had some doubts as to the wisdom of this, but it was the view of the responsible officers that it would have been too complicated to have had simultaneous elections for both District Councils (which had to be held) and Council Negri. I think this did not do full credit to the political instincts of Bornean peoples. They took readily to politics, and I doubt if they would have been confused at having to vote at the same time for both Local Government Councillors and Members of Council Negri.

The Information Office was heavily involved in preparations. We put out multilingual guides both to the elections and to politics. I have often wondered how much impact they made. It is very difficult to get the reaction of the consumer on such occasions. The guides were widely distributed, our hope being that literate members of the public would use them to explain what was happening to the illiterate members of their families and communities, but it was a bit like firing a shotgun in the dark.

The elections were contested by three main groups and by many independents. SUPP had the best party organization and stood by itself. It looked at one time as if the other five parties would stand as the Sarawak Alliance. But negotiations among the parties were very complicated and at times acrimonious. Eventually PANAS stood on its own apart from the Alliance. PANAS was led by the Datu Bandar, Abang Haji Mustapha, who came from one of the old, established families of Malay chiefs and who had achieved high office under the Brookes and the Colonial Government.

Previous elections in Sarawak had shown a remarkable tendency for a proliferation of candidates and consequent vote splitting. One of the principal tasks of my department was to advise against this practice. Vote splitting obviously benefitted SUPP and, indeed, there was good reason to believe that it would be encouraged by that party or elements in it as a deliberate and politically understandable ploy. The Information Office came in for some criticism for allegedly interfering in the political process. The view of the critics seemed to be that the race should go to the strong and that the Government should not advise the weak.

The elections went off well. There was a high turnout and polling was honest and orderly. Fewer Chinese registered as voters than did the Native peoples, but this was in no way due to any interference by the Government. I think it derived from a reluctance on the part of some older Chinese to become involved. SUPP won twenty-five percent of the votes cast in contested wards. If all wards had been contested, the percentage would probably have been rather less because non-SUPP parties predominated in uncontested wards. Nevertheless, the voting gave a fairly accurate picture of the proportion of those who demanded independence before Malaysia rather than independence through Malaysia.

The three-tier system led to an unedifying scramble for seats on the Divisional Advisory Councils, the electoral colleges for Council Negri. In the scramble, the Alliance showed itself to be more adroit and better financed than SUPP. The ultimate result was that SUPP only gained five of the thirty-six elected seats in Council Negri. This was not a fair result. SUPP should have had more, though it would not have affected Council Negri's endorsement of the entry into Malaysia.

Abdul Rahman Yakub, the outstanding Sarawak politician. After service in the **Federal Ministry**, he returned to the state to become Chief Minister and later Governor. He was successful in bringing the communist insurgency to a peaceful end.

The elections were followed by much squabbling within the Alliance as to who was to lead it and who was to become the first Chief Minister. The Federal Government wanted the post of Chief Minister to be filled by Abdul Rahman Yakub, a former Crown Counsel. Abdul Rahman Yakub is a Melanau, a man of uncommon ability and industry, who had made his way in the government service the hard way. As a boy he had not received the education to which his talents entitled him, but he entered the Native Officers service, continued his studies, and eventually obtained legal qualifications in England.

Abdul Rahman Yakub had, however, chosen a most unsuitable ward in Kuching and had been defeated in the elections. The Federal Government wanted the Governor, Sir Alexander Waddell, to appoint him to one of the three nominated posts in Council Negri but Waddell, a man of principle, declined to nominate to Council Negri anyone who had been defeated at the polls. He stoutly resisted the pressure and eventually Kuala Lumpur backed down. Abdul Rahman Yakub was given a cabinet post in Kuala Lumpur and his nephew, Abdul Taib Mahmud, also a lawyer, who had received a complete education in postwar Sarawak and Australia, was nominated to Council Negri and made a Sarawak Minister. He had not stood in the elections.

The Governor appointed Stephen Kalong Ningkan, a 2nd Division Dayak and the leader of SNAP, as Chief Minister. Stephen Ningkan had joined the police just before the war. He had spent most of the postwar years in Brunei working as a Hospital Assistant with the Shell Company. He was a strong-willed and ambitious man who had built up his party from the most modest beginnings.

A 2nd Division Dayak having been made Chief Minister, there was considerable pressure from 3rd Division Dayaks for Temenggong Jugah, who had long played an important role both in his own Division and in Sarawak affairs generally, to be made Governor. Jugah was a former Penghulu from Kapit District. He was a very shrewd man but uneducated. He was not acceptable to Kuala Lumpur as Governor. The Governor has to take part in the deliberations of the Council of Rulers—the Sultans—and it is unrealistic to expect the post to be held by a non-Malay. Jugah was, however, given a post as Federal Minister for Sarawak Affairs.

The post of Governor went to a widely experienced Malay, a former administrative officer, Datu Abang Haji Openg who, since his retirement from the government service, had been President of the Majlis Islam, the body regulating Muslim affairs in Sarawak. He had traveled extensively in Sarawak, spent many years in Iban areas, and spoke Iban fluently. He was a kind and popular man, who had, incidentally, given me a pass in my Higher Standard Malay examination for government officials in 1950, though I am afraid that in doing so he showed more kindness than discrimination.

Political development had also been proceeding in the state of Brunei. Here, in 1956, a party had been formed called the Brunei People's Party (Parti Ra'ayat Brunei or PRB) under the leadership of a part-Arab part-Malay called Sheikh Azahari. Although not actually born in Brunei (his place of birth was Labuan Island), Azahari had long been the most prominent political figure in Brunei. He was an erratic, emotional, and at times unbalanced man, but he also possessed some charisma and visionary fervor. He was a frequent visitor to Indonesia. The PRB gained widespread support in the state and when District Council elections were held at the end of August 1962 as part of a plan by the Sultan to move gradually towards self-government, the party swept the board. It won all the uncontested seats and every contested seat except one, the winner of which subsequently joined the party. The District Councils were to appoint sixteen members to a thirty-three-member Legislative Council. The balance of seventeen would have consisted of nominated and ex-officio members.

This move towards democracy was too limited to satisfy the PRB. Its aims were to form a Borneo Federation consisting of Brunei, Sarawak, and Sabah under the leadership of the Sultan. Azahari and his party were opposed to Malaysia and were on close terms with the SUPP in Sarawak.

The Sultan's government had enjoyed full internal self-government since 1956. It was wealthy and reasonably well administered though the bureaucracy was cumbersome and slow moving. The Sultan was no money-squandering oil sheikh. The large revenues derived from oil were honestly accounted for, and money was spent generously on schemes for the social betterment of the people. The state had good medical services and schools and was unique in Southeast Asia in having old-age pensions. There was some corruption but its degree was not significant. But despite these favorable factors, the Government lacked popular appeal. Political power remained firmly in the hands of an aristocratic oligarchy which failed to provide effective leadership.

The opposition of the PRB went as far as to send a number of young men to Indonesia for military training. This was done secretly by sending men over into Indonesian Borneo along old and deserted tracks running through North Borneo. Once in Indonesia, the Brunei men were sent for training to a place called Malinau about halfway between the border and the oil center of Tarakan. The training may have been a largely local initiative taken by the Indonesian military commander in East Borneo, a communist sympathizer. The movement was not accurately known to the Sarawak police, though there had been rumors of such movement for some time in 1962.

It seemed so incredible to me that when, in early December 1962, the Brunei newspaper *Borneo Bulletin* published what turned out to be an accurate and well-informed article on the subject, I was outraged. I thought it would be quite impossible for such movement to Indonesia to take place without becoming widely known in Lawas District through which I thought the trainees had to pass. I addressed a stern letter to the editor charging his newspaper with alarmist, irresponsible, and inaccurate reporting. The Brunei rebellion broke out the very next day. Fortunately, I was able to have my letter retrieved from the post office. I shudder to think what the editor would have done if he had received my letter after the rebellion was over.

In fact, the movement over the border and some local military-style training had been reported by the Resident, Dick Morris, and by his predecessor, Bob Young, both of them capable and experienced officers. But no police reinforcements had been sent to Limbang nor had anyone in the Secretariat bothered to tell me.

The rebellion was in fact extraordinarily ill-planned. Both the Chairman (Azahari) and the Secretary-General (Zaini) were out of the country. SUPP claims that their party and the PRB were in the course of sending delegations to the United Nations to protest the formation of Malaysia. The rebellion was not against the Sultan's authority, but the key to success lay in securing the person of the Sultan and this the rebels failed to do. Consequently the Sultan was able to appeal for British protection, which only he could do. The police in Brunei Town were able to withstand the uprising, though the rebels were more successful in the Seria/Kuala Belait oilfield area. Once the Sultan had made his appeal for British help, the rebellion was bound to fail.

But it spilled over into the adjoining areas of Sarawak. In Miri the Resident 4th Division, John Fisher, was given a warning on the very morning before the rebellion broke out. The warning was given under somewhat dramatic circumstances. Fisher received a telephone message from a man he did not know who said he had some important news to give him. The Resident should meet him at a certain oil rig. Fisher went there and a Malay he met by the rig told him to expect serious trouble and warned him to be on his guard. He gave no details. Fisher was a shrewd and experienced officer. The warning had the ring of truth and came on top of other rumors of trouble. Acting on his own initiative, he had the police placed immediately in a state of readiness and key points secured. Miri would have been attacked that night, but the news of the preparations made by the police put the rebels off balance. They delayed the attack but overran the small government station of Bekenu and the subdistrict of Sibuti, which lay to the south of Miri. The area was recaptured a few days later by a force of Greenjackets and Sarawak police.

A much more serious situation developed in Limbang, the headquarters of the 5th Division. Limbang is only about ten miles from Brunei Town as the crow flies. It lies along the river bank hemmed in by a range of hills. The recently arrived Resident—an Australian, Dick Morris—was uneasy. There were reports of military training and movement to Indonesia, and at the end of November some Malays were arrested on suspicion of belonging to an illegal organization, the so-called North Borneo National Army (TNKU). Morris noted an unaccustomed air of sullenness in Limbang. But there was only a small police detachment in the station and even if it had been a large one, the terrain makes it a difficult place to secure. The rebels overran Limbang and captured Morris and his wife. The Police Station was bravely defended by its occupants and four of them were killed. The remnants held out until Morris was forced at gunpoint to order them to surrender.

It took a force of Marine Commandos to recapture Limbang and they lost five men in the process. The Morrises were confined in the Hospital, which was in the thick of the fighting. When rescued, Morris explained who he was to the Marines and proceeded to resume duty as Resident. It constituted one of the pluckier and less known episodes of the British record in Borneo.

Limbang was noteworthy for more than a display of resolution by the Resident. Two men who behaved with special distinction were a Hospital Assistant and a retired Postmaster. The Hospital Assistant was a quiet and gentle man called Edin, who emerged as the natural leader of the demoralized group of civil servants and their families, while the retired Postmaster, Omar, donned his Red Cross uniform and insisted on his right to visit the prisoners and see that they were cared for.

Indonesian aid to the rebels had not extended to the provision of arms. They had only shotguns and weapons they had captured from the police—the Marines were killed in an initial burst of fire from a captured Bren gun. But it took a force of highly trained Marines several days to drive the rebels out of the town area. The fighting on the rebel side, both in Limbang and elsewhere, was almost entirely carried out by Kedayan, one of the smaller groups of Bornean peoples, traditional retainers of the Sultan of Brunei and said to be of Javanese origin. The Kedayan carried on the struggle for some time and their losses were considerable.

Harrisson, the old guerrilla maestro, had hurried off to organize an irregular force to contain the TNKU remnants. The people of the Baram were delighted to oblige. Temenggong Oyong Lawai Jau, with tongue in cheek, complained to Fisher that he should have been allowed to take Brunei Town while he was about it and so fulfill the ambition of his ancestors. The TNKU remnants were probably no great threat. A more important achievement by Harrisson was to write an excellent and lively introduction to Borneo for the use of British troops.

If Azahari had intended to proceed to New York, he changed his mind and he and Zaini remained in Manila. Azahari announced that he was the Prime Minister of the Unitary State of North Borneo and became heavily involved with shady and opportunist Philippine political figures who sensed some benefit for themselves in the situation. He eventually went to Indonesia and largely faded from view.

Zaini was persuaded to return to Brunei. The British authorities succeeded in making contact with him in his favorite nightclub through a schoolmaster who knew him well and who was brought to Manila especially for the purpose. Zaini was taken out of Manila and brought to Hong Kong and then back to Brunei, where he threw himself on the Sultan's clemency. It was understandable that he might be detained for a time, but in fact the Sultan's clemency consisted of detention without trial for ten years, until Zaini and some others succeeded in escaping to Malaysia. The British performance here was poor, for having persuaded Zaini to give himself up, Britain was under a moral obligation to see that the Sultan's vindictiveness was mitigated, and it had ample means of bringing pressure to bear. But life was very comfortable for British High Commissioners in Brunei, especially if they agreed with everything the Sultan, Sir Omar Ali, did.

Azahari, despite his connections with SUPP, had little effective support in Sarawak. His principal supporter was a Malay Education Officer—the first Sarawak Native to gain a University Degree, in Edinburgh. On the outbreak of the rebellion this officer, Ahmad Zaidi, was the Divisional Education Officer in Simanggang. But although he sympathized with Azahari, with whom he shared the same visionary view of a Bornean Federation, Ahmad Zaidi had done very little to organize opinion in Sarawak. He was detained for a time and then released. He defected to Indonesia on Malaysia Day 1963 but did not play an important role. Some years after the end of Confrontation he was allowed to return to Sarawak where he became a State Minister and later Governor.

The most serious aspect of the Brunei rebellion was that it served to crystallize Indonesian and, to a lesser extent, Philippine opposition to Malaysia. The Indonesian Communist Party, the PKI, had condemned Malaysia as a neo-colonialist plot at the end of 1961, but this standpoint had not received widespread support. The outbreak of the Brunei rebellion seems to have taken Indonesian official and unofficial opinion by surprise. But expressions of sympathy quickly built up, and this was stimulated still further by Malaysian comments on the part apparently played by Indonesia in training the rebels. From this point on, relations between the two countries and between Britain and Indonesia rapidly deteriorated. The term "confrontation" was first used in relation to the dispute by the Indonesian Foreign Minister on January 20, 1963. From a fairly vague concept, it developed until it came to represent most measures of hostility short of an actual declaration of war.

Philippine opposition to Malaysia arose from certain claims by the heirs of the Sultan of Sulu in regard to North Borneo. This territory was originally held by the Sultanate of Brunei, but early in the eighteenth century all but parts of the west coast passed to the Sultan of Sulu, who ceded it to the founders of the British North Borneo Company in 1878. The area ceded included part of what is now Indonesia.

The last acknowledged Sultan of Sulu died in 1936. The eventual dispute hinged on whether or not the area had been ceded in perpetuity.

After the Pacific War, the Philippine authorities gave some thought to the claims but never raised the matter. The heirs of the Sultan, however, sought to obtain a financial settlement from North Borneo and in so doing employed Philippine lawyers of doubtful reputation. One of the lawyers passed the papers on the subject to a lively weekly journal, *Philippine Free Press*, which shortly before the inauguration of President Macapagal on January 1, 1962, published an article entitled "North Borneo belongs to us." This article, coupled with the progress being made towards the formation of Malaysia and consequently towards change in the area, precipitated considerable press interest in the subject, and the claim was formally taken up by the Philippine government. President Macapagal was also familiar with the background of the claim. He was a former Head of the Legal Division of the Philippine Department of Foreign Affairs and had, in 1946, advocated that a claim be made.

In many ways it was an extraordinary one because it enjoyed absolutely no support from within North Borneo. Nevertheless, the Philippine people are proud and sensitive and blessed with a plenitude of lawyers and an uninhibited press. The wealth of North Borneo also aroused the cupidity of influential Philippine politicians. The British government would probably have done well to have taken the claim more seriously than it did. Talks in London early in 1963 made no progress, and the Philippines moved into a position where its opposition to Malaysia ran closely in parallel with Indonesia's and where it sought a solution in a purely Southeast Asian context. High-level consultations in Manila among Malaya, Indonesia, and the Philippines led to an agreement that Indonesia and the Philippines would accept Malaysia if an impartial UN assessment confirmed the support of the peoples of Sarawak and North Borneo, though this was qualified by the Philippine statement that its position would still be subject to the outcome of its claim on North Borneo.

These complicated events inevitably made some impact on everyday affairs in Sarawak. As a result of the Brunei rebellion, precautionary measures had been taken by the move of substantial British forces to Sarawak. In Kuching it was a very impressive spectacle, with vehicles and equipment being flown in from Commando Carriers by helicopter and landed on the Race Course. It was also a very businesslike performance. Nothing impressed me more than the efficient professionalism of the services. War service had not fully prepared me for this. The services mastered the problems of fighting in Borneo quickly and easily.

Relations with local people were excellent from the start and at all levels. At a rather high level, I remember asking John Fisher, during a telephone conversation, how he got on with the Director of Borneo Operations, General Walker. The line to Miri was not the best of telephone lines, but over the static came the booming reply, "Eats out of me hand, old boy, he's me brother-in-law." In the 1st Division we had Marines and a cavalry regiment, the Royal Irish Hussars. The commanding officer of the Hussars, John Strawson, was a particularly thoughtful and pleasant man. One of his officers, David Brookes, was attached to my office and greatly endeared himself to the Information Office staff. The British presence was a great blessing in more ways than one, for January 1963 saw Sarawak hit by unprecedented floods, and the presence of so many energetic servicemen and especially of their helicopters greatly facilitated relief operations.

For a time there was, from the security point of view, comparative calm. But we saw the beginning of a movement which did great harm to Sarawak and to the

Chinese community. This was the movement of numbers of young Chinese over the border into Indonesia. In the 1st and 2nd Divisions such movement is a simple matter. Quite a number of these young people were picked up by border patrols and brought back, but you could do nothing with them. It was useless to shut them up. Many leading communists had by now been placed in detention, but the offense of wanting to go to Indonesia without a passport was hardly a criminal offense in the case of the would-be border crossers. They were impervious to advice or the pleas of their families. When released, they simply tried again and were generally successful the second time. In Indonesia, they were cared for by the Government and the PKI and given military training, which they eventually put to use when they returned to Sarawak.

The calm was shattered in April when a sudden Indonesian attack overran the isolated police post at Tebedu, which immediately adjoins the border south of Serian in the 1st Division. The raiders, numbering about seventy-five, consisted of irregulars—Indonesian Dayaks and other local people who had been given some military training —accompanied by some Sarawak Chinese and a stiffening of Indonesian regular soldiers. This was followed by a number of other minor incursions along the border. The Indonesians claimed that they were the work of members of the TNKU.

I was at Nanga Entabai in Kanowit District with Hedda on a visit to John Wilson when Tebedu was taken and had immediately to return to Kuching. Here I was given the task of announcing to the public in a radio talk that all shotguns in the hands of non-Natives were to be handed over to the Government. This, of course, was primarily aimed at the Chinese because their weapons were most likely to fall into the hands of the communist movement, which had now formally called for armed struggle, but it also included guns owned by Europeans, including my own. The guns were handed in very promptly, though it was rather a painful thing to have to do. Quite a number of Native-owned weapons, however, fell into the hands of the SCO, and members of the movement were able to obtain ammunition, which was much more difficult to control. The SCO made good any shortage of shotguns by making their own. These were fearsome instruments made out of lengths of iron piping, but they worked, and for purposes of assassination and intimidation they were perfectly effective weapons.

The attack on Tebedu and some subsequent border incidents in the 2nd Division were particularly harmful to morale in Simanggang. There was near panic among the European families in Simanggang when a British Army officer gave his opinion in the Club that if he had his way, he would have all the European women and children out of the place. He was one of the few military idiots to surface during Confrontation.

The final agreement to establish Malaysia was signed in London on July 9. The provisions regarding the Borneo territories caused few difficulties, but there was some hard, last-minute bargaining by Singapore. And when all seemed settled, Lee Kuan Yew demanded a further provision, that the agreed-upon $150 million in loans by Singapore for the development of the Borneo territories should carry a condition that half the labor force on any development scheme financed from these loans should be drawn from Singapore. The hard-pressed Tunku gave Lee an undertaking in writing to this effect, written on the back of an envelope. It was sharp practice on Lee's part. He knew perfectly well that such a condition would never be acceptable in Borneo and that the Tunku had no authority to give such an assurance. Thus Singapore ensured that its undertaking to provide $150 million for the development of the Borneo territories was not worth the paper it was written on. It may have seemed smart business to Singapore but it was hardly the way to win friends.

It was at this time that an unenthusiastic Brunei finally rejected the Malaysia proposals. What the Sultan really wanted from Malaysia was that the new Federation should, with some modification, stand in the same relationship to Brunei in the future as had Britain in the past. This would have been impossible for Malaya to contemplate, because it would have meant giving Brunei a status denied to all the other states. A considerable degree of special consideration was offered, but this did not go nearly far enough to satisfy the Sultan. A supplementary reason was a small-minded decision taken by the Sultans of Peninsular Malaysia to the effect that the seniority of the Sultan of Brunei in the Conference of Rulers should date from the establishment of Malaysia and not from the date of his accession to the Brunei throne. This would have made the Sultan of Brunei the most junior member of the Conference, although historically Brunei was one of the most important of all the Malay states and the Sultan had acceded to the throne in 1950. It ignored the fact

Sir Omar Ali Saifuddin, the former Sultan of Brunei, shortly after his ascent to the throne

that Malaysia meant the creation of an entirely new nation and not merely the expansion of Malaya.

The last days of colonial Sarawak saw the UN inquiry which had been agreed to in Manila. The mission itself was readily set up. It was composed of two sections: one, under the mission leader, Mr. Michelmore, an American civil servant, covered Sarawak. The other, under a former Czech businessmen in Shanghai, went to North Borneo. Indonesia and the Philippines were to be allowed to send observers but demanded the unreasonable number of thirty each. The wrangle about the number of observers held up the work of the mission. In the meantime, it was announced that Malaysia would come into being on September 16 instead of the hoped-for August 31, the anniversary of the formation of independent Malaya. Eventually, a compromise was reached on the number of observers. The Philippines and Indonesia agreed to limit themselves to four observers and four "clerical assistants" each. Then there was further delay while Indonesia demanded that it should be allowed to use its own aircraft to bring the observers, a demand which was firmly turned down by the British government. Finally they arrived by RAF VIP aircraft.

Limitation on the number of observers and a refusal to have Indonesian aircraft flying over territory which was already under Indonesian attack were both reasonable stands to make in the face of a difficult situation. Further instructions that the Indonesians' luggage was to be strictly checked on arrival, however, seemed to me to be going too far. It would have been very embarrassing and probably counterproductive. I persuaded my colleagues who had been charged with this disagreeable task that it would be best quietly to ignore the instructions which had come from the Colonial Secretary, Mr. Duncan Sandys, who was then in Kuala Lumpur. The Indonesians, under Major-General Otto Abdurrachman, were given a courteous reception, and they too behaved correctly and caused us no difficulties. They were told that they could not use their radio transmitter—apart from any other reason, its main lead had been removed in unloading by the resourceful John Seal—but we sent all their numerous messages with great expedition to Jakarta without charge. The arrangements for the UN Mission tour were skillfully coordinated by Peter Ratcliffe. If they had come to make trouble they found they had no means of doing so, because Indonesia enjoyed no support in Sarawak.

The "clerical assistants" caused some amusement. Rarely can there have been a more muscular body of clerks. When they finally took their departure, Peter was joking with one of them, a powerful, thick-set man who had insisted on carrying a very obvious pistol. He was not supposed to but presumably felt more comfortable that way. "You're a very funny man," said the Indonesian. "And you're no clerk," replied Peter. The Indonesian beamed and emitted a throaty chuckle. "No," he said. "I command a battalion."

The delays caused by Philippine and especially by Indonesian procrastination held up the work of the UN Commission. The favorable report which it produced only just preceded the inauguration of Malaysia, and neither the Philippines nor Indonesia accepted the Commission's findings. It seems unlikely that they ever intended to in the first place.

These tortuous proceedings came to an end on September 15 when the British Governors finally took their departure from North Borneo and Sarawak. In Kuching, Sir Alexander Waddell inspected his last guard of honor outside the old Brooke Courthouse and after saying goodbye to his successor, State Ministers, and many

Sir Alexander bids farewell to his successor, Tun Abang Haji Openg

others, embarked on the frigate "Loch Killisport" which was docked at the Steamship Company's wharf opposite the Astana. The Governor stood on the bridge while the ship moved slowly out into the stream and steamed downriver. The Constabulary band played "Auld lang syne." It was exactly 124 years and one month since James Brooke, in the "Royalist," had first anchored off Kuching town on August 15, 1839.

9

THE LAST LAP

The inauguration of Malaysia in Sarawak did not get off to a very auspicious start. The new Governor, Datu Abang Haji Openg, almost collapsed during the inauguration ceremony. It was understandable. He was not in strong health; it was a moment of great emotional stress for him; and he was a very religious man who had been occupied with his devotions for most of the previous night. Another, slighter cause for embarrassment was the difficulty experienced in breaking the Governor's standard. In doing this, the appropriate flag—in this case the State flag—is hauled to the masthead tied in a neat bundle by the lower guide rope. A sharp pull on the latter should see the standard flutter open. It was a regular feature of Queen's Birthday Parades, when the operation was done skillfully and efficiently by a policeman, but on this occasion the Royal Navy insisted on doing the honors and there was a painful delay while the sailors struggled to get the flag open.

Otherwise the celebrations went off well. One satisfied spectator was Mr. Duncan Sandys, the Commonwealth and Colonial Secretary. He looked like a well-pleased midwife who has brought a difficult accouchement to a successful conclusion. When the full history of the formation of Malaysia comes to be written, I think the part played by Sandys, and especially the crucial support which he gave the Tunku in Kuala Lumpur immediately prior to its formation, will be found to have been highly significant. He was a strong-minded and determined politician who, as much as anyone, was not prepared to be pushed about by President Soekarno.

From here on, however, Malaysia, and especially Sarawak, was to suffer from an increasing level of Indonesian hostility. The British military operations in Borneo in support of Malaysia were directed from Labuan by Major-General Walker, a gifted and able soldier. He was a rather natty figure with a life-long connection with Gurkhas. He had commanded a battalion of the 8th Gurkhas in Burma, a regiment which his grandfather had once commanded. He was recognized as an authority on jungle warfare and commanded the 17th Gurkha Division in Malaya. He also held the honorific post of Major-General Brigade of Gurkhas.

In the latter capacity, just prior to the outbreak of the Brunei rebellion, Walker was involved in hostilities with the War Office over the future of the Brigade, which consisted of eight battalions and supporting units. He learned of a plan to prune severely the number of Gurkha battalions in the interests of economy. He was in fact told this by General Hull, who was about to become Chief of the Imperial General Staff. Walker, apart from being a devoted Gurkha officer himself, was concerned by the apparent intention to reduce so drastically Britain's most skilled body of military manpower in Asia. With perhaps more zeal than discretion, he not only alerted

Portrait of a successful midwife: Duncan Sandys at the Malaysia Day celebrations in Kuching

officers of the Brigade to the problems which they were likely to face, but also advised the King of Nepal of what was proposed (the King had been told nothing) and enlisted the support of the American Ambassador to Nepal, who thought the cuts would be harmful to the stability of that country. He sent a copy of the document he had given senior officers of the Gurkha Brigade to a former Chief-of-Staff Far East Land Forces and Colonel of one of the Regiments, who in his turn passed it on to three other former Gurkha Colonels. These officers were Field Marshalls Harding, Templer, and Slim. The general consensus of these eminent men was that Walker had been most disloyal, as indeed he had been, and Slim passed a copy to General Hull. Walker was not universally popular among British service officers, but even his opponents would have to admit that his capacity for getting into trouble in furtherance of what he believed to be a good cause was of a very high order.

Fortunately for Malaysia, the drastic scaling-down of the Gurkha Brigade did not proceed, at least during the next critical few years, and Walker gave good and distinguished leadership at the start of the Borneo operations. But although his lobbying activities were smoothed over, the War Office did not forget, and when Walker's term as Director of Borneo Operations came to an end, he did not, at the time, receive the Knighthood which he might have expected. Just to emphasize the point, General Lea, Walker's successor, was knighted.

The commanding officer in the key West Sarawak area was now Brigadier Patterson, another Gurkha officer, a dedicated, almost ascetic soldier. He had very different ideas than his predecessor, a Marine, who had wanted the border areas evacuated for a distance of five miles to allow his troops a zone in which they were free to fire on anyone. Some exposed Dayak communities in the 2nd Division had already been moved in accordance with this policy, but Patterson, more experienced in jungle warfare and Southeast Asian conditions, considered that the effect of this was to deprive his forces of their eyes and ears, and he countermanded the policy. But even so, Indonesian cross-border forays were difficult to stop. As Patterson put it to one visiting journalist, "The best I can hope to do is to lose more slowly."

Eventually the impossibility of a successful defense of Malaysia operating entirely within the borders of the country came to be appreciated, and the British government accepted the need for cross-border counter-strikes. These were

Two of the soldiers: Major General Tan Sri Abdul Hamid,
Malaysian Chief of Staff, and Brigadier Patterson

conducted under strict conditions and in complete secrecy. The Indonesian commanders found that their own much longer lines of communication were under attack. During the latter half of Confrontation, nearly all the fighting was taking place on the Indonesian side of the border.

A most remarkable aspect of these cross-border operations, which were known as Operation Claret, was the tight security that was successfully maintained. Hundreds of British and Gurkha servicemen knew what was happening but not a word leaked out. I myself was never brought into the secret—there was no reason why I should be—but I came to realize what was happening because from my local knowledge I knew that some of the events described could not have taken place inside Sarawak.

It presented a nice problem in newspaper ethics. Some journalists might claim that the news should have been made public, but this would not have been in the interests of any of the parties involved. It would inevitably have raised tensions still further. The Indonesians would have had to try to respond in one way or another. The Indonesian commanders, for their part, never made public what was happening, possibly because their competence would have been questioned in Jakarta if they had. In any case, Indonesians are tough soldiers and respect toughness in others. The British forces were only doing to the Indonesians what they would, in similar circumstances, have done themselves.

I think that some of the best British journalists, some of whom were frequent visitors to Borneo, realized what was happening, but if so, they recognized that it was not in the national interest to report the operations, even though it would have been a magnificent news story. Where so many held their tongue, it has seemed somehow disappointing that the first account of Operation Claret should appear in General Walker's semi-autobiography, *Fighting General*, by Tom Pocock.

The cross-border operations were greatly stepped up under Major-General George Lea, who replaced Walker early in 1965. Lea was another masterful and impressive soldier. In Kuching, Brigadier Cheyne replaced Patterson. Both Lea and Cheyne had sound foundations to build on. It was interesting to notice the differences in style between the Brigadiers in Kuching. Patterson had been entirely different from his Royal Marine predecessor Brigadier Barton. Cheyne was different again from Patterson. Where Patterson was calm and relaxed, Cheyne was high-strung and ever on the move. They both achieved the same results but in a different way. Poor Cheyne was to die of an incurable throat ailment not long after the end of Confrontation. He was a great loss to the Army.

The British operations in support of Malaysia never seemed to arouse any opposition in Britain. The high regard in which Malaya and the Tunku personally were held in Britain played a large part in this. Service in Borneo even seemed to have some glamor attached to it. On leave in 1965, I remember seeing an old recruiting poster for the Argyll and Sutherland Highlanders, who had their regimental center in Stirling Castle, reading, "If you join up before September there is still time to serve in Borneo." The services' Public Relations organization was both efficient and enlightened. They handled scores of correspondents, some of them far from easy people, and they wrestled successfully with testy soldiers in the field who disliked frequent and time-consuming visits by correspondents. There can, however, be no greater military mistake. The sympathetic journalist is a soldier's best friend, or nearly so. One especially imaginative idea of the services' Public Relations was to bring out the *Daily Mirror* cartoonist JAK, who did a memorable series of drawings of Sarawak for that paper, drawings which were both kind and funny. Casualties never reached a point where they could have swung the balance of public opinion in the other direction. By the standards of Vietnam, the loss of life was trivial. This was partly due to luck and partly to good and careful management. Total Commonwealth losses were 114 killed and 181 wounded, but not all the losses were sustained in action.

Many different units served in Borneo. At peak periods there were 17,000 Commonwealth servicemen there. The ground forces included Australian and New Zealand servicemen; a number of battalions of the rapidly expanding Malaysian Army; various British battalions, Royal Marine Commandos, and Gurkhas; Naval and Air Force units from the various countries; and large numbers of Malaysian police. The para-military Police Field Force often played a military role and generally failed to get the recognition it deserved. The Field Force says, with some justification, that it provides "soldiers on the cheap." They did good work during Confrontation.

This multi-unit, multinational, and multiracial force worked surprisingly smoothly together. Some frictions were inevitable but as seen by me, they were minor in nature and never impeded operations. The Commonwealth forces enjoyed the advantage of unified and skillful command, first class intelligence, and the fact that the forces were operating in a friendly environment amongst friendly people. The Indonesians were woefully misinformed about the true conditions in Sarawak and Sabah. They assessed the situation in what had been British Borneo by erroneous extrapolation from their own colonial experience.

The performance of the Commonwealth units was not entirely uniform—this would have been too much to expect—but the general performance was remarkably high. There can be no doubt, however, that the biggest load of all was carried by the Gurkha battalions, which undertook tour after tour in Borneo. Their professionalism and military efficiency was outstanding, and by their high standards of personal conduct, they quickly earned a position of exceptional respect. One aspect of the Gurkha Brigade which was not always appreciated was that the men were the lowest paid of all the security forces in Malaysia. By agreement with the Indian government, the Gurkhas in the British Service could only be paid the equivalent of Indian Army salaries. The British government sought to mitigate this by providing good social amenities but their actual pay was pitifully small.

The Gurkha Brigade has always been, even in the old British Indian Army, something of a closely knit little world of its own. For British officers, it was almost as much a vocation as a profession of arms. There was a strong corporate spirit and very strong bonds of mutual respect and affection between the British officers and the Gurkhas themselves. The latter feature was not peculiar to the Gurkha Regiments, but it was perhaps most strongly developed there. In some ways, it had an inhibiting effect on the careers of British officers, who tended to remain in the Brigade and not move out into the wider sphere of professional activities for which their talents often fitted them. In 1963 I met an officer whom I knew in 1943 in India when he was a Lieutenant with the 2nd Gurkhas. He was still only a Major but seemed content.

The formation of Malaysia saw the departure of a considerable number of British civil servants under the terms of the Malaysia Agreement. Those who wanted to leave, for family or other reasons, were given generous severance terms by the

British government. As the Colonial Empire diminished, the generosity of terms given British officers for loss of career prospects increased, and Sarawak and Sabah were two of the last. There was also, apart from the interest in helping to bring Malaysia through its initial phase, considerable inducement offered to expatriate officers to stay on for as long as their services were wanted.

In Sarawak, the periods of additional service offered those who were willing to stay on was four years for administrative officers and six years for technical officers. In Sabah the periods were longer—six and ten years respectively. We thought the Sabah periods unrealistic and this indeed proved to be the case. The services of officers could still be dispensed with by the State Government, and the Sarawak assessment proved to be much the more accurate one.

I was one of those who stayed on, and from being Head of my own Department, became part of the Federal Department of Information within the Ministry of Information and Broadcasting. The change of status presented few problems. I was indeed treated with the greatest consideration by my Directors and by my Minister, as well as by my other colleagues. I had come to know many of them during the pre-Malaysia days when we held a number of meetings which had established a basis for mutual understanding, but the treatment I enjoyed went well beyond what

My first Malaysian Director, Encik Sopiee, with Peter Ratcliffe,
the Sarawak Director of Broadcasting

I might reasonably have expected. My first Director was Mohamed Sopiee bin Shaikh Ibrahim. He was a most lively man who had received his higher education at the London School of Economics, had served with Malayan Missions at the UN, and had helped to form a Pan-Malayan Labour Party. Sopiee was a tremendous personality, a man of fire and imagination.

When Sopiee left to take up a post in London, he was succeeded by Syed Zainal Abidin, a much more quiet and gentle but equally able Director who had worked his way steadily up the organization from modest beginnings as a Field Officer. His sudden and premature death from a heart ailment was a great loss for his country. I had less to do with the Minister, Senu bin Abdulrahman, but he was always most kind. He was an original man who, after an early career as a teacher and a young man in politics just after the war, decided to further his education. He did this by working his way as a sailor to the United States where he jumped ship and, as an illegal immigrant, worked his way through the University of California. He had been Malaya's first Ambassador to Indonesia. I enjoyed a most pleasant relationship with my new Asian colleagues. They were men of ability and experience who had generally worked their way up the ladder in their Department and were far better qualified in some aspects of information work than I was.

The good relationship which I enjoyed was no isolated case. It was the general experience in Sarawak that the relationship between the remaining expatriates and their Malaysian colleagues was always cordial. In this respect we owed a particular debt to the first Federal Secretary to be appointed to Sarawak, i.e., the senior Federal officer in the state. This was the charming and helpful Tunku Mahomed, one of Malaya's top civil servants. Some political problems affecting senior expatriate officers eventually arose in Sarawak, but our relations with our Federal colleague always remained good. For this the tactful and constructive work of Tunku Mahomed and his successors was largely responsible.

Sarawak was also fortunate in the appointment of a Secretary for the newly formed State Security Executive Committee, which coordinated security activities. It consisted of state cabinet ministers, civil servants, policemen, and servicemen. The Secretary was David Wilson, a former Australian regular soldier and Malayan civil servant who had become a Malayan citizen and a convert to Islam. He had served throughout the first Emergency in Malaya and later with the United Nations in West Irian. He was experienced both in security work and in the way Kuala Lumpur did business. A stickler for principle and a man who loved an argument, he did valuable work, which in my view was not always fully appreciated.

Sarawak retained a number of senior expatriates, including those holding the important positions of State Secretary, Financial Secretary, and Establishment Officer. This was essential to provide a bridging period of continuity, especially at a time of massive British reinvolvement in the security field. The State Secretary was Tony Shaw, who had come to Sarawak originally from the Malayan Customs Service. He had played an important coordinating role during the Malaysia negotiations. He had a somewhat vague manner behind which lay a clear and perceptive mind. He was a good-natured man but could be resolute when the need arose. Generally he was at least two moves ahead of everyone else.

John Pike, the Financial Secretary, came to Sarawak shortly after I did and followed in my footsteps to Sarikei, Binatang, and Lawas. His financial acumen inevitably led him into that field. He had been responsible for negotiating for

Tony Shaw (center) talking to a senior Malayan official (right) and
Datuk Teo Kui Seng, a leading Kuching Chinese personality

Sarawak very favorable financial terms for entry into Malaysia. He was by nature more cautious than Shaw. Together they made a very effective combination.

The Establishment Officer was John Williams, an enormous man who had seen more of British withdrawals than most people. Not only had he served in Nigeria and Singapore in the immediate pre-independence and pre-self-government periods in those countries, but he was one of those unfortunates who had to withdraw across the Sittang River in Burma in 1942 after the bridge across that river was blown up by our own forces. He was one of the last Senior Administrative Officers to leave Sarawak.

Many other expatriates played important roles during this interim period. The list is too long to enumerate here. But a group of enlightened policemen played an especially important part under their able and popular Commissioner, Roy Henry. He was a large and sociable Scot who had served in Malaya. He was one of those brave men who are constitutionally unable to swim but do not let this deter them from traveling in longboats and launches which are liable to capsize or run aground. He was also an accomplished mimic. It was only a little time before I left that I discovered that one of his best party pieces was of me, some years earlier, on the telephone thinking that he, Henry, was a drunken Kelabit disturbing my rest in the early hours in a police quarter not far from our house across river.

Inevitably, the senior expatriate officers were drawn into advising the state politicians and in helping them to present their ideas. I myself was called on to write many speeches. This is a reasonable thing to ask civil servants to do, but it had some dangers. No matter how one tried, the thinking of an expatriate official would not correspond entirely with that of the Minister. The practice introduced a slightly unreal element into some public utterances. So long, however, as the State Government saw eye to eye with the Federal Government, work of this kind presented no problems. The situation was to change when political difficulties arose between the two tiers of government.

A new kind of activity in which I became involved was so-called Psychological Warfare. This is not a term which I like because of its lack of precision. A great many forms of political activity, information work, and propaganda are capable of being given the label, and the term—psywar for short—is much used by baffled soldiers and politicians. Psychological warfare can be defined as a non-violent means of fighting declared and undeclared wars or of combating subversion, a method which is intended to weaken the enemy's will to resist, to win over the civil population, to sustain the public's willingness and determination to carry on the struggle, and to win and retain the support of world opinion. We obviously had a situation in Sarawak in which psywar was called for, both in combating Confrontation and in opposing the communist movement. Inevitably the Information Office was regarded as the appropriate organ of government to coordinate psywar.

The foundations of psywar are often fairly obvious. If you want to weaken an enemy's will to resist, you must have a reasonable alternative to offer him and he must also be under pressure. If you are not winning the battles, you will not win psywar either. You must be able to get your message to him, by dropping leaflets or by conventional broadcasts. You must ensure that the behavior of the security forces is exemplary. Nothing helps your opponents more than misbehavior by your own men. Good deeds by the armed services are a valuable sort of activity, which help retain the support of local people. Nothing is more damaging to enemy morale than the knowledge that local opinion is against him. The Government needs to be popular, honest, and socially progressive. If this is not the case, your opponents will be greatly strengthened. Agrarian discontent of whatever kind is one of the most fertile fields for hostile exploitation. In sum, there must be clearly demonstrated moral superiority on your side.

Such considerations are not all within the competence of an Information Department, but we were involved in trying to make government attitudes better known to the people through the establishment of a large field staff and by such activities as civic assemblies. We were also involved in much joint activity with the armed services.

Malaysia was fortunate in commanding the services of one of the world's leading authorities on psywar, C.C. Too. He operated within the Prime Minister's Department almost entirely on his own. He had no back-up organization but he provided theoretical and practical guidance. He was an inspired expounder and lecturer. Anything worthwhile that I learned on the subject of psywar, I learned from him.

Combating Indonesian propaganda was comparatively easy. There was no support for Indonesian claims that Malaysia was a neo-colonialist plot, except among that section of the Chinese population who were influenced by communism and among some rural Malay and Melanau communities which had grievances over the granting of timber rights. The communist movement was an entirely different matter. In some Chinese communities there was undeniable frustration over land, particularly in the Lower Rejang. Here the Chinese immigrants in the earlier part of this century took up empty swamp forest and planted rubber. The rubber did fairly well and the planters prospered, but the soils were unsuitable peat. The yields of rubber have declined, the land is unsuitable for replanting, and the planters and their numerous descendants have limited alternative outlets and, in particular, very little alternative land. As you fly over the canopy of rubber trees in the Lower Rejang and around Sibu you peer down through gaps in the canopy at the farmhouses. It would be hard to imagine a more claustrophobic and frustrating environment. This is the sort of area that is associated with the communist movement in Sarawak.

Not all communism in the state stemmed from land problems, but the underlying land problem played a significant part. The Chinese were confined to a Mixed Zone of some 4,000 square miles and could obtain title to land nowhere else. But by no means did they have all of the Mixed Zone—probably little more than a quarter. The rest belonged to Natives. Outside the Mixed Zone was a smaller Native Area where only Natives could obtain title. The rest of the land outside the Forests was Interior Area and Native Customary Land where Natives could work the land but could not secure title. The result of this was that the Chinese were short of land and Native Land had little value. This had been the situation since Brooke times.

I had hoped that our main psychological effort would be devoted to this question of land. Unfortunately, the Colonial Government had moved very slowly to solve land problems. It was not until 1962 that the problem was considered by an expert committee. The committee recommended that the classification of land into Zones and Areas should be abolished, that all land should be held under title, and that Natives should be allowed to sell land to Chinese under supervision. This would have had several results. More land would have become available to Chinese, and the value of the main capital resource of Natives would have become much greater. Widespread and extortionate illegal renting of land by Natives to Chinese would have become a thing of the past. Unfortunately, these recommendations were evolved too late for anything to be done by the Colonial Government, and it was too difficult a subject to be tackled by the new State Government. Land reform became a political issue and the position today remains much as it was under the Brookes.

These were serious and worrying subjects, but there was some lighter relief in our work in the Information Office. Lightest of all perhaps was the problem of royal portraits. While Sarawak was a colony, the British Colonial Office was always generous with the provision of handsome color prints of the Royal Family. We were always distributing them and they formed a popular form of adornment for houses, shops, and schools. One especially popular photograph was that of the Royal Family on the lawns of Balmoral, complete with the royal corgis. The corgis puzzled some Dayaks who had never seen such odd looking dogs and assumed them to be small pigs!

After the establishment of Malaysia, my Head Office in Kuala Lumpur started to send us quantities of equally good photographs of the King and Queen of Malaysia. These in turn we issued methodically to all outstations for distribution to the public. But an unexpected problem arose. I was to find that it was one thing to get people to put up royal portraits, but quite another matter to get them to take them down again.

This was not due to any fervent attachment to the British Royal Family. They just happened to like the pictures. The result was that visiting Malaysians were continually being confronted by pictures of British royalty, which was embarrassing for me as the only expatriate in the Information Office in Sarawak. I did my best to anticipate these problems but they kept turning up in unexpected places. The Tunku was confronted by a picture of the Queen at a meeting in a Malay house in Kuching, my own Minister by one in a Malay school on the coast. Worst of all, Tun Razak, when opening a new land scheme, was confronted by one in a brand new cooperative store. My colleagues were very nice about it all but it was embarrassing. And I had not the heart to point out that when I was in the Baram, the Kelabit houses were festooned with photographs of Soekarno and that in Lawas, I distinctly remember seeing some fine old lithographs of the last Sultan of Turkey, Abdul the Damned.

As was to be expected, we had a state visit by the King of Malaysia. The King, or Yang-Di-Pertuan Agong, is one of the Rulers of Peninsular Malaysia elected for a term of five years by his fellow Rulers. The King who visited us in November 1964—with his very elegant and photogenic wife, unbelievably a mother of ten—was the Raja of Perlis. I had never been close to the planning of a VIP visit before. At the best of times it calls for meticulous preparation, but on this occasion very detailed security precautions were required as well.

I myself composed a draft address of welcome to be read by the Deputy Chief Minister. It was not one of my most successful efforts and was rejected as being totally unsuitable. Otherwise my main problems were with the police. In Sibu, only the day before the arrival of the Royal couple in the state, I discovered that a police order had been issued that no photographer was to approach within thirty paces of the King. This was crazy. It would have meant that no good photographs could have been taken in Sibu, while no such restriction was being applied in Kuching. I had a fierce argument with the police and conveyed my dismay to my Director in Kuala Lumpur, but the order remained. However, to my relief, when the King and Queen eventually arrived in Sibu, things grew a little confused. Indeed they grew so confused that in the hurly-burly, the photographers came into the closest proximity with His Majesty; the problem for the photographers was to get far enough away to take photographs. So the day was saved and I forgave the police. The King was a very pleasant and urbane gentleman and the Queen was charming.

After the formation of Malaysia, the rate at which rural development was to be carried out was accelerated. The Information Office was expected to publicize this. Prominent among the new programs were several land schemes of the kind that had long been established in Peninsular Malaysia. These involve the systematic planning and planting of development areas, complete with village settlements and all amenities, such as schools and water supply. Much of the cost is borne by the Government and the balance is regarded as a loan to the settlers, each of whom receives a house, several acres of land properly planted under estate conditions with high-yielding material, and another plot for growing fruit and vegetables. The settlers provide the labor for establishing the scheme and are paid for it. They do not have to start repaying the loan element until the crop planted has come into production.

These schemes are largely the brainchild of Tun Razak. They are well organized and well thought out. It would be hard to imagine a more efficient way of modernizing the countryside or any other way in which capital could be injected

Rural settlement—new style.
View over the Land Development Scheme at Melugu in the 2nd Division.

into the countryside for the benefit of the countryman to parallel but not replace the activities of private enterprise. The schemes do, however, suffer from certain drawbacks. They are expensive and, because they are efficient, they cater for relatively small numbers of settlers. From 1956 to the end of 1974, for instance, the very efficient Federal Land Development Authority (FELDA), charged with these schemes in Peninsular Malaysia, had settled no more than 30,100 families. This constitutes a considerable achievement but is not a large total in terms of the whole population. A more serious objection is perhaps that these large and impressive schemes tend to divert attention and funds away from dispersed rural extension and other activities which bring improvements to villages outside the ambit of the new schemes. The latter can never hope to cater for more than a minority of the rural population.

Sarawak presented considerable problems for the introduction of these new schemes, as the soils are unusually poor and there was little unencumbered land where they could be undertaken. In Peninsular Malaysia, where little shifting cultivation was practiced, there were and still are large areas of potentially agricultural land still covered with forest and untouched except for timber extraction. In such areas, land development schemes could start from scratch. In Sarawak such areas were few and far between, except in very remote parts of the state or in mountainous or swampy country. Elsewhere the various indigenous peoples had practiced shifting cultivation on a very wide scale. Before a Land Development scheme could be started, it was first necessary to negotiate the surrender of customary rights, a costly and time-consuming business. Even where land was supposed to be unencumbered, as in parts of the 4th Division, it was often found that enterprising and energetic Dayaks had already moved in. Even if their claims to be there were more than doubtful, they could not be summarily ejected.

I have paid a number of visits to Land Development Schemes in Peninsular Malaysia and they are most impressive. But they have not been notably successful in Sarawak. The state's Land Development Board, the counterpart of FELDA, successfully established rubber schemes in all the Divisions but they have not done well. Partly this is due to the fact that Dayaks, who made up a large proportion of the settlers, are individualists and not readily brought into schemes calling for cooperative effort and some degree of regimentation. Oil Palm schemes in the 4th Division have shown greater promise, but even here difficulties have been encountered in finding the right kind of permanent settler for the schemes.

Development had always received special attention in the Information Office, and there was no difficulty in stepping up this work to publicize and explain the increased volume of development. In addition to the major schemes, there was much emphasis on Minor Rural Development. The aim of these schemes was to try and ensure that every community received some benefits under the Development Plan. For communities living outside the scope of major development schemes, it was sought to provide some tangible evidence of the Government's interest, whether it was a village water supply or a new landing stage or a footpath or a supply of fire extinguishers. The idea of such minor schemes is sound but, unless maintained, some of them, particularly any form of footpath construction, are quickly overwhelmed by natural growth or washed away by the rains. Communities might cooperate in building such things, especially if it meant a cash grant to see that the scheme was undertaken, but once completed there was much less interest in keeping the new facilities in a good state of repair.

On several occasions I accompanied Sarawak Ministers on tour and was sometimes able to bring Hedda along as the official photographer. One tour took us to Lawas and up the Limbang with the Chief Minister, Stephen Ningkan, to visit the house of Pengarah Ngang, the Dayak Chief of the area. It was interesting to see the Chief Minister in action. He had a rapid-fire style of speech delivered with great emphasis. The tour was to include a visit to Bareo in the Ulu Baram and then to spend the night with Temenggong Oyong Lawai Jau at Long San. But Ningkan, without good reason in my view, decided at the very last moment not to proceed on this part of the journey and sent the State Secretary and the Residents of the 4th and 5th Division and myself in his place. This was highly inconsiderate, because the Temenggong had called in all the leading figures of the Ulu Baram to meet Ningkan. The Temenggong was understandably annoyed and offended when we arrived by a Malaysian Airforce plane without the Chief Minister. Whether the Temenggong thought that the expatriate officers were in some way to blame I do not know, but he made us suffer for the omission. The party that night was the most boisterous one in all my experience of Sarawak. The pilot of our plane was a British attached officer, but flying with him was a young Malay Pilot Officer. I thought he looked a little startled.

162 *Fair Land Sarawak*

Another such journey took us to Long Jawi, a large but isolated Kenyah house far up the Balui tributary of the Rejang, with the Minister for Sarawak Affairs, Temenggong Jugah. Long Jawi had been overrun by an Indonesian force some time before and a number of local Border Scouts as well as Gurkhas had been killed. The visit was to make relief payments to the relatives of those killed. After a pleasant evening's entertainment in Kapit, we flew to the naval helicopter base at Nanga Gaat in the Balleh and from there to Long Jawi. The Navy had established very good relations with the Dayaks. Our pilot, a young Marine called David Rowe, stood almost in the relationship of an adopted son to Jugah. His Dayak name was Bubu.

We had quite a large party for this trip and with a full load of fuel the big Wessex helicopter would have had difficulty in taking off from the normal helicopter pad. Bubu therefore flew us up in two groups to another pad on a little hillside where we all piled in and could then take off and be airborne.

The people at Long Jawi had only moved into Sarawak during the war and they had been much upset by the attack made on them. Their assailants had suffered severely because troops had been flown in behind them and they were ambushed on

One of the Long Jawi widows whose husband was killed by the Indonesians

their return journey, but this did not save the Border Scouts who had been captured. They were taken a little way upriver and there slaughtered—apparently a return to an old and bloodthirsty ritual.

My special recollections of Long Jawi were of Jugah addressing the people of the longhouse and later, when we were entertained in the traditional manner, dancing the ngajat, of seeing the wall behind him festooned with pictures of the British Royal Family. And, of course, the young 6th Gurkhas then garrisoning the area. Several off-duty soldiers attended the presentation and subsequent party. They were called on to dance and replied that as good soldiers they could not possibly do anything like that. They gave a demonstration of arms drill instead. But as the evening wore on it became apparent that not only had they been dancing in Long Jawi, but that they had been teaching the Kenyah girls Gurkha dances too.

Temenggong Jugah and Bubu (Lt. David Rowe)

The Gurkhas had been teaching the girls Nepali dances

But the Temenggong thought they should learn some ballroom dancing too.
Note the pictures of the wrong royalty on the wall behind.

We were allowed to fly in a number of different kinds of helicopters. They were indispensable during Confrontation. There were never very many available but they were operated very efficiently, and the Indonesians never understood how few there were. For anyone like myself, who has walked a great deal in Borneo, there is a special magic carpet quality about helicopters. I could never come to take them quite so much for granted as the men who operated them. Sometimes I thought their nonchalance went too far. On one occasion I accompanied our Minister for Works and Communications, Datuk Taib Mahmud, and his wife Puan Leila on a visit to Lundu. We flew back in an RAF Whirlwind helicopter with an RAF Warrant Officer returning to Kuching from ground staff duties, who sat in the doorway without a safety belt and with his legs dangling in the void. I felt quite sick the whole way back to Kuching and felt sure this was not in accordance with RAF Standing Orders.

The RAF did tend to be rather strict about rules and regulations. One of the more unfortunate examples of this occurred on the day the rebellion broke out in Brunei and it was essential to rush two companies of Gurkhas to Brunei from Singapore and to get them there before dark. They very nearly did not get there in time because of delay caused by RAF ground staff. The aircraft and aircrew were ready to go, but the despatching staff were only narrowly prevented from weighing all 200 Gurkhas individually and having all their difficult names correctly recorded on the right manifest forms. I felt that the dangling Warrant Officer was not acting up to some of the traditions of the service.

In many ways the period of Confrontation was an exhilarating one. There was much work to be done, and one could hardly avoid reflecting on the fact that the Indonesian border was only thirty miles away. But at the same time there was a sense of purposefulness and confidence. Most people, though not all politicians, worked together well. The presence of so many troops, who had to be supplied, accommodated, and provided with staff of various kinds, and the expansion of local security forces meant that business was good and there were plenty of jobs. And the external pressure meant that the period of transition from British colony to state of Malaysia took place under the influence of a strongly unifying factor. It provided a breathing space while the new relationships between the State and Federal Governments could be ironed out and become established. It was hateful to know that lives were being lost unnecessarily, but apart from this I have no doubt that Confrontation was beneficial to Malaysia. If Indonesia had desisted from armed intervention, the early years of Malaysia would have been far more difficult.

The withdrawal of Singapore from the Federation in 1965 took everyone by surprise but caused few problems in Sarawak. After a brief honeymoon period, there had been a steady deterioration in relations between the Federal Government and Singapore. There was too little compatibility between the two for a permanently smooth working relationship to be established. Singapore had worked hard, though not always very harmoniously, for the establishment of Malaysia. But between 1961 and 1963 there were enough differences, often expressed on the Singapore side with a bluntness which was hurtful to the Malay leadership in Kuala Lumpur, to ensure that there was perilously little goodwill left once merger was complete.

Almost immediately after Malaysia Day, elections were held in Singapore. These were contested by the Singapore Alliance, the local equivalent of the governing coalition in Malaya. The election resulted in an overwhelming PAP victory and the Alliance failed to win a single seat. This was disturbing for Malaya's dominant United Malays National Organization (UMNO), which saw its three previously held constituencies won by the Malay candidates of a non-communal party. Such a development struck at the very foundations of politics in the peninsula. UMNO reacted violently and wildly. The PAP, not a body of men given to turning the other cheek, responded strongly too.

If PAP had remained a purely local party, little harm might have resulted, but the party decided, apparently in contravention of an unwritten agreement with the Tunku, to contest the elections in Peninsular Malaysia in April 1964. In the outcome, the PAP was almost as unsuccessful in the peninsula as the Alliance had been in Singapore. In July and September 1964 there were communal riots in Singapore, which were probably sparked off by Indonesian infiltrators. But UMNO agitation over alleged discrimination against Malays in Singapore, unemployment amongst Singapore Malays arising from Confrontation, and resettlement plans affecting a Malay area all played their part in building up tensions. The PAP was not prepared to accept the rather simplistic role for Singapore envisaged by the Tunku of a prosperous city-state which concentrated on commerce and did not seek to play a national role. It saw itself rather as the spearhead of a forward-looking, non-communal Malaysia, but this was regarded by Malays, fearful of the large Chinese population and determined to retain political control in what they regard as their own country, as an attack against themselves.

The situation was not helped by the partial and somewhat lecturing attitude adopted by some organs of the British press. It has always been a problem in Malaya and later Malaysia that foreign journalists find it easier to see things through Chinese eyes than to comprehend the complex fears and ambitions of Malays. They generally have far more social contact with Chinese, and they do not find it easy to establish a genuinely balanced viewpoint. The result sometimes has been that material is written which is unbalanced and at times painfully patronizing in tone towards Malays.

In Australia, early in 1965, I was to watch some of the mutual exasperations at work. Lee Kuan Yew came down on an official visit, which naturally received much attention. The Malaysian High Commissioner—an old political opponent, Lim Yew Hock—refused to meet him, although Lee was willing to do so. Lim departed on a speaking engagement to some far place. Lee gave a talk to a crowded National Press Club. It was Lee at his brilliant best, statesmanlike, tactful, convincing. He dealt with questions in a masterly way, including those from an Indonesian reporter whom he kindly and politely shredded to pieces before gently putting him back in his place. It was a masterly performance highly beneficial to Malaysia. But every seat in the crowded dining room had had placed upon it by Lee's unofficial staff a bundle of collected Lee speeches, largely devoted to criticizing the government of his own country and propounding the Lee vision of how Malaysia should be run.

Just when the departure of Singapore from the Federation first came to be discussed is not clear, but it was not a decision that was suddenly arrived at, nor did the initiative come entirely from the side of the Tunku. Relations deteriorated to the point where the possibility of serious communal disturbances became very pressing, and the Tunku and his closest advisers concluded that the only solution lay in separation.

I have often wondered how close Malaysia came to complete disintegration at this time. A prime reason for the establishment of the Federation had been to accommodate Singapore. It is unlikely that Malaya would ever have contemplated entering a Federation with Sarawak and Sabah alone. If in August 1965, the Tunku had wanted to, it would have been possible to opt out of the Federation, leaving Britain to worry about Sarawak and Sabah and the large British forces then in those states. There were many people in Peninsular Malaysia of all races who had no enthusiasm for the costly commitment to the outlying Bornean states, and I doubt whether total withdrawal would have been politically damaging in Peninsular Malaysia. It would simply have left Britain to pick up the pieces of one more unsuccessful Federation.

But I have no reason to believe that the idea was ever considered. The leaders of Peninsular Malaysia were honorable men who had come to regard the sometimes troublesome people and politicians of Sarawak and Sabah as their fellow countrymen. The Tunku's government did not, however, keep the Bornean states informed of the impending departure of Singapore, though when the new Federation was formed, Sarawak and Sabah had been treated as equals of Malaya and Singapore. This failure to consult caused some anguish in the Bornean states. Donald Stephens, the Chief Minister of Sabah, was particularly upset. In Sabah there were even some mutterings of secession. The failure to consult was also disliked in Sarawak, but the State Government behaved with sense and maturity. It called for an objective assessment of the situation, including an assessment of Sarawak finances. The assessment showed clearly that it was in the best interests of Sarawak to support the Federal Government and this was done. The State Government lost little time in making its position clear that the new situation did not affect the state's policy and position within Malaysia.

Having withdrawn from Malaysia, Singapore went on to make a considerable success of life on its own. There was initially a good deal of residual friction, much of it—though not all—originating in Singapore. If Singapore could needle Kuala Lumpur, for instance by publishing material critical of Malaysia in the official review, *Singapore Mirror*, it generally did so. Singapore leaders are oddly prickly. Despite immense abilities, they seem unsure of themselves at times, and this is reflected in a defensive aggressiveness that is often unjustified. They tend to be very sensitive about their own feelings but far less so about the feelings of others. Internally Singapore is well and honestly run; it is authoritarian, pragmatic, and somewhat humorless. The Government comes in for plenty of criticism, especially from academics, but heaven help Singapore if the academics ever have the running of the place.

While the withdrawal of Singapore caused no serious problems in Sarawak, internal political problems proved to be far more intractable. The Sarawak Alliance, as the governing pro-Malaysia alliance was known, was a somewhat uneasy combination of four parties, but only three of them—SNAP, BARJASA, and the SCA—were represented in the six-man State Cabinet, and three of those posts were held by members of SNAP. The fourth party, PESAKA, was represented in the Federal Cabinet, as was BARJASA by Temenggong Jugah, Minister for Sarawak Affairs, and Abdul Rahman Yakub, who held several appointments as Assistant Minister and Minister, ending up as Minister of Education.

The proliferation of parties and interests had made the selection of a Chief Minister difficult. It was logical to have a Dayak Chief Minister since the predominantly Dayak parties, SNAP and PESAKA, held more than half the seats in Council Negri. Despite SNAP being the smaller of the two, its leader, Ningkan, had the burning ambition and the clear idea of exactly what he wanted, which was largely absent in the case of other Dayak members of the Council. His position, however, depended largely on there being some degree of Dayak unity. His relations with the SCA were good, but relations with BARJASA were much poorer. The outstanding Sarawak political figure, Abdul Rahman Yakub, was in Kuala Lumpur, and Ningkan's relations with him, never good, tended to deteriorate. Ningkan had drive and personal ambition; he was prepared to seek advice on many matters and to use it with discrimination; he was a competent chairman who was prepared to listen to the views of others and to take sensible decisions. But he was quick-tempered and a poor parliamentarian; he tended to see power as being something which belonged to him as of right, and some aspects of his personal conduct left him open to criticism.

The State Government did well initially. The Deputy Chief Minister, James Wong, who had stood as an independent in Limbang and subsequently joined SNAP, and Teo Kui Seng, the nominated SCA member, were capable businessmen with considerable Local Government experience. A second Dayak Minister (for Local Government), Dunstan Endawie, was a steadying influence on Ningkan. The two BARJASA members were Awang Hipni, a leading Melanau personality from Matu District, and Abdul Taib Mahmud, a young Australian-trained lawyer and the nephew of Abdul Rahman Yakub. Taib showed himself to be a capable Minister, but felt that he was not given the responsibilities for which his intellectual attainments fitted him. Another important figure until October 1965, when he left to read law in

Stephen Ningkan, Sarawak's first Chief Minister, with his brother, Simon Ningkan. Simon was killed in the Indonesian attack on the 17th Mile Police Station.

England, was the Chief Minister's Political Secretary, a shrewd, hard-headed Foochow Chinese called Ting Tung Ming. The opposition consisted of SUPP and PANAS. The latter party, though it supported the establishment of Malaysia, had been offended at some of the political manoeuvres which had taken place and had quarrelled with BARJASA. It withdrew from the Alliance shortly before the elections.

The State Government handled the business of government competently, but rivalries and differences were too great for political calm to continue indefinitely. Ningkan's style offended many; he spent a disproportionate amount of time outside the state and did little methodical traveling within it. Although he was not alone in this, he demanded some pomp and circumstance when he traveled: welcoming arches, flag-waving schoolchildren, and formal entertainment. Native members of the Alliance felt that he was too closely linked to Chinese business interests. Ling Beng Siew, a wealthy Sibu businessman, and Wee Hood Teck, a Kuching banker, played a prominent part. There were competing demands for timber licenses.

Timber was the cause of much that went wrong in Sarawak. In colonial times the exploitation of timber had been on a considerable scale, but the Forestry Department sought to ensure that it was exploited on a basis of sustained yield, i.e., that the amount cut annually in any forest was the same as that forest's regeneration capacity. The Forest Officers were gentlemen and botanists but not well suited to dealing with rapacious businessmen. The Colonial Government was, however, capable of saying no to the importunate. The mainly Chinese timber men made a great deal of money but exploitation was limited.

With the advent of Malaysia, the authority for issuing timber licenses passed to the politicians. This largely coincided with surging demand for timber, higher prices, and the availability of far more sophisticated means of extracting timber from jungle areas which had previously been little touched. The demand for timber areas greatly increased and this led to corruption over the award of forest areas to big business.

In addition to big business, groups of Natives made numerous requests for timber areas. They could rarely work the areas themselves. If awarded an area, they simply sold it to a Chinese businessman who stripped it of its merchantable timber. Most of the increased output was in the form of logs, which bring the least benefit to the people of the state. Any ideas of sustained yield were largely forgotten. A few people grew very rich, including some Native Chiefs who claimed vague and shadowy "rights" to forest areas, though such rights had never been conceded by the Brooke and Colonial Governments. There was dishonesty, corruption, and jealousy at every hand. The only Minister to call for orderly and properly planned long-term extraction of timber was Taib Mahmud, but his views carried little weight.

The Chief Minister was the object of criticism, and at the same time he became estranged from much Native opinion through his often autocratic behavior and his frequent absences from the state. There were rumblings of discontent in 1964. There was quarrelling between SNAP and PESAKA and this was encouraged by BARJASA. Matters came to a head in 1965 over the Land Bills.

There was a genuine need for reform of the land laws, and the State Government sought to implement the recommendations of the Land Commission. This was attacked as a sell-out to the Chinese. A compromise agreement about the Bills was reached at a meeting of the Sarawak Alliance Council, but this apparent agreement was a case where yes really meant no. The Bills had to be withdrawn. The opponents of the Bills then formed a Sarawak Native Alliance under BARJASA leadership, which excluded SNAP. The Ningkan Government was very close to collapse. However, SNAP and PESAKA were still able to talk to each other, and after intensive negotiations in Sibu, in which Ling Beng Siew played an important part, a new government was formed without BARJASA or PANAS—essentially it was a Dayak-Chinese Alliance. A few days later, both the excluded parties joined the Government, which now had an enlarged membership, the three ex-officio members standing down.

Ningkan remained as Chief Minister but showed few signs of having learned much from the crisis, especially the need to preserve Dayak unity. His personal conduct continued to give offense; his popularity and standing declined. Wee Hood Teck came to play an increasingly obtrusive and disliked part in the affairs of government and spent much time in the Chief Minister's Office with Ningkan. Companies in which he was interested were given certain concessions, and he was said to be trying to have his bank, the Bian Chang Bank, made the Government Banker and so given control of the state's surplus balances. There were defections from SNAP to PESAKA.

The situation was complicated by differences with the Federal Government over the continuing role of senior expatriate officers and over the national language. The presence of a number of expatriate officers, especially the holders of the offices of State Secretary and Financial Secretary, were becoming an irritant in Federal-State relations, though in fact all the administrative officers were due to leave not later than 1967.

The position of the expatriates was inevitably affected by the steady improvement in relations between Malaysia and Indonesia after the abortive coup in Indonesia on the night of September 30, 1965. This resulted in the destruction of the PKI but did not lead to an immediate cessation of Confrontation. It did open the way to improved relations and led to the official termination of hostilities by the Bangkok Agreement of June 1, 1966.

The National Language (Bahasa Malaysia) was due to be introduced as the official language in Peninsular Malaysia in 1967, and there was some federal criticism of the Sarawak government for allegedly dragging its feet over increasing the use and teaching of Malay. There were in fact many real difficulties in doing this in a state where Malays were in a substantial minority and where the availability of Malay language teachers was very limited. But the criticism and an unfortunate tendency for Federal politicians to refer to Malaysia when they meant Peninsular Malaysia aroused fears among Dayaks that the provision of the IGC Report, which provided a minimum ten-year period for the full introduction of the National Language in Sarawak, was going to be ignored. The Chief Minister responded to this domestic problem unwisely by suggesting that Peninsular Malaysia might defer the introduction date to 1973 to enable the whole of Malaysia to move in the matter together. This gave great offense to the Federal Government and did Ningkan much harm.

Matters came to a head in June 1966. By this time, a majority of the Sarawak Alliance members of Council Negri, who constituted a majority of elected members in the Council itself, had aligned themselves against Ningkan. They refused to discuss matters in the Sarawak Alliance Council, but the way was set for them to prepare a vote of no confidence at the next Council Negri Meeting, which was to take place on June 14. The Federal view, however, was that Ningkan, having lost the confidence of the Sarawak Alliance, could be dismissed by the Governor without

Datuk Penghulu Tawi Sli, Sarawak's second Chief Minister

recourse to Council Negri. An additional, though less publicized, reason for the Federal position was that if the issue had been debated in Kuching, some of the dissidents might well have been induced to change their minds and won over to the support of the Chief Minister. In any case, the Alliance members declined battle in Council Negri, departed for Kuala Lumpur, and returned after the Council Negri session with a high-level delegation of the National Alliance Council. This was led by the Minister for Home Affairs, Tun Ismail, and included the Federal Attorney-General, the Inspector-General of Police, and the Director of Special Branch. It was with some difficulty that the police were persuaded not to send in a Riot Squad as well.

This large party descended on the unfortunate Governor, who was eventually persuaded to dismiss Ningkan. "We have acted," said Tun Ismail, "strictly in accordance with the law. If Ningkan does not accept this, let him test it in the courts." Ningkan in defeat behaved with a dignity that he had not always demonstrated in office. He took legal action, claiming that the Governor's action was unconstitutional. The public responded calmly, though there was much sympathy for Ningkan, whose popularity, which had been at a very low level, shot up.

The new Chief Minister was another 2nd Division Dayak, Penghulu Tawi Sli, a former government clerk from Simanggang. He was a small, kindly man, lacking Ningkan's fire but possessing enough ambition to want to lead. His family had long played a prominent role in the Simanggang area. His differences with Ningkan were of a personal kind; they had few policy differences. The new State Cabinet was a weaker one than its predecessor. The most powerful member of the Cabinet was Taib Mahmud, who became Minister of Agriculture and Forests.

The change of government led to the departure of the two most senior expatriate officers, Shaw and Pike. They were on cordial terms with the new Chief Minister, but there was Federal pressure for them to go, and the political problems which had arisen made their continuation in office embarrassing. Their tasks in the transition

Tony Shaw's successor as State Secretary, **Tan Sri Gerunsin** Lembat, with his wife, Puan Sri Racha

process were completed. Shaw left at the end of August and Pike a little later. Pike's place was taken by an experienced Chinese officer, T'en Kuen Foh, who had been my colleague when I was Development Secretary. He had long financial experience, but the new State Secretary, Gerunsin Lembat, was a broadcaster and educationist. It was not easy for him to take over as Head of the State Civil Service, but he adapted quickly and successfully to the new post.

In the Information Office, we did our utmost to promote the new Chief Minister, but there was great public interest in the outcome of the Ningkan court case. There was never, in the view of most local lawyers, much doubt about the outcome. The Federal Attorney-General did not appear to argue personally the case which he had propounded. In Court, the Federal case appeared weak. The Judge, Mr. Justice Harley, found that Ningkan's dismissal was unconstitutional and that lack of confidence in the Chief Minister could only be demonstrated by a vote in Council Negri. Ningkan's opponents now demanded that Council Negri be recalled so that they could propose the vote of no confidence, which they had failed to do in June. Ningkan declined. Under the Constitution there was no requirement for the Council to meet until December.

The next few days were politically hectic. Although outside the realm of politics, calm prevailed throughout the state, Ningkan's opponents set out to create an impression of emergency. The Council Negri members in opposition to him were reduced to a state of panic by a few threatening telephone calls and were kept away from contact with the public. Some minor disturbances—window smashing and stone throwing—were engineered. Ningkan was largely denied use of the Broadcasting services. On September 15 the Federal Government declared a state of emergency, claiming that there was a threat to national security from the communists. This was a little hard on Ningkan who, whatever his failings, was bitterly anticommunist and whose own brother, a police officer, had been killed in action the previous year when a combined Indonesian-SCO force overran a Police Station seventeen miles from Kuching. A White Paper was issued which was based on a proposed supplement to update *Danger Within*, drafted several months earlier. The Sarawak Constitution was amended to enable the Governor to recall Council Negri. This was duly done on September 23—the SNAP and SUPP members boycotting the meeting—and Ningkan was out of office again.

For a second time he sought redress through Court action, claiming that the declaration of emergency was fraudulent. In the Malaysian Federal Court, his claim was rejected by a split two-to-one decision, and this was upheld in 1968 in the Privy Council. Whatever the legal arguments, the prolonged litigation effectively ended Ningkan's political career in Sarawak. He withdrew from the political arena while his case was being fought in the courts and he never made up the lost ground.

Stephen Ningkan had his limitations as a leader, but he was not a negligible figure and in many ways he played a positive role in the early days of Malaysia. He played his part according to his lights. I doubt whether anyone else would have done better during those early days when Sarawak was settling down into its niche in Malaysia. He was genuinely multiracial in outlook, and if he leaned heavily on Chinese support, it was because he had no other resources on which he could depend. He knew his own people and felt that they expected that, as Chief Minister, he would command personal resources far greater than those derived from his salary. He respected the integrity of the public service and did not put his hand in the public till. I think history will look more kindly on Ningkan than some of his contemporaries.

One of the last public occasions at which Ningkan presided was a farewell parade mounted by detachments from Commonwealth units who were now withdrawing from Sarawak. It was an occasion I will always remember. There were detachments from the Royal Marines, the New Zealand Regiment, and Gurkhas, with the Constabulary Band playing. It seemed especially appropriate that the Marines took part. They were first in Sarawak in 1843 with Keppel. It was a perfect late afternoon. One of the officers on parade was a tall, one-armed Royal Marine who saluted with his left arm. It was a very pleasant occasion and afterwards the State Government entertained the participants with beer below the Secretariat building. Thus ended the Indian Summer of our confrontation. For me this marked the final end of the British role in Sarawak.

The British withdrawal was unfortunately marred to some extent by pettiness at a low level in the handover to Malaysian forces. The British effort in Sarawak had been so well done that it was painful to discover the willingness of a few to spoil the ship for a ha'porth of tar. The handover could have been done more gracefully and more generously. There were, for example, instances where simple furniture and other items were burned or auctioned for a song rather than be handed over to the Malaysian services as a contribution to their well-being and comfort. This was not due to ill will on the part of responsible soldiers but to unimaginative pennypinching devised by some military babu and carried out with glee by that type of moronic individual who exists in every organization and who enjoys following stupid orders to the letter, especially when it upsets others. There was some unnecessary rancor as a result, and the savings to the British taxpayer were negligible.

It may be wondered what kind of impact political troubles had on an expatriate officer like myself. They caused one distress because one was on friendly terms with the protagonists on both sides. One was disconcerted by their ruthlessness. A particularly unpleasant feature was the criticism—bitter, unfounded, and unfair—directed at the Judge who found for Ningkan and at Dr. Sockalingam, the Speaker of Council Negri. Both men did what they believed to be right in the best tradition of their offices. Both were accused by deliberate rumor and innuendo of personal bias. But on reflection, I came to conclude that this was an experience that Sarawak politicians had to go through and a lesson that had to be learned about the harsh reality of politics.

The expatriate officers in Sarawak did not come under severe attack at any time before or during the political troubles of 1966. There was occasional sniping by Federal politicians and in the Malay press of Peninsular Malaysia. The expatriates gave the local politicians the degree of support they thought was expected of them within the context of making Malaysia work, and this meant giving advice on Federal-State relations which was not always welcome to the center. It would have been dishonorable and wrong to wash our hands of all responsibility for advising inexperienced state politicians in such matters. No doubt at times we made mistakes, but on the whole I think we achieved the right balance, and by the time we left, the machinery of government was working smoothly, and the State-Federal relationship at the working level was reasonably well established.

Such sniping as there was sometimes upset people but in fact it was generally mild. Quite early on such criticism was put into perspective for me by the State Chairman of the Public Service Board, the late Dickie Wilkes, who came to Sarawak after a long career in West Africa. Discussing some hurt expatriate reactions to a rather unkind statement by a Federal politician, he said: "My dear Alastair. These people here are being silly. When I was in West Africa I was accused in the local press of every crime in the calendar including murder and buggery. I assure you the expatriates here have very little to complain about."

Sometimes the criticism did not even refer to Sarawak. I remember once, when visiting Kuala Lumpur, there was some criticism by the Tunku of expatriate activity, which I took to be an unjustified reference to Tony Shaw. I said as much to my Director, Syed Zainal. He was quite pained. "Oh no, no," he said, "not Tony Shaw." And then added rather sorrowfully, "Lord Head." It was unfortunate that Head, the man of stature who sacrificed a political career for his principles at the time of Suez, never established an entirely harmonious working relationship with the Malaysian leadership. He was sent out to provide strong and authoritative British representation in Malaysia during Confrontation. He took over from a mediocre man, Sir Roger Tory, who, as viewed from Sarawak, seemed at times to regard himself as a supernumerary member of the Tunku's staff. Tory was much more popular in Kuala Lumpur than Head.

I never to my knowledge came under personal attack. I can only once remember being admonished by my Minister. This was for having failed to call out Public Address vehicles when there was a disturbance in Kuching between Malay Service

The end of the British presence. The final parade in Kuching.

Major General Ibrahim, the first Malaysian Director of Operations in Borneo, with Royal Marines after the parade

Corps troops and local Malay civilians. He was, of course, quite correct in saying that this should have been done. The incident had caught me totally unprepared. But by the last quarter of 1966, the point had been passed where as an expatriate I could be of much further service to my Ministry. The Federal Information service has an important political role for which an expatriate was unsuitable. It was, therefore, very amiably agreed that I should depart, and I handed over to my colleague Taibi Ali at the end of the year. Most of the other remaining expatriate administrative officers and policemen left soon after. By the middle of 1967, all had left, which was almost exactly what had been planned in 1963. Our relationships with both our State and Federal colleagues remained cordial to the end and with the passage of time, remain in retrospect, no less cordial. Hedda and I left in the same way as we had first arrived, by ship, steaming down the Sarawak River on a rainy day and out through Muara Tebas into the South China Sea.

BIBLIOGRAPHY

There is a substantial body of literature devoted to Sarawak. The following list is only intended as a guide.

EARLY WORKS

Beccari, Odoardo. *Wanderings in the Great Forests of Borneo; Travels and Researches of a Naturalist in Sarawak.* London: Constable, 1904.

> The author was an eminent naturalist who worked in Sarawak between 1865 and 1868.

Furness, William Henry. *The Home-Life of Borneo Head-Hunters.* Philadelphia, Lippincott, 1902.

> Despite its rather tiresome title, this is an excellent book, largely about the Baram. Much better than the contemporary works of Charles Hose.

Keppel, Henry. *The Expedition to Borneo of H.M.S. Dido for Suppression of Piracy: with extracts from the journal of James Brooke, Esq., of Sarawak.* London: Chapman and Hall, 1846.

> This is the book which put Sarawak on the map. Consists largely of the writings of James Brooke. More of his voluminous writings are to be found in several other works.

St. John, Spenser. *Life in the Forests of the Far East.* London: Smith, Elder, 1863.

> A first class work of observation and early travel.

HISTORY

Brooke, Anthony. *The Facts about Sarawak.* 1946. Singapore: Summer Times, c1983.

> Gives the anti-cession case. It was by no means a negligible one.

Brooke, Sylvia. *Queen of the Head Hunters.* 1970. New York: Morrow, 1972.

> All the Brooke women were devoted to Sarawak in their way and wrote about Sarawak extensively. This, the autobiography of the last Ranee, is the final chapter. Good for a giggle and a bit more. In some ways it is rather a touching work.

Great Britain, Commission of Enquiry, North Borneo and Sarawak [Cobbold Commission]. *Report of the Commission of Enquiry, North Borneo and Sarawak.* London: H.M. Stationery Office, 1962.

Inter-Governmental Committee (Great Britain and Malaysia). *Malaysia, Report of the Inter-Governmental Committee.* London: H.M. Stationery Office, 1963.
   This and the preceding title are key documents in the formation of Malaysia.

Leigh, Michael B. *The Rising Moon: Political Change in Sarawak.* Sydney: Sydney University Press, 1974.
   An odd title but a very comprehensive work on the development of politics in Sarawak.

Pringle, Robert. *Rajahs and Rebels: The Ibans of Sarawak under Brooke Rule, 1841-1941.* Ithaca, NY: Cornell University Press, 1970.
   An important and well-researched book looking at Brooke rule from the Iban point of view.

Reece, R.H.W. *The Name of Brooke: The End of White Rajah Rule in Sarawak.* New York: Oxford University Press, 1982
   Excellent work on the final years of the Brooke dynasty.

Runciman, Steven. *The White Rajahs: A History of Sarawak from 1841 to 1946.* Cambridge: Cambridge University Press, 1960.
   The interest that Sarawak has always aroused in outsiders is illustrated by the fact that it was possible to get such a distinguished historian as Sir Steven Runciman to write its history when the Colonial Office was encouraging the production of such material. It is based entirely on European material but is essential reading.

Sandin, Benedict. *The Sea Dayaks of Borneo before White Rajah Rule.* 1967. East Lansing, Mich.: Michigan State University Press, 1968.
   The former Curator of the Sarawak Museum, himself an Iban, writes on the early history of his people as passed down by word of mouth from generation to generation.

PEOPLE

Freeman, Derek. *Report on the Iban.* London: Athlone Press; New York: Humanities Press, 1970.
   Revised edition of an important work first published in 1955.

Freeman, Derek. *Some Reflections on the Nature of Iban Society,* Canberra: Department of Anthropology, Research School of Pacific Studies, Australian National University, 1981.
   A masterly and most readable essay on this extraordinary people.

Geddes, W.R. *Nine Dayak Nights*. 1957. London: Oxford University Press, 1961.
   A charming account of the Land Dayaks of the 1st Division.

Harrisson, Tom. *The Malays of South-West Sarawak before Malaysia: A Sociological Survey*. London: Macmillan, 1970.
   A long and untidy book but the only major work on the Malays of Sarawak.

Jensen, Erik. *The Iban and their Religion*. Oxford: Clarendon, 1974.
   Needs to be read with a critique by Freeman in the *Sarawak Museum Journal*.

Ju-K'ang T'ien. *The Chinese of Sarawak; A Study of Social Structure*. London: Department of Anthropology, London School of Economics and Political Sciences, 1953.
   Gives the background of the Chinese communities in Sarawak.

Morris, H.S. *Report on a Melanau Sago Producing Community in Sarawak*. London: H. M. Stationery Office, 1953.
   The only work devoted to the Melanau.

Morrison, Hedda. *Life in a Longhouse*. 1962. Singapore: Summer Times, c1988.
   Photographic account of everyday life in Iban longhouses.

Richards, Anthony. ed. *The Sea Dayaks and Other Races of Sarawak*. Kuching: Borneo Literature Bureau, 1963.
   Brings together a number of interesting early articles which appeared in the Sarawak Gazette. Mostly on the Iban.

Wright, Leigh, Hedda Morrison, and K.F. Wong. *Vanishing World, the Ibans of Borneo*. New York: Weatherhill, 1972.

CONFRONTATION

Mackie, J.A.C. *Konfrontasi: The Indonesia-Malaysia Dispute, 1963-1966*. Kuala Lumpur and New York: Oxford University Press, 1974.
   Comprehensive except on the military side.

Pocock, Tom. *Fighting General: The Public and Private Campaigns of General Sir Walter Walker*. London: Collins, 1973.
   General Walker is no Lord Roberts when it comes to humility but the book is important for throwing some light on the military side of Confrontation.

MISCELLANEOUS

Cramb, R.A. and R.H.W. Reece, eds. *Development in Sarawak: Historical and Contemporary Perspectives*. Melbourne: Centre of Southeast Asian Studies, Monash University, 1988.

Dickson, Mora. *Longhouse in Sarawak*. London: Gollancz, 1971.

An uncritical account of the work of John Wilson illustrated with charming drawings by one of Wilson's assistants, Arthur Thwaites.

Dickson, Murray. *A Sarawak Anthology*. London: University of London Press, 1965.

A perceptive collection of 120 extracts from good writing on Sarawak.

Harrisson, Tom. *World Within: A Borneo Story*. London: Cresst, 1959.

The first part is a sympathetic if rose-tinted account of life in interior Borneo before the arrival of Europeans; the second part is the story of that part of the SRD Operations for which Harrisson was responsible.

Lee Yong Leng. *Population and Settlement in Sarawak*. Singapore: D. Moore for Asia Pacific Press, 1970.

A useful human geography though already somewhat out of date.

Morrison, Hedda. *Sarawak*. London: Macgibbon, 1957.

Photographic record of our first nine years in Sarawak. Several later editions have been published in Singapore.

Report of the Land Committee. [Kuching?]: 1962.

Important for understanding the land problems of Sarawak.

Sarawak Gazette. Kuching.

Except for the war years it has been appearing ever since 1870 and contains a vast amount of interesting material.

Sarawak Information Service. *The Danger Within. A History of the Clandestine Communist Organisation in Sarawak*. Kuching: Sarawak Information Service, 1963.

An interesting account of the development of the communist movement in Sarawak. It has been updated twice in official publications—The Communist Threat to Sarawak, Kuala Lumpur, 1966, and The Threat of Armed Communism in Sarawak, Kuala Lumpur, 1972.

Sarawak Museum Journal. Kuching.

First class scientific periodical devoted entirely to Borneo. Its high standing is the main monument to the work of Tom Harrisson in Sarawak.

Smythies, B.E. *Birds of Borneo*. Edinburgh and London: Oliver and Boyd, 1960.

Comprehensive and standard work.

www.ingramcontent.com/pod-product-compliance
Lightning Source LLC
Chambersburg PA
CBHW082147230426
43672CB00015B/2858